T0072395

DR. ANA NOGALES'
BOOK OF LOVE,
SEX, AND
RELATIONSHIPS

DR. ANA NOGALES'
BOOK OF LOVE,
SEX, AND
RELATIONSHIPS

A GUIDE FOR LATINO COUPLES

Dr. Ana Nogales *with Laura Golden Bellotti*

BROADWAY BOOKS | NEW YORK

First trade paperback edition published 1999.

Designed by Chris Welch

The Library of Congress has catalogued the hardcover edition as:

Nogales, Ana, 1951–
    [Book of love, sex, and relationships]
    Dr. Ana Nogales' book of love, sex, and relationships : a guide for Latino couples / Ana Nogales with Laura Golden Bellotti.
        p.   cm.
    Includes index.
    ISBN 0-7679-0118-5 (HC)   Spanish ed.: ISBN 0-7679-0120-7
    1. Hispanic Americans—Life skills guides.   2. Hispanic Americans—Communication.
3. Hispanic Americans—Sexual behavior.   4. Hispanic American women—Psychology.
5. Hispanic American women—Attitudes.   6. Man-woman relationships—United
States.   7. Hispanic American families—Psychology.   I. Bellotti, Laura Golden.   II.
Title.
E184.S75N64   1997
305.868073—dc21   97-27659
                                                                            CIP

ISBN 9780767901192

146712470

To all Latinos living in the United States

CONTENTS

Acknowledgments   ix

Introduction   xi

1 | Living Between Two Worlds   1

2 | Culture Clash en Nuestra Casa   23

3 | Communication Es Mucho Más Que Conversation   50

4 | Latino Lovers Under the Sábanas   79

5 | Taking It Out on Each Other   108

6 | Helping Our Children to Value Themselves   134

7 | What Our Family History Teaches Us   168

8 | ¡Socorro! We Need Help!   196

9 | Relationship Success Stories:
     Blending the Best from Both Worlds   231

10 | The Ten Most Frequently Asked Questions
      About Amor, Sexo, and Relationships   257

Index   279

ACKNOWLEDGMENTS

I would first like to acknowledge the two countries to which I am so grateful:

> . . . Argentina, where I was born to immigrant parents, for giving me my "espíritu latinoamericano." I love Argentina, and I love being a Latina.
> . . . the United States of America, for allowing me the opportunity to become a part of the Latino community here, to join with others whose roots are in Latin America but who now make their home in this wonderful country where many cultures can live together. I am grateful to all the people in this country—Latinos and non-Latinos—who welcomed me and my family with the understanding that together we can create a United States of America where we all feel at home.

I also want to thank my family . . .

My husband, Alex, for his love and for building with me the relationship we share, which has inspired so many of the insights expressed throughout this book.

My three daughters, Eleonora, Gabriela, and Natalie, the Latina women who are my pride, and who are using the opportunities this country has afforded them to become everything that I always wanted them to be.

My mother, whose hard work and perseverance toward her goals have been a constant inspiration to me.

My dad, for being a dreamer, which enabled me to construct a dream for my own life.

My brother and sister-in-law, Bruno and Quela, and my sister and brother-in-law, Norma and Oscar, who have always been supportive to me in many, many ways.

I want to extend my profound gratitude to my agent in Los Angeles, Betsy Amster, whose idea it was to write this book, who trusted that I could do it, and who opened a new door for me.

A warm thank you to my agent in New York, Angela Miller, for her strong support and dedication to this project.

A heartfelt thanks to our editor, Janet Goldstein, for believing in the book and for providing her wise and enthusiastic editorial guidance.

I have a special thank you for my collaborator, Laura Golden Bellotti, for being my second brain, thinking with me, feeling with me, and putting into words the concepts and ideas and the spiritual love that I want this book to express.

Lastly, I am very grateful to my clients and my television and radio audiences, for sharing their experiences with me. I know that their stories will encourage and inspire the readers of this book.

—Dr. A. Nogales
February 1998

INTRODUCTION

I wrote this book especially for you. Whether you are single or have been married for years, whether you are a third-generation Latino or a recent immigrant, regardless of the kinds of concerns you may have about your relationships—you are the person I had in mind when I wrote this book.

In the many years I have been a psychologist, newspaper columnist, and talk-show host, I have never come across a self-help book about love and relationships that was addressed specifically to the Latino reader residing in the United States. Being in a love relationship is always a challenge, because two people's personalities, feelings, expectations, and dreams are intermingled—and are often at odds. As Latino-Americans, we face additional challenges when it comes to relationships: our cultural values frequently clash with those of the mainstream culture, and we must cope with a unique set of social pressures. These special circumstances can't help but affect how we relate to the people we love.

Having dedicated my professional career to helping those in the Latino community with their concerns about family, marriage, intimacy, and "living between two cultural worlds," I knew that a book about relationships specifically for Latinos was needed. And I felt that if I shared with you the compelling stories people have told me about their personal lives, as well as the advice and strategies I have given to them, this would be enormously helpful to you. I hope you find this to be true.

I bring to this book my own experiences as well—my experiences as a single person, as a married woman, as a mother, as a psychologist, as a community member, and as an immigrant. When I came here almost twenty years ago from Argentina, I felt a deep connection to the country in which I grew up, and my identity was closely tied to it. It was a culture shock and an adjustment for me to meet so many different kinds of Americans and so many different kinds of "Latinos." I married a Mexican-American man whose parents were immigrants from Mexico. Their background was quite different from mine, but we also had many things in common. I learned from their experiences, and my husband and I both continue to learn from one another. The people I have had the privilege to work with in the Latino community of Los Angeles have also opened my eyes to various life situations and relationship issues, and these revelations have touched me in a profound way.

Working as a Latina psychologist in this country, adapting to a new culture, reaching a deeper understanding about marriage and love with my husband, and helping my children grow up in our diversified community—each of these has expanded my awareness and understanding, and throughout this book I will share with you the insights I've come away with.

I am assuming that the reason you picked up this book may be any one or several of the following:

❦ You want to explore how being Latino and leading a "cultural double life" affects your relationships with those you love.

❦ You are happy in your marriage but would like to make it more intimate and more meaningful.

❦ You're having some persistent problems with your spouse (or boyfriend or novia), and you want to understand what the causes are. You'd like to learn from your disagreements and find out what to do to make things better—so you can grow closer to one another.

❦ You want to better adapt to the pressures we face as Latinos and to prevent the kind of desperation that can jeopardize relationships and lead to infidelity, domestic violence, or substance abuse.

❦ You would like your sexual life to reflect who you are as a loving, sensual, sensitive person, so that you and your mate can experience greater intimacy on both a physical and spiritual level.

❦ You need some advice on how to help your children take advantage of the opportunities this country affords them while at the same time making sure that they live by the cultural values we cherish.

We will be talking about all these topics—and much more—in this book. We will get to the heart of how Latinas and Latinos are reacting to changing concepts about what it means to be a man or a woman; why some Latino men feel proud that they restrict their wives from working outside the home—and why so many Latinas, on the contrary, feel proud to be earning a salary; how sex can be a more fulfilling experience as partners reach a new level of closeness and understanding; why some Latinas find "macho" men attractive . . . but only when these men respect a woman's right to be the person she wants to be; why some wives are unhappy with their husbands even though the husbands are doing all they can to provide a good living; what to do when your expectations for a better life are shattered, and economic or social pressures take a toll on your family; and how to live "between two cultural worlds" without losing your Latino identity.

In every chapter, you'll listen to personal stories told by those whose families are very similar to yours and mine and whose situations will be very familiar to you. Every Latino reader will recognize him- or herself in both the individual struggles and the success stories in this book. And throughout, I will offer you my professional insight, practical advice, even some optional exercises and techniques that you might wish to take advantage of.

Sharing our stories with those we trust is a very beneficial experience. I hope that in reading this book, you will be encouraged and strengthened to look at your relationship and to deepen it, to resolve the issues between you and your partner, and to develop the closeness you desire.

Sinceramente,
Dr. Ana Nogales

To protect the privacy of the individuals whose stories are used in this book, all names have been changed with the exception of Henry Barbosa and Antonia Hernandez, whose real names are used.

LIVING BETWEEN TWO WORLDS

Sometimes *I almost feel like the Clark Kent/Superman character—dashing into a phone booth to secretly change his identity when his friends aren't looking. One group of people sees me one way, and to others I'm a very different person. With friends at work, I'm Michael—just another nice, single guy who works in sales. I speak English without a trace of an accent, flirt politely with women in my office, and get razzed by coworkers for always ordering healthy salads for lunch. With my large extended family, I'm Miguel. The one who made it through college and has a great job. The one who makes a pig of himself on too many albondigas and taquitos. The one who is taking too long to find a wife because he wants to be certain she's the right one. Although I feel comfortable in both situations, it's almost like pieces of myself are missing when I'm playing one role or the other.*

—Miguel/Michael, age 29

When *I first came to this country in my twenties, I didn't even know what a "date" meant. When someone asked me, "Do you date?" I had no idea what they were asking. I needed to learn so many things about the way men here approach you, what kind of invitations they're giving you when they ask to see you. Do they want to take you out on a date, or just have sex, or have a relationship, or get to know you? What is the language of romance? I had to learn the whole thing all over. . . . And the diversity here is so great that what is fine for* *another person is not fine for you. You don't belong to a close-knit group of people like you did in your own country, where you're not only a part of a huge family but you also have the same friends for the last six years of school, and you feel like a family with them too. You know you fit in. There, the rules are always the same. Here, everybody has their own rules.*

—Marta, age 35

Whether we were born in the United States or have lived here only a short time, as Latinos we inhabit two distinct worlds. One is the world of our parents, grandparents, and great-grandparents. This is the culture we hold in our hearts. The culture that embraces large families and close ties to aunts and uncles, cousins, and sisters-in-law. The culture that values tradition, loyalty to old friends, and a sense of belonging to the community.

We also dwell in the multicultural world of the United States, an environment so diverse that it is almost impossible to define. It is a world where the opportunity to pursue your dream is supposedly granted to every citizen. Where striking out on your own is hailed as heroic. Where women and men are more equal than anywhere else in the world. And where the individual is nearly always valued over the group.

Like Miguel, many of us grapple with the feeling that we have two separate identities. We sense that when we move from one "world" to the other, we must somehow alter parts of ourselves in order to be accepted. And we wonder what we're gaining and what we're giving up in the process. How does this "cultural double life" affect our relationships, our love life, and the well-being of our families?

Some of us are immigrants like Marta, who can still remember longing for her country of origin even as she thrilled to the possibilities inherent in her new home. Not yet as adept at bridging the two worlds as Miguel, Marta has had to familiarize herself not only with a new language but also with an entirely new set of cultural ground rules. Accustomed to socializing in groups, she had to learn how to act with a man on a first date. Dependent for so long on the emotional support of her close-knit group of friends and family, she had to discover ways to establish new connections so that she could feel that she belonged. The adjustments she has had to make reverberate in her marriage, her role as a mother, and her interaction with relatives and coworkers.

As for me, I often feel that my identity is both "aquí y allá." Two distinct aspects of myself have been joined as one person. For example, although I never listened to tango music or folk music in Buenos Aires, when I first came to Los Angeles, I had this need to listen to "my" music, so that I could feel more in touch with who I am. And I always felt so happy when another driver would see my I LOVE ARGENTINA bumper sticker and honk and wave enthusiastically. In that instant, I wasn't so alone—someone from my country was driving down the very same freeway! Even now, when I get on the plane to go back to Argentina for a visit, I feel that in some sense I can finally relax, like taking my shoes off. But after I've been there a few weeks, I can't wait to come back. Because my home is here now, my roots are now here. So what ultimately defines me as a person is neither there nor here; it is both here and there—aquí y allá.

It's the same for my husband. He's first-generation Mexican-American, educated here, but he tells me that culturally he feels "in the middle"—having been raised with both the United States and Mexican cultures as strong influences. And he has had to go through a lot of conflicts to find a cultural balance that he's comfortable with.

In this chapter we will explore the struggles and the ambivalence we Latinos experience as we attempt to live between two worlds. As we gain a better understanding of the bicultural fabric that underlies our lives, we'll begin to see how it influences the way we relate to those we love and care about.

EL SUEÑO AMERICANO: THE AMERICAN DREAM

How often we have heard relatives tell their stories about what they thought the States would be like before they actually arrived here in this most celebrated of countries. All immigrants, no matter where they're from, have an almost Disneyland vision of how their lives will be transformed in the country that boldly proclaims itself to be the land of opportunity.

That vision is based partly on reality and partly on hope. What we immigrants want to believe about the United States is that those of us who are determined enough can earn good money and enjoy a comfortable lifestyle; that even poor people can work hard enough to one day own their own business or send their children to college; that the principles of democracy on which the country was founded will assure newcomers the same chance granted to natives to get ahead and provide well for their families. For women, there is the additional promise that we will be given the same educational and economic opportunities as men.

Certainly there is some truth to each of these assumptions. But as we all know, succeeding in this country is not as easy as the immigrant imagines it to be. There is a tremendous discrepancy between the glossy, media-created images of the "all-American good life" and the tough economic and social pressures most of us in the Latino community must face.

Not only do we newcomers find ourselves living between the two worlds of Latino culture and mainstream United States culture, but at the outset we must also live between the luminous world of our "American dreams" and the world we actually find when we arrive here. Often disappointed by how our hoped-for life is at odds with the reality of our daily existence in the United

States, many Latino immigrants wonder if "back home" sometimes made more sense than "living in the USA."

Like many Latino immigrants—Argentines, Nicaraguans, Sal-
vadorans, Cubans—Ernesto came to the United States for political reasons. As a refugee, he appreciates not only the economic
opportunity this country has afforded him but the political and religious freedoms as well. Coming to this country over twenty-five
years ago meant coming to a land where he could talk freely,
where he didn't have to feel afraid that if he said the wrong thing,
it might cost him his life—or that of a relative. Still, he misses
much about his native Argentina. He recently went back for a
school reunion, at which he was asked to give a speech about what
it was like living in the United States.

> As I started talking, tears came to my eyes. I knew that all my
> old friends were envious of me. I have a good life in the United
> States, I have a successful career, my children were raised in the
> States and have become successful too. But I told them in my
> speech, "All of you wonder what would have been if you had left
> like I did. You complain that you don't have the things I have. But
> what you do have is each other. Most of you kept the friendships
> you had since you were children, the valuable friendship you are
> sharing here today. Your children were close to their grandparents,
> aunts, uncles, cousins. You share a life in common. You have a
> history together. Just by walking in the streets, you meet your
> friends. And you give each other a hug, with a lot of pleasure, a lot
> of love, and a lot of memories of the good times you had together.
> Over coffee you share what's going on in your life. If you're in
> trouble, you call each other. I have acquaintances and neighbors,
> but I don't have anybody to call when I have really good news to
> share or something sad to talk over. I don't meet anybody in the
> streets with whom I go back years and years. So who lives better?
> You who have each other? Or me, who has all these wonderful
> things, but who is essentially alone?"

Flora, a fairly new immigrant from Guadalajara, Mexico, also talks about what she misses, as well as some of the jarring experiences that have made her think twice about remaining in the United States.

In Mexico, we didn't have much, but now I think maybe I didn't appreciate some of the things we did have. Like the importance of our family and the closeness we had together. Here our home is nicer; we live in a nice apartment in a pretty good neighborhood. But I worry about the problem of gangs and the influence on my kids. I see them behaving in a way that I never taught them, and it frightens me. Also I don't see my husband as much, because we both have to work to be able to afford the rent. I was raised where the family sat down together to eat the evening meal, and we can't do that here, because my husband works at night. I hope our decision to improve our lives and raise our family in this country turns out to be the right one.

Luis, Flora's husband, is also concerned that his family may be sacrificing too much in order to achieve the dreamed-of "good life":

We had to leave both our families behind. My brother recently moved here, but Flora and I both miss all our relatives very much. I think living near them would make a big difference in bringing up the kids. I always had aunts and grandparents and older cousins watching me when my parents weren't around. I know Flora could use the help. Here everyone seems to be on their own. I miss the feeling of being part of a large family, of knowing that there was always someone there to help you out, no matter what you were going through.

Luis and Flora struggle with the life changes they have had to accept in order to live in this country. But they're also already enjoying a piece of that dream that compelled them to move here in the first place. They each earn more money here than Luis did in Guadalajara. Their children have learned English and are doing well in school. Luis hopes to one day open his own car-repair shop. And Flora is taking classes at a local adult-education school in preparation for eventually becoming a teacher. Their reservations and worries are ultimately outweighed by their achievements and future plans. And their unrelenting dreams.

BLENDING IN VERSUS ROOTS

For those of you who were born in this country—either to immigrants or to first-, second-, or third-generation families—a divided sense of identity and loyalty is often at the core of what it means to be Latino. Proud of the strides your family has made in this country, and aware of the culture your forefathers and mothers brought with them, you are likely to regard your cultural roots with love and respect. But, quite naturally, you also feel much more "American" than either your immigrant counterparts or your elders who have closer ties to traditional Latin values.*

It's probably hard for you to picture yourselves living in the country from which your relatives originally came. You may look at cousins who still live there with a kind of sadness, because you feel more privileged living here. Whereas your parents or grandparents might ask themselves how you would have turned out had they remained in their home countries, you probably never ask

*Geographically, the Americas include Canada, the United States, Mexico, and the countries in Central and South America. Given common usage among Latinos and throughout the world, we've used the word "American" in this book to refer to people of all ethnic groups—including, of course, Latinos—living in the United States, and the term "Americanization" to refer to the process by which one becomes more culturally like the majority of those who live in the United States.

yourself that question. For all of this country's problems and short-comings, you feel this is where you belong.

At times, you may wonder if certain Latino attitudes that your family shares hold you back from the life you want. Still, there are traditional cultural values you don't want to deny. But it isn't always easy integrating the Latino way into the American lifestyle we feel comfortable with.

Rita, a second-generation Mexican-American, typifies the ambivalence felt by many of today's upwardly mobile Latinas. Twenty-six, married, and in her third year of law school, she is the embodiment of the American dream. But she also acknowledges the trade-offs she has had to make to pursue her goals:

> Most of my friends from high school have two or three kids already. As much as I love what I do and can't wait to practice public-interest law, I feel a twinge every time I'm invited to another baby shower. And so does my mom. Children are the focal point of Mexican families, and I feel that I am disappointing her in some way because Jerry and I have decided to wait to have kids until my practice is established.
>
> I saw so many girls in my neighborhood who wanted to go on to college but never did because they got married and pregnant right out of high school—or pregnant first and then married. And I think many of our mothers have a kind of unspoken desire for us to put marriage and family as our first priority, ahead of college— even though they say they want us to get ahead. Maybe it's a mistrust of so-called liberated women, a feeling that somehow it's not feminine to have a career. But I didn't want anything to prevent me from following through with my plans for my own life.

Rita becomes sad when she discloses that some members of her family feel she has somehow betrayed her "roots" by striving to become "more than just a wife and mother." She values the importance Latinos place on family but doesn't think women should be forced to forgo meaningful careers in order to be full-time moms.

Unlike her mother and her aunts, Rita feels comfortable with the idea of sharing child-care responsibilities with her husband. "That's one of the many reasons I was attracted to Jerry," Rita confesses. "Because he doesn't think it's a threat to his masculinity to be involved with a woman who wants an equal relationship. Unfortunately, too many Latino guys are still caught up in the macho thing."

Rita's comments touch on one of the most volatile areas distinguishing traditional Latino values from modern American beliefs: the role of women. Again and again, I hear from women who complain that their boyfriends or husbands cannot accept that "times have changed" and that women should be treated differently. The changing role of women is affecting our relationships and families in many, many ways, and this issue, more than any other, is causing Latino couples to seriously question their cultural roots. Although "blending in" with mainstream American culture is sometimes seen as "selling out" our Hispanic traditions, when it comes to affording women the same chance as men to have a satisfying life, many of us feel that those traditions must finally yield to a more equitable code of behavior.

Victor agrees. A first-generation Cuban-American, he says that he appreciates the ways women have joined men in the workplace and are more equal in social situations. He prefers dating women who are career-oriented, and he claims he inherited this preference from his mother, who was a registered nurse. But Victor must often defend his opinions at family gatherings, where a number of his uncles and cousins like to spar with him on this topic.

There are many times when I've brought girlfriends to family events at mi abuela's house, and my Uncle Manny and Uncle

*Roberto call me over to tease me about them and knock my taste
in women. It usually has to do with the fact that I tend to choose
women who are strong and outspoken, who aren't afraid to
disagree with me—or with my male relatives, on occasion. This
really rubs my uncles the wrong way! To them, the man must
always show the woman that he's boss, even if she knows more
about something than he does. I enjoy my uncles and usually
humor them, letting them have their say. And, believe me, this has
gotten me into a lot of trouble with girlfriends after we leave the
party!*

Enjoying the company of his opinionated uncles as much as he
enjoys dating dynamic women, Victor would never wish to give up
one in favor of the other. His love of family and his penchant for
male camaraderie are as much a part of who he is as is his respect
for women. But as his story confirms, leading a cultural double life
means that Victor must justify his uncles' behavior to his girlfriends, and accept the ridicule of his beloved tíos.

A SENSE OF BELONGING

Feeling that we belong to a welcoming community is a crucial part
of our Latino tradition. Much more than is the case for mainstream Americans, our identity is grounded in membership to our
family, to our church, to our cultural community. We tend to view
ourselves in relationship to others. We cherish the close connections that bind us to those we respect and love. And we depend
on their emotional support for our sense of strength in who we are.

Traditionally, our families have always been large, and they give
us a built-in sense of identity. You belong to the Gonzales family,
you belong to the Guerrero family, the Nogales family. And this
group of people is so big that you don't need to incorporate many

friends. Cousins and sisters-in-law and nephews are your friends. There are so many family members that you can socialize among yourselves and never be wanting for companionship. There is a gratifying sense of community just within your own family. In the film *Fools Rush In*, this closeness within an extended family was accurately depicted in the family of the character played by Salma Hayek.

Latino relatives sustain each other in so many ways. As members of large extended families, we often find that we don't need to reach out for solutions to social or psychological or economic dilemmas; answers are found within the family structure. There is always someone to talk to, to lend you money, to introduce you to a nice single guy.

Unfortunately, the extended family doesn't always exist in the States. Many of us have immigrated here without our families or with only a very few members, and consequently we experience a great emptiness as we adapt to life without our relatives close by. We feel isolated and lonely at first, until we figure out ways to compensate for the family structure we left behind.

Then, too, the extended family is foreign to the contemporary way of life in the United States. When most people here speak of family, they are referring to a much smaller group of people than the families with which we are familiar. They mean their "immediate" family—husband, wife, and one, two, or three children. Grandparents, aunts, uncles, cousins often live thousands of miles away. The "nuclear family" may go to visit Grandma and Grandpa for a week at Christmas time, or aunts, uncles, and cousins may get together for a family reunion once in a while, but socializing with dozens of relatives at a time on a regular basis is not the rule.

In fact, many people in this country never see their own parents or siblings, even if they live in the same city, having severed relations with them for one reason or another. While much lip service

is paid to "family values," many Americans tend to value their independence and the freedom to "do their own thing" more than
loyalty to their family, no matter what the cost.

In addition to depending on close family ties, Latinos have traditionally turned to the Catholic Church for a sense of belonging.
Beyond its purely religious role, the Church has always provided a
deep feeling of security and community. It is a gathering place, a
comfort, another form of family.

The Church often plays an especially crucial role in the life of
new immigrants, helping them overcome feelings of isolation and
unfamiliarity. It gives them a comfortable sense of belonging that
they probably experienced as part of a large family in their native
countries. They know they will be taken care of by the group, that
the church community will give emotional support to its members, and that as individuals they will find others who share a similar background.

Even if they didn't go to church very often back home, here in
the United States the Catholic Church provides immigrants with
a foundation for their new lives. It offers a social network as well
as a sense of unity and identity, which newcomers in an over-
whelmingly diverse environment frequently lack.

But does the Church continue to be an integral part of most
Latinos' lives once they are established here? Or does "Americanization" bring with it a tendency to look elsewhere for a social and
spiritual foundation? Long a mainstay of Latino culture, is the
Church's prominence beginning to erode?

First of all, there are hundreds of Christian denominations in
this country, whereas in Latin countries the Catholic Church has
long been dominant. As with every other aspect of the American
lifestyle, we are faced with a dizzying array of choices when it
comes to our religious orientation.

There is also the problem that Catholic doctrine conflicts
with modern American mores and attitudes at times, as we see
in the context of such issues as equality between the sexes, divorce,

birth control, and of course, abortion. Again, as Latinos, we face another instance of being caught between two worlds. Many feel torn between their long-standing cultural ties to the Church and strongly held convictions they have acquired as the result of acculturation. Does this mean that allegiance to the Catholic Church, an aspect of Latino identity so long taken for granted, is being gradually edged out by our new culture? Not necessarily.

Like Sandra, a Puerto Rican professional woman, many contemporary Latinos learn to accommodate both sides of their divided system of values.

I grew up in the Catholic Church and cannot imagine my life without it. It's part of who I am, even though I disagree with a lot of what the Church stands for. Like their adamant position against women priests. Every other religion has women in positions of authority now. Isn't it time they followed in that direction? And in terms of my own life, it was heartbreaking for me when I went through my divorce, knowing the Church disapproved of my actions. Yet I had to be true to my own feelings, and staying married to someone I no longer loved was not possible for me. Recently, it was even more heartbreaking when I couldn't remarry in the Church. And as for birth control, very few of my friends who are Catholic go along with the Church's ban on everything except the rhythm method. And I don't either. But for all its faults, I still feel the Catholic Church is like home. It's in my heart, it's where I belong.

EXPRESSING OURSELVES

There is another, more subtle difference between the Latino and mainstream American character that is especially noticeable when it comes to our love and family relationships. This distinction has to do with how we express our feelings. Whether our ancestors come from Mexico, Central America, Puerto Rico, Cuba, South America, or Spain, we have the reputation of being warm and emotional people. Of course there are the stereotypes that understandably make us cringe—"fiery Latin bombshell," "hot-headed," "Latin lover." But it's true that there is an undeniable warmth, if not fire, to the Latino spirit.

How does this warmth come across in our interactions with acquaintances and with those closest to us? We are generally open and friendly to people we meet for the first time. We welcome friends into our homes and treat them like family. We are physically demonstrative when we love someone. We are not afraid to hug and kiss our children—even when they're adults.

But on a deeper level, we tend to express our love for our spouse and family through our actions rather than in words. A loving husband and father provides for his wife and family, remains loyal to them, and rarely considers divorce an option. A wife and mother demonstrates her love by taking care of her husband and children, providing a welcoming home to which they can return each day for comfort and security. And children show their love by respecting their parents and staying in close contact with them even when they're grown.

While mainstream families in the United States may share some of these behaviors, there is a discernible way in which the expression of love—and of feelings in general—differs between many Latinos and typical "Americans." Mainstream psychological thinking, especially in the last twenty years, holds that telling loved ones how you honestly feel is of the utmost importance in a relationship. The closer you are to someone, the more important it is to be open with them, divulging emotions, fears, secrets. But the notion of sharing your inner feelings with someone else, even if that person is the one who is closest to you in your life, is not common in Latino families.

There are many reasons for this resistance. First of all, Latino men generally consider it a blow to their pride to reveal any fears or anxieties they may be experiencing. Giving an appearance of confidence and strength is crucial to their identity as men. And since expressing their feelings requires becoming vulnerable, Latino men are understandably reluctant to do so, either with women or with other men.

Usually, Latina women raised in the traditional way have also been taught to keep their thoughts and feelings somewhat to themselves, although to a lesser extent than men. As little girls, we are expected to respect our elders and show our love for them by our behavior, by obeying them and doing what is right. Expressing to parents our doubts or frustrations, telling them what's really going on in our lives, is not the norm. So when as adults, we become involved with a man, we are not in the habit of verbally expressing our deepest or most troubling feelings. And because we're aware of the difficulty men have communicating with us, we often give up the effort to "share" our feelings before we've even tried.

This does not mean that Latinos never express their emotions. It means that we don't usually do so in words. Often clients ask, "Why is it important to say 'I love you,' when I show her that I love her?" Many avoid saying the words "I love you" or "I need you" or "I want [or desire] you," because they believe that to do so is almost a form of belittling themselves. If they have to say the words, they contend, it means that they're incapable of actually being a loving person.

Sometimes, words feel not only unnecessary but also too powerful, as if they contain a kind of force or magic we're afraid of. As if by uttering something so personal we will be compelled to act in a way that is not natural. Words have a lot of implications, containing many meanings, and we don't want our intentions to be misunderstood by misusing such power.

There is also the question of Latino reserve or modesty. In our cultures, we tend to think that naming certain things that are considered very private is improper. This view goes along with our custom of keeping very personal matters to ourselves. Certainly love is very personal, but there are other areas of our lives where the same principle applies. For example, some women refer to the menstrual period simply as "eso"—"that"—considering it indelicate to use a more explicit term. Similarly, using words to name or label our emotions, even when they're positive, feels improper to many of us.

The experience of Cristina, a friend of mine whose sister recently came to visit her from San Antonio, perfectly exemplifies the differences between how Latinos and non-Latinos in the United States tend to express their feelings.

> I told my friends how happy I was that my sister was coming to stay with me for a few weeks. All my Hispanic friends came to visit her, to welcome her, to get to know her. One went and bought her favorite cookies, so she could share the favorite treats with my sister. Another one brought my sister avocados, because in San Antonio this time of year you cannot find good avocados. Everything related to food, because eating together in Latin cultures is so important. Serving food is a way of serving love.
>
> My Anglo friends, on the other hand, didn't show up. They wanted to give me the "space" to visit with my sister alone; they didn't want to disturb our time together. After my sister left, they called and wanted to talk about how the visit went—which was, I guess, their way of expressing their friendship and affection for me.

Although we are a warm, open, hospitable people, who look for and celebrate the passion in life, we usually express how we feel through our actions rather than our words. In subsequent chapters, we will be exploring how this particular characteristic affects our interaction with the opposite sex, our sexual relations, and our relationship with our children.

LATIN FORMALITY MEETS AMERICAN CASUAL

In most Latin American countries, there is still no significant "middle class"; you belong to either the high economic class or the low one. Most people look toward the upper classes as a model, and what they see in the dress and demeanor and behavior of the privileged class is a distinct formality. The Latino tradition, even in this country, tends to incorporate this bias toward a certain kind of formality. We try, as much as possible, to carry ourselves as people who are proud and well-bred.

Pride is the key word here. For one thing, you represent your family, so you don't want to be "la vergüenza de la familia" (the shame of your family). You don't want to be looked down on, because you want to reflect your family in a positive light. This involves the concept of "el qué dirán" (what will people say). Being formal means being very conscious of how you look in the eyes of others, behaving appropriately, demonstrating that you are cultured and educated. You want to be regarded as a distinguished person because that appearance contributes to your own pride and that of your family.

When you behave more formally, you show others that you value yourself. You are identifying yourself with "the best." You are accomplishing what is expected of you by your community and by the society at large. Being formal means that you are reliable and dependable; you project a strong, conservative image. You are not vulnerable. This tradition goes for women as well. A woman who adheres to this code of formality puts forth the image of someone who holds her head high, has pride in herself.

If you are informal, your behavior says to others that you don't really value yourself. If you break the code of formality and allow yourself to look like an eccentric, others will look down on you and wonder about your family, your breeding, your educational and economic status.

"Acculturated" Latinos in this country are more relaxed when it comes to these standards, but we still tend to be more formal than our "mainstream American" counterparts. For many of us, living between two worlds means that we retain the tradition of formality enough to preserve our sense of pride, but we also allow ourselves the casual impulse that so defines the lifestyle in the United States.

Alicia is a case in point. In her personal life she is very informal, laughing heartily at a good joke, speaking openly on any topic that arises, showing up at family barbeques in shorts and sneakers. But in her professional life as a social worker in the Latino community, she is a different person. She must conduct herself with a certain formality and reserve. She dresses conservatively, always wearing suits to work and to civic functions, and carries herself with the kind of ceremony that shows that she acknowledges herself as a professional. "I must play the role the community expects of me," she explains. "If I don't dress and behave in this way, I won't be taken seriously."

She tells an amusing story about meeting with a colleague in his office and being "absolutely shocked" when he stood up to shake her hand . . . because he was wearing tennis shorts! "I appreciate the openness of many of my non-Latino friends. I like the honesty that often goes along with their more informal way of presenting themselves and communicating. But there are circumstances where I personally draw the line. It's just not the way I was brought up."

THE MACHO THING VERSUS THE LIBERATED MAN

Dealing with the differences between Latino "macho" behavior and the more "liberated" outlook shared by many women and men in the United States is another aspect of living between two worlds. Latina women frequently tell me that they wish their boyfriends or husbands would become more "Americanized" in this area. And Latino men counter that their girlfriends and wives are becoming less feminine, less loving, and too "liberated."

Latino men did not invent machismo. Nearly every culture in the world respects and glorifies male strength, tenacity, and superiority over women. The Latin incarnation of masculine power and pride, however, is legendary.

Some point to the roots of machismo in the Western Hemisphere as dating back to Native American cultures, which encouraged and inspired men to die fighting. In the Aztec world, Tlacaélel, the adviser to the Aztec kings, was revered as the "embodiment of power on earth." He advocated that warriors seek a "famous death" by distinguishing themselves in warfare, becoming known as men likely to die courageously, and ultimately dying in the midst of battle. By giving their life in this valiant and public way, men would be assured a place in heaven. According to Miguel León-Portilla, author of *Aztec Thought and Culture*, and Earl Shorris, author of *Latinos*, the word in Náhuatl for this ideal state in which to die is the passive form of the verb "mati" (to know), which is "macho" (to be known).

After Spanish and other European invaders brutally crushed the various Native American civilizations, machismo took on a very different quality. The conquistadores had not only enslaved other men, they had also taken any woman they desired. In this process of conquering and imposing their own will and values, they brought their kind of machismo to the indigenous people, as well as to a new race of people that subsequently emerged: the mestizo. The indigenous and mestizo population had become a beaten-down, oppressed people. And unfortunately, their own acts of machismo were often a reaction to their powerlessness— attempts to prove their manhood in the context of a new culture that had stolen it from them.

In its contemporary form, machismo continues to mask the powerlessness felt by many Latinos in this country. Faced with economic struggles, the barriers of language and racism, and the growing equality of women, Latino men act out their need to be strong, to "be known," to have a self-image of which they can be proud. Some engage in harmless verbal combat, boasting to other men about their business or romantic conquests. Others, with less hope and less to lose, clash with invented rivals in a more dangerous and concrete way, joining gangs and dying for a sense of honor.

Perhaps the saddest and most despicable way in which machismo is manifested is in outbursts of domestic violence. A man's code of honor has been grossly perverted when he must beat his wife or children in order to validate himself as a human being.

There is also the macho game of romantically ensnaring and then abandoning women. As Ilan Stavans, author of *The Hispanic Condition*, put it, "Possessed by doubt and insecurity, the macho spirit finds recreation in challenge: testing its romantic strategies, pondering its physical presence, counting its victims."

Even Latino men who are secure and successful and acculturated to mainstream American values find the machismo style tempting. Acting macho is, after all, part of their heritage—passed down from one generation of fathers to the next. And in its more benign forms, it is not always unattractive to females. Modern women may say that they are put off by macho guys, but many are still secretly impressed by the "strong, silent type" or the grandiose romantic or the man who takes control.

And certainly not all non-Latino men in the United States are the models of liberated behavior. Women from every ethnic background continue to struggle with macho attitudes at work, in social situations, and in the home. But, by and large, the way of life in the United States incorporates equality in the workplace, active parenting by both fathers and mothers, sexual freedom for women, and a number of other accepted modes of conduct that fly in the face of machismo.

Throughout this book, we'll be talking about how Latino women and men are coming to grips with "the macho thing," and we'll look at why our Latino upbringing usually means that we must struggle with this issue on a deeper level than most mainstream Americans.

WHERE DO WE STAND?

It's hard enough for couples in the 1990s to weather the usual storms of love relationships—finding the right person, dealing with issues of trust, control, and compromise, keeping their sex life alive and satisfying, confronting the betrayal of infidelity. But those of us who are Latino-Americans must also add to the mix the question of our cultural identity, which influences every aspect of our personal life. The social customs in our country of origin; the roles we learned from our parents; the attitudes of our grandparents, which we may disavow but which are still with us on a subconscious level—each of these factors affects who we are and how we relate to the people we love.

In this chapter, we've begun to look at some of the differences between the mainstream United States and Latino cultures that form the backdrop for the relationship issues we'll be discussing. As you scan the following lists of cultural characteristics, you will probably be able to think of a number of other ways in which your own life divides along cultural lines. Most probably you identify with some of the values on both lists. Neither list represents the right or wrong way to be. Both sets of values are worthy qualities of which we can be proud. The important thing is to learn from both cultures and to blend cultural values in a way that best suits who you are.

In Latino Culture . . .	In Mainstream United States Culture . . .
❦ "taking care of" your mate proves your love	❦ "sharing feelings" is essential to being close
❦ family, including extended family, is always your first priority	❦ you define family as "nuclear" or "immediate"
❦ belonging, feeling part of a group is an important aspect of your identity	❦ independence and "striking out on your own" are valued over group involvement
❦ formality is a way of showing pride in yourself	❦ informality makes you more approachable, more "democratic"
❦ single people usually socialize in groups	❦ single people usually "date" in couples
❦ elders are treated with respect	❦ youth and vitality are celebrated
❦ traditional male-female roles are more prevalent	❦ more equal roles for men and women are accepted by many

Of course, each of us has a unique personality, family history, and set of personal concerns. But as Latinos living in the United States, we also share at least some aspect of a "cultural double life," and it is this living in two worlds at once that both challenges and enriches our personal relationships.

CULTURE CLASH
EN NUESTRA CASA

In the typical Latin fashion, I was raised to be a pleaser. First to please my parents, then to please a man, to be the peacekeeper at home, the one that takes care of the husband and children and everybody. When I first took a job, it was just to contribute to our family income. But then I started my own custom drape business, and it just took off. I began to make really good money and my husband quit his job to help me manage the business. Now I have a lot of employees working under me, I work a lot of extra hours . . . and I also have a lot of extra problems I never had before. Like the resentment my husband feels about my success. He tells me I've become too pushy, too businesslike, that I'm not the same woman he married. He wants me to still be the typical housewife whose main purpose in life is to please her husband.

—Gloria, age 42

I am proud of Gloria, I really am. She's made something of her life. But she has changed in the process, and not all of the change is good as far as I'm concerned. It's fine that she's the boss at work, and I don't even mind that at the office, technically, she's my boss, too. But at home she has to learn to turn that off and take care of the family needs. Become the caring, loving woman I fell in love with.

—Ralph, age 45

Although the issues Gloria and Ralph are contending with are
not unique to Latino couples, their problems are definitely col-
ored by the cultural values with which each grew up. Their struggle to determine which set of cultural standards should be used to
gauge their expectations, their behavior, and their relationship is
one most of us can easily relate to. Like Gloria and Ralph, we notice that our relationships can become strained when we try to integrate both the Latino and mainstream values we've become
accustomed to. These two distinct cultures often pull us in opposite directions, forcing us to seriously question what is right and
wrong in a love relationship, in a marriage, in a family. It is this
playing out of the "culture clash" beneath our own roof that is the
focus of this chapter.

"IF I BECOME SUCCESSFUL, WILL YOU STILL LOVE ME?"

In Gloria and Ralph's case, the clash is centered on the appropriate behavior and role a modern wife ought to assume. It is difficult
for Ralph to articulate his feelings about how Gloria has changed
since she's had her own business, but his emotions center on feeling threatened and fearful.

He says he resents the fact that Gloria works long, extended
hours, because he thinks she should be at home with their children, who miss her and need her. What he really means is that he
needs her to be there for him. He is worried that her success is de-
priving him of her attention, and he is critical of how she has chosen to change her life. Ralph feels that Gloria's new life as a
businesswoman prevents her from being the loving wife and
mother he expects her to be.

> She used to throw her arms around me and prepare my favorite
> foods when she knew I'd had a particularly hard day. Now we
> have a housekeeper, so Gloria rarely cooks during the week. The

cooking is done by our housekeeper who has become the "ama de casa," while Gloria acts like a boss, ordering the kids to set the table and me to help out in the kitchen. But more than that, it's her attitude. She's lost her softness, her femininity.

For Ralph, home has become an extension of work, where his wife is the boss, again giving the orders, and where he is no longer the recipient of special attention and love. Now, whenever he's pleased with the food, he doesn't feel it's a meal that has been cooked with love; it's merely the work of an employee. So the special moment of sharing the family meal is not the same. And more important, he has come to doubt Gloria's love for him.

Gloria contends that Ralph's expectations are simply out of line with today's standards and that he is criticizing her as a wife because he's intimidated by her success as a career woman. But she also admits to feelings of guilt.

I enjoy having my own business, and I want Ralph to accept that, but at times I have this guilty feeling that I'm not being the woman I was raised to be—the loving and nurturing one who is there for everybody. It's not that I want to avoid being a caring mother or a wife, it's that it's not always easy for me to zero in on what Ralph is needing when I come home. I love him, and I want to show him that. But it's hard for me to switch gears after being this strong person all day, and then to suddenly turn into the caretaker. I realize I need to learn to relax and enjoy my home life more, but Ralph has to accept this new part of who I am now, too.

Both Ralph and Gloria are caught between conflicting cultural images of the perfect woman. Women in the Latino community are brought up to be helpers. First, they are expected to help their mothers, their grandmothers, their younger sisters and brothers. When they grow up, they are supposed to take care of their husband and children, see that the household runs smoothly, and be the "peacemakers," as Gloria puts it. But in this country, where there are so many new opportunities for women, many Latinas are discovering that in addition to being competent mothers and housewives, they can also be competent workers, great supervisors, outstanding professionals, successful entrepreneurs, like Gloria, or even United States congresswomen, like Loretta Sanchez. What they see in mainstream American women that they want for themselves is self-fulfillment, success in a career, and economic independence.

But when Latino men, like Ralph, experience life with women who are making changes and becoming more independent, the change frequently has a debilitating effect on their image of themselves as men, especially if they were raised with the traditional male role firmly implanted in their mind. Your girlfriend's or wife's success in a career outside the home is often interpreted by other men as your own weakness. You must not be "man enough" if your woman surpasses you in any way. This kind of macho thinking maintains that a strong man will make certain that his woman never exceeds his own accomplishments, never usurps his rightful position as head of the household. The equation, not alien to non-Latinos but even more common among Latinos, is simple: a strong, accomplished woman diminishes the stature of the man she's with. A successful wife is a threat to a husband's pride.

A man's fears are also tied to the fact that our capitalist society values people according to what they do and how much money they make. So if a woman starts earning more than her husband, she is automatically viewed by some as being more valuable than he is. Added to this point of view is the fear, felt by many Latino men, that if a woman becomes financially more successful than her husband, she will leave him for someone who is more equal to her.

A successful wife, or any wife who becomes a breadwinner, often has fears of her own. The greatest one is that her husband will no longer love her, because her new role will render her unlovable. And if she is not loved, she is not a real woman. Intrinsic to being a woman in our culture is being loved by the man who has chosen you. The teachings of the Catholic Church reinforce this belief by implying that a woman's role is to love and receive love and be protected by her man. If a woman is able to "protect" herself by providing for herself economically, she risks being perceived as something other than a "real woman."

There is an additional fear when a woman starts earning a decent income: being in some way alienated from her family. In some Latino families, earning good money, whether you're a man or a woman, is perceived as becoming too "Americanized"—a betrayal of your roots. Family members may look upon a financially successful person as someone who is going to forget about the family. A woman faces a kind of double jeopardy in this regard. She is perceived as having abandoned her roots by, first of all, excelling where her relatives may not have succeeded, and secondly, by taking on a role that is considered an exclusive part of the masculine domain.

When Gloria and Ralph face each other with their various accusations and grievances, therefore, they bring to their arguments not only their unique personalities and personal history together, but also the cultural biases they've inherited from both their families as well as from the larger United States society in which they live. Gaining an understanding of why they feel the way they do and what influenced them to hold the opinions they profess is the first step toward finding a solution to their conflict.

Gloria and Ralph love each other, but Gloria's success has created dramatic changes in their relationship. As the result of her economic independence and the confidence that success has fostered, Gloria has become more "Americanized" when it comes to her expectations of what a relationship should be. She wants Ralph to love her for the person she has become, not for the caretaker she used to be. Ralph is trying to adjust to Gloria's new role, but he wants to be reassured that she still needs him and loves him—and respects him as a man. Both continue to struggle with the fears brought on by their changing lifestyle.

It will take time for Ralph to realize that Gloria's new role as a breadwinner doesn't threaten her role as a woman. Rather, her increased self-esteem is likely to make her feel more confident as a woman. Becoming successful doesn't mean that you have to leave your family behind or exercise control over others. Instead of feeling afraid and threatened by Gloria's success, Ralph can turn his fear into an invitation—an invitation to get to know a new part of Gloria and to celebrate her success with her.

Facing our fears means transforming them into challenges or invitations to learn more about ourselves and those close to us. Being open in this way is what leads to personal growth.

❦ Exercise
ARE YOU AFRAID OF YOUR WIFE'S OR YOUR OWN SUCCESS?

Remember I told you there were going to be some practical exercises in this book? Here is the first one, for both you and your spouse (or your novio/novia) to complete. Your answers will help you to clarify what you are feeling.

Men: (¿sí o no?)
1. Am I afraid that if my wife works outside the home, she will meet others with whom she will have more in common than with me—and that these new affiliations may lead her to be unfaithful?
2. Am I afraid that if my wife earns more money than I do, she will gain all the power in the family—and I will feel less of a man?
3. Am I afraid that if my wife spends too much time at her work, I won't get enough of her attention?
4. Am I afraid that my wife might become so successful that she won't appreciate me?

5. Am I afraid that if my wife becomes a career woman, she won't be the same family-oriented kind of woman my mother was?

Women: (¿sí o no?)

1. Am I afraid that if I become too successful, I'll betray my culture and family—and feel isolated and lonely?
2. Am I afraid that if I change too much and become too successful, my husband will think of me as tough and unlovable?
3. Am I afraid that if I spend more time on my career, my husband will retaliate by having an affair?
4. Am I afraid that if I do what it takes to become successful, I will lose the feminine, loving, nurturing qualities I also value?

If you feel ready, you can explore your answers with your partner. The goal is not to eliminate these feelings but to acknowledge your fears and to turn them into challenges and possibilities. Every relationship involves changes, and even positive changes can lead to feelings of fear and insecurity. But isn't it true that when we view our change-related fears in a more positive light, we can often see new choices that might actually make us happier?

A man like Ralph may come to realize, for example, that if his wife works outside the home, she will be more confident and feel better about herself and that this change will make her more pleasant to be around. So he learns that her change will actually benefit him as well.

A woman like Gloria, who faces the fear that her success will alienate her partner, could discover that he will be as proud of her as she is of herself. On the other hand, she may find that her success makes him pull away from her altogether but that she can survive being alone and can even meet new people who will accept her for who she is. Either way, she faces her fear and remains true to herself, allowing for the kind of relationships that will accommodate the person she has grown to be.

"IF YOU LOVE ME, YOU MUST LOVE MI FAMILIA TAMBIÉN"

A caller on one of my talk shows recently phoned with an urgent problem that brought her to tears as she told it. It seems that her brother was moving to the United States from El Salvador and wanted to live with her and her husband for a while. She had been married only a few months, and her husband, a second-generation Chicano, was vehemently opposed to his brother-in-law's moving in. Willing to lend him money and help him find a job and a place of his own, the husband was not willing to share his home with his wife's brother. The caller felt pulled in both directions. She understood her husband's feeling that they "needed their privacy" at this early stage in their marriage, but there was no way that she could turn her brother away. "He's my family," she pleaded. Unfortunately, her husband's point of view concerning who should live under the same roof differed considerably from hers.

It is customary in our countries of origin for us to welcome extended family members into our homes to live with us, should the need arise. Incorporating another relative into the household is not considered a big deal; it is even seen as a way to enhance the family's strength and cohesiveness.

One reason families are so important in the countries we've left behind is that the political environments are usually so unstable, and there must be a sense of stability somewhere or you wouldn't be able to cope. Families must be strong and provide that sense of enduring community. Such is certainly the case in El Salvador, where my talk-show guest was from.

Extended families are also the source of our emotional security and well-being here in the United States. Perhaps because we live within a larger culture, with which we don't always feel comfortable, big families give us a feeling of safety. Knowing that we're part of a large group of relatives takes the sting out of being a "minority." We want to be close to our own people. We need that.

In big cities, families often live close to each other—sometimes in the same building, sometimes down the block or a few blocks away. Even in poor families, when someone gets married, parents somehow make room for the young couple. In richer families, a home is made for the couple on the parents' property or nearby. It's the sense of wanting to preserve a tightly knit clan, keeping in close touch with one another, supporting one another. The mentality is that one more member of the family doesn't matter— "Donde come uno, comen dos" (Where one can eat, two can eat just as easily). That generosity of spirit is instinctive in Latinos.

On the other hand, the sense of privacy that so concerned my guest's husband is something people in the United States are very protective of. Privacy isn't a luxury; it's a necessity. Married couples need it, as do young single adults—even teenagers! Couples—especially newlyweds, like the Salvadoran woman and her Mexican-American husband—need their "space," and infringing upon it is considered neither proper nor courteous in the mainstream American culture. Asking a recently married couple if you can live with them indefinitely is not acceptable in this country.

In the United States, the phrase "single-family home" describes precisely who is meant to live within it: one family, consisting of a husband, a wife, and their children. Siblings do not live with each other once they're married, nor do adult children normally live with their parents.

Latinos who are more acculturated to the way things are here often find it hard to accept the fact that their parents or grandparents grant such a significant role to extended family members. They may enjoy the holiday parties with dozens of cousins, aunts, and uncles, but when the party's over, they want to go home to their own private "bachelor apartment" or "single-family dwelling." They want to be free to live their lives the way they design them, without interference from this great-aunt or that elderly cousin. They may choose to have special friendships with certain relatives, but they don't want their entire social life dominated by family members. And they don't want unsolicited advice from well-meaning relatives who do not share their aspirations or values.

Culture clashes within our homes can arise over just such issues. Hector, a thirty-year-old Puerto Rican from Manhattan, made a decision to leave his job as an electrician, take out a loan, and go to school full-time to study broadcasting. His wife of less than a year, Yolanda, endorsed his plan and agreed to postpone starting a family, so that she could continue working and supporting them while he attended school. But her family didn't like this idea at all, and they didn't keep their disapproval to themselves. Yolanda explains.

When I called to tell my folks that Hector had been accepted in the program, my dad screamed at me to put Hector on the phone. Then he screamed at Hector for about a half-hour straight, telling him he was nuts to jeopardize our security like this, to force me to support both of us, and to put off having children just so he could pursue some "dream fantasy," as my father put it. Hector tried to be polite and justify himself to my father, but when he got off the phone, he was really mad, and we ended up getting in a huge fight.

I tried to explain to him that my parents worked hard to get where they are. When they moved here from Puerto Rico in the 1950s, they struggled at whatever jobs they could find so that my sisters and I would have a more or less middle-class life. The fact that Hector would want to quit a job and give up a secure income to try something risky like learn how to become a disc jockey—with no guarantee that he'll find work—doesn't make sense to them.

Although Yolanda was behind her husband one hundred percent, she also defended her father's outburst. She saw it as concern rather than meddling. She understood that her father's behavior came from a place of love, that her parents only wanted the best for their daughters and were worried that this change in Hector's plans would put Yolanda at economic risk.

The history of Hector's parents is actually similar to that of Yolanda's mother and father, but they are much more accepting of their son's autonomy, and they trust him to make his own decisions. For this reason, Hector perceived his father-in-law's tirade as overly critical, intrusive, and inappropriate.

What Yolanda and Hector had to come to an understanding about was that their families are quite different, even though they come from the same culture. Yolanda's parents are much more Latino in their thinking; Hector's consider themselves to be fairly mainstream American in their outlook. The couple is therefore bound to clash when it comes to the issue of how much influence their parents ought to have in their lives.

The role of the extended family is very different in the United States from what it is in Latin countries, and Yolanda's family still holds on to the classic Latin belief that families stick together, no matter what. This means that members of your extended family not only share in your joys but also help out in any way they can when you are having a problem. Regardless of the fact that your children are adults living on their own, or married with a spouse who is technically only an "in-law," as parents you continue to be involved in their lives.

With respect to parents of a young Latina who has recently married, the ties are particularly strong. It is commonly said that a man may leave you, but you'll always have your parents and your brothers and sisters. So a young woman's family tries to be very supportive of her in her first years of marriage. At the same time, the son-in-law is considered to be almost on probation, not totally accepted until he has proven himself. It's as if the wife's family must make absolutely sure that he's going to do right by her before they give their stamp of approval.

Usually, a newlywed will take this attitude into account and do nothing to ruffle his in-laws, but Hector felt that his career plans didn't require the authorization of his father-in-law. Obviously, Yolanda's father felt differently. His feeling of connection to his daughter is as strong now as it has always been, and he considers it his duty to continue to look after her best interests.

Yolanda's sisters also feel as connected to her now as they did growing up. They see each other at least once or twice a week and talk on the phone daily. This, too, is often cause for Hector's consternation.

> I love my sisters-in-law. They're a lot like my wife, so how could I not love them? But I don't necessarily want them hanging out here every weekend, and for a while that's what it seemed was happening. They'd come over on Saturday for coffee or Sunday for lunch and then just kind of stick around for hours. It was like I never had the chance to be with my wife alone on the weekends. I finally had to confront Yolanda about this. She was hurt at first— claiming that I didn't love her sisters. I do love them, but I love my wife more. And she's who I married!

Yolanda views the situation from a different perspective. Having grown up in a household where relatives were always dropping in unannounced and staying for hours, she sees nothing wrong in her sisters' spending time with her at her place on the weekend. As is the case in many other Latino families, Yolanda's relatives feel at home in each other's residences, not just when they're invited for a special occasion but anytime. For them, "Mi casa es su casa" is not merely an empty cliche. It describes what they sincerely believe. "Hanging out" never requires an invitation—or even a phone call. Aunts, uncles, sisters, and brothers just show up. They may stay for a drink or a meal, or they may just drop in on their way home to catch up on the day's events or the family gossip. Whatever the circumstance, it's not like having company over. They're just part of the family. It's no big deal.

Yolanda is especially close to her sisters and considers them her best friends. Having to restrict their freedom to drop in whenever they want to feels wrong to her, as does Hector's apparent jealousy.

> *It would never occur to me to think that my sisters visiting with me in any way infringes on my relationship with Hector. I mean, it's not as if they're in competition with him. They're my family—and my closest friends. I would never be against Hector having his brother or close male friends come by and spend time, have a few beers, whatever. As far as I'm concerned, your home isn't just for the two of you, it's for your family and friends, too.*

Differences of opinion about the appropriate roles extended family members ought to play are bound to arise in Latino households. We come from a culture in which families are more involved in each other's lives than they are here in the United States. Usually, this is a wonderful bonus in our lives, but problems occur when what we take for granted as Americans clashes with these close family ties. Here are some of the ways in which the role of extended family members can create conflicts for Latino couples:

* rivalry/jealousy between spouse and in-laws;
* complaints that a spouse spends more time with his/her family of origin than with his/her own family;
* a sense of your privacy being invaded by extended-family members;

❦ lack of freedom to pursue your own goals because of pressure from extended-family members;

❦ differing opinions regarding family obligations.

Preserving close ties to our family of origin is so important to most of us that we need to do whatever we can to prevent bad feelings between that very special group of people and the new family we have created with our partner. While this harmony is not always easily achieved, we can set the right emotional tone by thinking about how lucky we are to come from a culture that values family so highly. Without the strong family ties that enable us to love and feel loved, our lives would not be nearly as rich. This doesn't mean that we can't make independent decisions or ensure the privacy we're entitled to, but it does mean that we can offer to our partner's extended family the same respect and warmth that we want our partner to offer to ours.

THE DOUBLE STANDARD—LATINO STYLE

Throughout this chapter, we've been discussing cultural attitudes in our Latino communities that can result in various relationship problems. This next concern, while widespread among the Latino population, is shared by women and men in every culture. Infidelity is not unique to Latinos, but those of us who believe that partners should be sexually faithful to one another often face a greater obstacle when it comes to this issue than do non-Latinos. The reason is that many Latinos still believe in the double standard—that it's okay for men to have affairs outside marriage but most definitely not okay for women. Not only do many married men feel that they have the right to engage in sexual activity with other women, they also believe that their wives ought to accept this behavior as normal, as part of what it means to be a man. Again, it's a macho thing.

Linda, a second-generation Mexican-American in her thirties, had to deal with the all-too-common problem of machismo and infidelity in her first marriage. She was brought up with traditional Latino family values that stipulated explicitly different roles for men and women. She was expected to marry and have children and was therefore never encouraged, as were her brothers, to have a career or a higher education. After high school, because she was the oldest child, Linda worked in order to help out with the family income. Then she married Eduardo, also a Mexican-American born in the United States. Eduardo was very domineering and believed that all decisions were to be made by him. He took the title "head of household" literally. Linda felt that their relationship should be more equitable but confessed that she might have been able to deal with the other aspects of Eduardo's macho behavior if it hadn't been for his infidelity.

> It really hurt me when I found out that Eduardo was having affairs. But what went beyond hurt to rage was that he felt entitled to have them! He hid them for a long time, he denied them. But when he finally admitted he was having sex with other women, he actually expected me to accept this about him. He told me a wife's role is to be home, to be with the children, to be a housewife, and that I had nothing to complain about because he always came home and was providing for me and my two daughters. I later found out that this kind of attitude was something he learned from his own family.

Eduardo's behavior had indeed been passed on to him, almost like a tradition or a family value. His mother had gone through the same kind of hurtful experience as Linda, but she put up with it throughout her marriage and never considered divorce. The Latino women of her generation were taught to look upon a man's extramarital affairs as something to be anticipated and tolerated.

Linda, on the other hand, who is much more acculturated than is her mother-in-law, could not simply look the other way. She has been exposed to a more liberated view of women, thanks to the women's movement, and she could not tolerate Eduardo's double standard. She said that she could never accept the habitual infidelity he felt entitled to indulge in.

But like so many women in her position, Linda's first inclination, when she discovered that her husband was having affairs, was to blame herself. She assumed that Eduardo's interest in other women had something to do with her own sexual inadequacy. Actually, the quality of their sex life had little to do with Eduardo's quest for sexual experience outside his marriage. In a sense, he was simply going through the same motions his father, grandfather, and great-grandfather before him had. He was proving his dominance over his wife, keeping up the image of being in control, and asserting his masculinity in what to him was a culturally acceptable manner.

As for their actual sex life, Linda said that Eduardo was as traditional in the bedroom as he was in other areas of his life. "He always had to be the one in control," she said. "So he was more or less in charge of when we had sex, how long it should last, and what kind of positions we used. He even told me when he wanted me to have an orgasm." Linda always felt that it was her responsibility to be available to Eduardo sexually, to fulfill his needs without really considering her own. She had been taught that a man's sexual needs were stronger than a woman's and that a wife's duty was to satisfy her husband.

Another aspect of the traditional Latino value system implies that it is a woman's role to be patient with her man, to help him change and overcome any bad habits. She is supposed to stick with him, right or wrong, no matter how much it might hurt her to do so. Fortunately, Linda had the strength of character to break with that tradition, as so many Latinas are doing these days. She refused to follow in the footsteps of her mother-in-law and accept a man's alleged "need" for extramarital affairs. "If Eduardo had said that he was sorry for his actions, or shown me that he wanted to change, I might have decided to give him another chance," Linda said. "But it was his arrogance, his insistence that he was entitled to behave in this way, even though it denigrated me and the whole idea of marriage. I just couldn't live with that."

It was only when Linda was faced with Eduardo's infidelity that she realized she could no longer be in a relationship in which she felt her own needs were constantly discounted. The "last straw" of infidelity actually proved to be a blessing, because it motivated Linda to seek a more fulfilling life for herself. In spite of her fears about going against her family's advice and about being alone, she divorced Eduardo and became more independent both economically and mentally. Knowing that she had to support herself and her daughters, she went back to school and then steered herself into a good career.

Once Linda started assessing what she wanted and needed from a man, she discovered that a good relationship is one in which both partners can be themselves, communicate freely, and derive pleasure and emotional support from each other. Here's what Linda has to say about her present husband, the changes she's gone through, and her attitude toward machismo:

> My second husband is also Mexican-American, and he's also traditional, but he's much more open to change. Most important, I'm a different person now. I'm proud of my career and the progress I've made. I stand up for myself more. But I must admit that I'm still attracted to strong men, to part of that "machismo" that Eduardo projected and that my present husband has in a more real way.
>
> My father set the standard for me, I guess. He was strong, someone you could depend on, someone who could make a decision, someone you could feel safe with. My present husband is strong in all those ways. But I've become stronger, too. Confronting my first husband's infidelity, going through with the divorce,

*starting out on my own taught me lessons about myself. I
remember my father telling me after my divorce, "M'ija, I don't
want to die without knowing you are with a man. You need
someone to take care of you." I know he meant well, but I told
him, "I don't need anyone to take care of me, Papa. I can take care
of myself."*

Usually, as Latino men become more integrated into American
culture, they relinquish their feeling of entitlement to habitual extramarital affairs. Still, this macho tradition lives on in some
Latino households. I think it's important to remember that men
are not just the product of their fathers, they are the product of
their mothers as well. Often, both parents instill in their little boys
the sense of being privileged in ways girls are not. Mothers, along
with fathers, can help prevent the "double standard" by teaching
their boys to respect girls and women and by sending their sons a
strong message: Women want loving, faithful husbands.

The Latino man's sense of entitlement to sexual relationships
outside marriage has been a fact of life for many generations, but
many men in our culture are now realizing that they don't need to
repeat the pattern they saw in their father's or grandfather's behavior in order to prove their own worth as a man. They have new
opportunities to show their maleness without hurting their wives
and children. Today, more and more Latino men are proud to be
faithful to their spouses, and they enjoy a closeness that is not possible when there is infidelity.

Another aspect of the double standard is that too often Latina
women are judged according to the madonna-whore, good
girl–bad girl stereotypes. Measuring a woman's character by how
closely she fits the virginal ideal, while steadfastly believing in a
man's right to be sexually promiscuous, is at the heart of the
Latino double standard.

Elizabeth, a single mother in her late twenties, told me that
she's reticent even to date men because of the pressure to have

sex. Becoming sexually involved with a man would mean that she would lose her ability to speak her mind and be herself in a relationship. She explained to me that she realizes that many Latino men not only don't respect women who have sex outside of marriage, but they are also threatened by strong, outspoken women—another aspect of their double standard. Separated from her husband, Elizabeth says that her first priority is her children, not male companionship.

> *Celibacy is very important for a woman. My sisters don't feel this way, they're much more open about sex. But I think once a woman has sex with a man, she stops being herself with him. She's afraid to be honest about what she believes and what she wants because she's afraid of being left by a man she's already had sex with.*
>
> *My husband is the only man I've had sex with, and he taught me everything I know. But that's okay. I think it's better to refrain from having sex than to do what a lot of American women do, which is give so much of themselves when they have a sexual relationship with a man. They open up a lot with a man, and men don't do that. So a woman leaves herself wide open for disappointment.*

What Elizabeth is saying is that women can retain more power within a relationship when they don't have sex with a man before marriage. They can remain stronger than women whose sexual involvement makes them more vulnerable. And feeling strong is important to Elizabeth. A third-generation Mexican-American, she has always believed that a woman needs to be self-confident and independent and never depend on a man for anything. In her family, many of the men were alcoholics, so the women had to rely on themselves to hold the family together. What is of the utmost importance to Elizabeth is that she is satisfied with herself. "My sense of pride," she says, "is what makes me a person."

Interestingly, Elizabeth's ideal man, as she described him to me, shares many of the qualities she values in herself. The key words are strength and self-confidence, but intelligence, vulnerability, and heart are equally important.

> I want a man to be strong. I see my ideal man as having strong features in his face but a softness in his eyes—because they are an extension of his heart. Hard-working hands, not afraid of hard work, but he doesn't have to use his hands, because he can use his brains. I want a man to be romantic, not afraid to be affectionate. And also to be his own man, self-reliant and independent. He should understand other men, which means not bragging or being competitive. It's more important that he compete with himself. He should be someone who doesn't have to put anyone else down in order to feel better about himself.

Linda also talked about strength when she described how her father "set the standard" for what she values in a man. But, like Elizabeth, she also spoke of developing her own strength, believing, as Elizabeth does, that women must rely on themselves for a sense of security and well-being. It seems that women like Linda and Elizabeth are emblematic of the way Latinas are blending aspects of Latino and American values to fit their experiences. Elizabeth and Linda are both strong women, committed to self-reliance, yet they are still attracted to the classic Latino image of a strong man. Their ideal man, however, combines that strength with the intelligence and sensitivity these women have also come to appreciate.

Elizabeth is mindful of the ways the double standard requires her to be more sexually restrained than either men or mainstream American women. But her belief in herself and her ability to "go for what I want out of life" illustrates how Latinas are in the process of changing a set of rules that has always proclaimed, "Men only, no women allowed."

FREEDOM OF CHOICE

Perhaps the most cherished aspect of being an American is our astounding array of choices, from our gigantic supermarkets stocked with an unparalleled variety of foods from all over the world, to our ability to settle anywhere in this vast and diverse country, to the privilege of making hundreds of personal decisions concerning how we wish to live our lives.

Our countries of origin seldom provide the breadth of choices this country does. And as Latinos, we often feel more comfortable with certain traditions that limit our choices. Living as close as we can to our families rather than moving away is one such tradition. Elizabeth's decision to limit her sexual activity to marriage is another. And the connection most Latinos have to the Catholic Church is yet another.

Carlos and Angela are a young couple whose cultural clash centered on Carlos' exercising his freedom of religious choice. Originally from Costa Rica, Carlos and Angela were married in the Catholic Church back home, and at that time they promised to baptize any children they might have. But after they settled in Los Angeles, the exposure to so many different cultures and religious traditions motivated Carlos to explore his spiritual beliefs. In the process, he abandoned his allegiance to the Catholic Church—a decision that created a serious rift between him and Angela. This is how Carlos explained the situation.

> *Being a Catholic was never a choice for me. It was part of my heritage that was never questioned by anyone in my family. But when I came here, I began to question a lot of things, including my religious upbringing. I could no longer accept the mandates of the Catholic Church or the sense of guilt they instill. A friend from work introduced me to the Lutheran Church, where I went for about a year. But something was still missing. Then I found that I*

felt much more sympathetic with Judaism, and that is what I have chosen for myself. This is okay with Angela, but she still wants to baptize our children in the Catholic Church, which I disagree with.

Angela doesn't consider herself very religious, but she finds that being Catholic is more than a religion. And for this reason, she feels strongly about preserving Catholic traditions for her children. Angela had this to say:

> *The Catholic Church is part of my family, part of my values, and part of my culture. So it's something I want to respect as a piece of my personal history. To give that up would mean giving up who I am. I want to pass on these Catholic values and culture to my children because I promised I would when we got married and because I would feel terribly sad if my children didn't have baptism and communion and everything else that goes along with being a Catholic. Carlos is entitled to choose for himself what church he wants to go to, but it's not fair that he deprive our children of something that is part of their cultural history.*

Religious differences is a new area of contention among Latinos. Since Catholicism is so dominant in our culture, and because most Latinos in the United States remain loyal to the Church, we are just beginning to face the kinds of compromises couples like Carlos and Angela must make.

Unfortunately, there is no magical formula by which husbands and wives can work out what's fair when it comes to their children's dual religious background. Such decisions are very personal and depend upon how much each spouse is willing to compromise, how deeply each feels about their religious beliefs and cultural values, and how similar or disparate the traditions are. Most religious leaders suggest that couples choose one faith or the other to teach to their children. They argue that trying to combine two religions (or even two denominations of the same religion) not only diminishes both traditions but also causes confusion in the minds of children. On the other hand, a more liberal strategy proposes blending aspects of both traditions and teaching children that both religions contain a basic faith in God and a belief in humanitarian principles. This approach involves informing children of the essential philosophies inherent in both religions, so that they can make an intelligent choice when they reach adulthood.

What Carlos' and Angela's dilemma points out is that new choices usually beget even more necessary choices. Not everyone feels comfortable with choices. Certainly it is simpler to stick to a path that involves fewer options and fewer decisions, because such a course requires less of the life traveler. But often it is the range of choices we're presented with that enlivens and enhances our journey.

WHERE DO YOU CLASH IN YOUR RELATIONSHIP?

As noted earlier, there are many influences affecting a couple's relationship—family history, economic circumstances, cultural factors, and each partner's own personal psychology. In these first two chapters, we have explored the ways that living between two cultures can affect your personal life. For example, such issues as the role of your extended family and the balance of power between men and women can create serious "clashes" in Latino marriages and relationships. Throughout the book, we will see how your unique family history can also affect the way you interact with your partner and children—and Chapter 7 will focus on learning more about your past in order to better understand your present relationship or marriage.

In the next four chapters, we will hear about the everyday issues today's Latino couples are grappling with—communication, sex, and parenting—as well as more serious concerns, such as infidelity, domestic abuse, economic stress, and racial prejudice.

But before we go any further, it will be beneficial for you to try to identify the specific "clashes" in your own relationship as accurately as you can, and to think about the kind of positive changes you would like to see happen. The following questionnaire gives you the opportunity to pinpoint the issues you're concerned about, so that, as we progress through the book, you'll be able to focus on those concerns that are most relevant to your life.

I use the words *spouse, husband,* and *wife* throughout the questionnaire, but many of these statements can certainly apply to novios or novias as well. Also, although the statements usually ask you to identify the problems you experience with your spouse, be clear about whose problem it is. Are you the one having difficulty "opening up" or listening? Are both of you equally guilty of being too critical? It is very common for one member of a couple to blame the other person. As you think about these areas of conflict, try to be as objective about your own behavior as you can.

❦ Questionnaire
WHERE ARE THE CONFLICTS EN TU CASA?

Rate your conflicts on a scale of 1 to 5. 1 signifies the conflict never occurs; 2 means it occurs only occasionally; 3 means it occurs about half the time; 4 means it occurs almost all the time; and 5 means it occurs all the time. If you assign a number 3 or higher, it is probable that you have identified a problem that needs your attention.

Cultural Clashes Regarding Extended Family

❦ I feel that my spouse's family interferes in our life too much.

❦ I feel that my spouse doesn't appreciate my family enough or show them the love and respect they deserve.

❦ We argue about how much time we should spend with our extended families.

❦ I feel that my spouse shows more love to his/her family of origin than he/she does to me and our children.

❦ My spouse expects us to contribute to her/his family's income, even though our own family's needs are great.

Cultural Clashes Over Male-Female Roles

❦ We argue about the proper roles for a woman and a man.

❦ My husband feels threatened because I have a job outside the home or a career that is more successful than his.

❦ My wife has lost sight of her responsibilities to her family ever since she started working.

❦ My husband doesn't feel that helping around the house is a man's job.

❦ My spouse doesn't spend enough time with our children.

❦ My husband is too macho.

❦ My wife is too bossy.

Other Cultural Clashes

❦ My spouse has become too "Americanized" and has lost touch with his/her roots.

❦ We disagree over the role the Church should play in our lives.

❦ My spouse often doesn't understand me or my family because he/she is not Latino.

❦ I have/my spouse has been the victim of racism, and this experience has taken its toll on our relationship.

Clashes in Communication

❦ My spouse doesn't really listen to me when I try to talk about personal issues. He/she is always impatient when I bring up certain subjects.

❦ My spouse has a hard time "opening up" and expressing how he/she feels.

❦ My spouse criticizes me when I try to express my feelings.

❦ My spouse always has to be right in any argument or discussion; we can never reach a compromise.

Clashes Over Sexual Issues

❦ My spouse always wants to have sex, even when I'm not in the mood.

❦ My spouse is often cold to me in bed, and I don't understand why.

❦ My spouse is not aware of my sexual needs and believes men ought to be "in charge" in the bedroom.

❦ My spouse doesn't tell me what gives her/him pleasure and expects me to know intuitively.

❦ Our sex life has become unexciting, and we don't know how to change the situation.

Clashes Over Infidelity, Abuse, Addiction, and Economic and Social Pressures

❦ My spouse is abusive to me and/or to our children.

❦ My spouse is addicted to drugs/alcohol and refuses to get help.

❦ My spouse feels that it is his right to have sexual affairs and that I must accept this way of life.

❦ I am/my spouse is under so much pressure regarding a work situation or a racial conflict that I am afraid I am/my spouse is beginning to take it out on the family.

Clashes Over How to Raise the Children

❦ We argue a lot about the best way to raise our children.

❦ My spouse doesn't spend enough time with our children.

❦ Our children are spending time with people who are a bad influence on them, and we don't know how to stop this behavior.

❦ We're worried about teen pregnancy, drugs, and gangs, but we disagree about what to do to prevent our children's involvement.

❦ Our children don't show enough respect to their elders.

Once we begin to confront these issues, we'll be better able to consider constructive solutions. Throughout the book, you'll hear about how others have dealt with these concerns, and I will offer suggestions, ideas, and advice for how you can deal with similar situations in your own relationship or family. The kinds of clashes listed above are the facts of our lives . . . let's face them together and learn how to create more harmonious relationships.

COMMUNICATION ES MUCHO MÁS QUE CONVERSATION

Alberto *and I are so alike in so many ways. We're both teachers, we enjoy the same music and books and movies, we laugh a lot, our grandparents even come from the same state in Mexico. But when we have an argument about something, we have very different ways of approaching it. He treats it like either a debate or a lecture, completely cut off from his feelings. I want us to talk to each other about how we feel, and to have him understand me.*

—Sylvia, age 32

Women *love to tell us that we don't know how to communicate our feelings! I don't hear this just from my wife, I used to get it from girlfriends, and from my sisters, too. What I want to know is, why does it always have to be their way? A guy has no problem communicating with another guy.*

—Alberto, age 30

Even when partners come from the same cultural background, they may still have very different perspectives. Each of us has a unique personality and a personalized set of values, beliefs, and needs. Each of us has been shaped by a distinct pattern of family dynamics, and our individual life experiences have influenced the way we think and relate to people. Our personal differences are what make life interesting, but they can also cause misunderstandings and conflicts.

The key to resolving conflicts within a relationship is threefold: learning more about yourself, so that you have a clear sense of your own feelings and values; listening to your partner's point of view, so that you can reach a solution which suits both of you; and being open to change—both within yourself and in the relationship. Honest and respectful communication allows you to work on each of these.

In this chapter we're going to answer Alberto's question—and that of many other men and women—once and for all: just what does it mean to "communicate your feelings," and why is that kind of communication so essential? And we're going to find out why openly expressing yourself, like Sylvia, is not the only thing you need to do in order to communicate effectively with your partner. Listening is equally important.

As each of you develops your self-awareness, and your communication and listening skills, you'll understand one another better and be better able to resolve your disagreements, both los grandes y los pequeños. And you'll also find that the closeness in your relationship is growing stronger, because open, respectful communication is what brings intimacy to a couple's shared life.

DO MEN AND WOMEN REALLY SPEAK DIFFERENT LANGUAGES?

Communication often means one thing for men and quite another for women, as Sylvia and Alberto so candidly confirm. Some say that this difference in communication styles is innate or biologically determined. Boys and girls, some experts believe, are "programmed" from birth to interact differently. I believe that the communication differences between the sexes are largely the result of the distinct sexual roles imposed by the culture.

In our traditional Latino cultures, men are expected to compete with each other, so that they can get ahead and provide for their families. Life for a man is like a race in which he must "win" over the others. In order to be successful in this race, he must hide his feelings, so that he doesn't show weakness or vulnerability. In terms of his family, a man is expected to use his life experience to guide his wife and children; he is expected to have all the answers to whatever problems or conflicts arise.

For women in our cultures, on the other hand, the world of connections is more important than is competition. Life is about being close to the people who are important to us; it is about community and intimacy. Women are expected to use their intuitive abilities to take care of everyone's emotional needs and to be the peacemakers in their families.

Keeping these traditional expectations in mind, it is not difficult to understand that for most men, communication means providing answers and supplying information; but for most women, communication means sharing thoughts and feelings. Let's take Alberto and Sylvia. She says that whenever she comes to him with a problem, not only does he become impatient with her, interrupting her before she is finished, but he also feels compelled to come up with a solution, rather than just listening to what she has to say.

> I've been very stressed out at work lately. The principal has been giving me a hard time, and I need someone's shoulder to cry on. I don't really want to cry, I just need someone to be on my side, to listen to me. I would hope that could be my husband, but Alberto doesn't understand what I need. He thinks he has to come up with some "immediate action" to solve my problem. And he gets angry when I don't take his advice. I'm not looking for that. I just want to talk things over with him, to get a little empathy and support. I want him to throw his arms around me and tell me

everything will be all right. That would give me the strength to figure out a solution on my own.

Alberto is baffled by Sylvia's criticism, because he believes that the appropriate response to his wife's complaints about her work is to help her figure out a plan of action for ways to deal with the principal. The problem between Sylvia and Alberto is that they have contrasting ideas about what it means to communicate with someone close to you. How can they get beyond this barrier?

The first step is to acknowledge the differences that exist and accept the fact that women and men frequently disagree on this issue. Instead of getting upset that Alberto reacts as he does, Sylvia can try to understand that he is responding out of love for her. His way of showing his support is not her way, but that doesn't mean he loves her any less than she loves him. Once Sylvia understands this, she can approach Alberto in a loving way to ask for what she wants.

I so often hear men complain that women expect them to be mind readers. "If she had told me what she wanted, I would have given it to her," they say. "But she thinks if I really loved her, I would know what she needs automatically!" When I reminded Sylvia of this statement, she said. "But if I have to ask him for a hug instead of advice, it wouldn't seem like it was coming from him." What I told her is that relationships are about learning from each other and that the only way Alberto can learn about Sylvia and what she needs from him is for Sylvia to tell him.

While men's and women's differing communication styles often present the kind of misunderstanding Sylvia and Alberto are grappling with, couples need not remain at an impasse. We must realize that we all have both "feminine" and "masculine" traits within us. We have the "feminine" attributes of intuition and sensitivity, which allow us to be creative and to connect deeply with other people, and we have the "masculine" traits of taking action and showing our strength, which allow us to get things done. If we stay rigidly within our traditional "masculine" or "feminine" roles, we limit ourselves and create unnecessary dependence on each other.

On the other hand, we can choose to develop those qualities that may be more apparent in our spouse than in ourselves and to learn from each other. In this way, we create a balance, within our own character and between us as a couple. Alberto, for example, can learn to develop the ability to be more empathetic, to be a better listener, and to express what he feels. And Sylvia can learn to be stronger and more forthright in asking for what she wants.

COMMUNICATION IS MORE THAN CONVERSATION

"I don't know what she wants," Ron complained to me on one of my call-in shows. "I talk to my wife, Tina, all the time about everything—about the children, about my job. I tell her what I do at work, what I do with my friends. So I don't know what she wants with this 'communication' she keeps bothering me about! Sometimes I think she's crazy." Tina grabbed the phone and spoke for herself. "I want to know more about what's going on inside him, how he feels about us, about how our relationship is going, about his plans and his wishes. But he doesn't get it!"

As we mentioned, many Latino men have been shaped by a culture that teaches them at an early age to be strong and autonomous, to avoid revealing any sign of vulnerability. When men like Ron are accused by their wives of not "opening up," not talking about their feelings, they often react with frustration and defensiveness. Because they were trained to be in control of their emotions, to be asked to abandon this training is an unsettling and scary demand. Rather than show that they're afraid of this kind of interaction, they get angry.

What had been happening with Ron and Tina was that they

were growing more and more distant, until finally Ron started thinking about divorce. The more Tina complained that he didn't open up with her, the further away Ron drifted. He withdrew from her and rarely talked to her at all.

Fear was at the root of Ron's withdrawal. His conversations with her never seemed to be enough for Tina, and yet the idea of becoming more emotionally intimate with her was completely unfamiliar to him. Although he couldn't acknowledge this, Ron's choices seemed equally frightening to him. Either he would not be able to give Tina what she wanted or he would be forced to engage in something he perceived as very threatening. His solution was to withdraw from Tina altogether.

As for Tina's part in the couple's communication problems, it seems that she did a lot of talking but wasn't a very good communicator. I could tell from the way she talked on my show that she had a lot to learn about what communication really is. She embellished what she had to say with lots of details and then repeated much of what she'd already told me. When I confronted her about this habit, Tina admitted that she was a "big talker." Even more self-revealing was her remark that "I think I talk too much in order to cover up what I'm really feeling."

Tina's long-winded one-way conversations overwhelmed Ron. They made him "disconnect" from what she was saying and prevented any meaningful dialogue between the two of them. Ron said, "She talks and talks, and I get tired of listening."

I told Tina that she needed to edit herself by determining beforehand exactly what it was she wanted to communicate. I told her that she should work on this step by first writing out the message that she wanted to communicate to Ron. Warning her that she might be tempted to write page after page, I told Tina that she should boil down what she has to say to one short paragraph. This process would force her to focus on the essence of what she needed to tell Ron.

Since Ron was having a problem expressing himself, saying that

"I tell her what went on during the day. I don't know what more to say. I don't know where to start," I gave him an exercise as well. He was to select a time every day when he and Tina would sit down together for fifteen minutes. He would use that time to communicate something simple to her. What he chose to say would be more than just a report of what happened during the day; it might be what he felt about what had happened that day. If he couldn't think of what to say, I told him, he should tell Tina what he was feeling at that moment. He should take deep, expanding breaths first, to relax himself and to get in touch with his own body, and then say what he felt as he looked at Tina, or what he felt looking at his children, or what he felt remembering something he had done in the past. These statements should be very simple, nothing "heavy" or momentous. In this way he would gain experience in spontaneously expressing his thoughts, ideas, reflections, feelings.

Like Ron, many men often think, "Oh no! My wife [or girlfriend] wants me to try to reach into my soul and talk to her about something so deep. This is going to be really draining!" For this reason, I told Tina that she would have to lower her expectations regarding the kind of conversations she wanted with Ron. Partners don't have to constantly discuss the deepest subjects or dramatically bare their souls in order to get close to each other. But as they begin to feel more comfortable with one another, they will find their communication becoming more effortless, more natural, more spontaneous. At that point, even a look into each other's eyes will communicate a lot.

Is communication within an intimate relationship something to be afraid of? Is it all about talking? What are the ingredients in healthy communication?

Communication is more than reporting what took place during the day. It is more than a conversation. It is the giving and receiving of each other's thoughts, feelings, doubts, joys. Communication enables you to understand each other, to work out solutions to your problems, to get closer. It doesn't mean seeking agreement on everything; but it does mean respecting one another. Communication holds relationships together by allowing for the free flow of emotions and ideas.

Beginning the process of meaningful communication involves effort, but it need not be intimidating. The goal is to honestly express what you want to say and to respectfully and attentively listen to what your partner has to say. Communication is not a debate or a chance to "win" an argument. Good communication opens the door to learning more about the other person and to feeling closer.

GUIDELINES FOR HEALTHY COMMUNICATION

I am so often asked to describe what good communication involves that I have come up with the following guidelines. As you read through them, try to truthfully consider how you usually communicate with your partner.

When You Are Speaking . . .

❦ Concentrate on a specific, personal issue. Don't make generalizations, such as "I always feel . . ." Talk about specifics, such as "Yesterday, I felt . . ." Also, don't generalize about other people, such as "Men always . . ." Focus on the two of you as individuals.

❦ Don't criticize or accuse the other person or make the other person feel guilty. No one likes to be judged, and criticism only makes the other person react defensively. Instead, use the phrase "I feel" to make statements about how your partner's behavior affects you. For example, "When you do . . . , I feel. . . ."

❦ Be honest. Even "kind lies" or "white lies" make us lose trust. We don't have to protect each other with lies, but we can be honest without being cruel.

❦ Be direct. Come right out and say what is on your mind, what you are feeling. Don't cloud the issue by talking about matters that are not relevant.

❦ Concentrate on the feelings behind the statements you are making. What are you feeling? Express that.

❦ Don't label your partner or engage in name calling, such as "You're such a liar . . ." or "You're crazy. . . ." Instead, describe the behavior that has made you upset and describe how you are feeling—for example, "When you don't tell me where you spend your time, it makes me feel angry and insecure."

❦ Express your feelings, but don't use them to intentionally harm the other person. Tell your partner that you are going to disclose your feelings and that your intention is not to hurt them but to explain how you're feeling.

❦ If you find yourself growing more and more angry, stop the conversation and say, "I need to stop here, because I can't control my anger. We can continue this conversation at such and such a time." Settle on a definite time to continue the conversation, then go off by yourself and write down or speak into a tape what is making you angry. What is the issue? Is it really what you've been talking about or does this issue remind you of something else that happened to you in the past? Or is your anger related to your partner's reactions during the conversation? The goal isn't to bury your anger, it's to figure out exactly what causes it, so that you will have greater control over it. Then, when you come back to the conversation, you will have a clearer sense of the specific issue you need to discuss.

❦ Don't monopolize the conversation or make a speech. Say what you have to say as clearly as you can, then give the other person an equal amount of time to talk.

❦ Don't say something merely to see how your partner will react.

❦ Don't inundate the listener with details, thereby forgetting the important things that need to be said. Concentrate on the main point you're trying to make.

❧ Don't change the subject. Stick to the issue that both of you have agreed to discuss.

When You Are Listening . . .

❧ Don't prejudge what your partner has to say. Try to keep an open mind, as difficult as that may be for you.

❧ Never interrupt or complete sentences for the other person.

❧ Seek to identify with and understand your partner. Put yourself in the other's shoes, however hard that might be.

❧ Make good eye contact with your partner as he is communicating with you. Don't look elsewhere when he's talking to you.

❧ Pay attention, not only to your partner's words, but also to her tone of voice, her emotional state, and her body language. Use these clues to deepen your understanding of what she's feeling.

❧ Indicate, perhaps by nodding your head, that you are, in fact, listening to the other person.

❧ Pay close attention to what your partner is saying, without jumping to a conclusion. Give yourself enough time to take in what they've just said and to understand their feelings about it, before you respond.

❧ If you find that you cannot listen any longer, tell your partner as much and explain why. Use "I" statements, such as, "I feel that this conversation is overwhelming . . ." or "I feel that this is too much for me at the present time." Then commit to continuing the conversation at another time by saying something like, "Let's get together later this afternoon [or tomorrow, at such and such a time], and we'll continue."

When You Respond to What Your Partner Has Just Said . . .

❦ Before you respond by stating your own feelings and thoughts, first acknowledge to your partner that you have heard what he just said by repeating the essence of what he's just communicated to you. Phrase your statement like, "I hear you saying that you feel . . ." or "If I understand you correctly, you are saying that. . . ."

❦ Don't draw conclusions for the other person. Respond on your own behalf, concentrating on how you feel about what he's just said.

❦ Never criticize your partner's feelings. You may not understand why your partner feels as he or she does, but there is no such thing as "wrong" feelings.

❦ Don't accuse your partner of not telling the truth.

❦ Don't ridicule the other person or use sarcasm or jokes in response to something said seriously.

After the Dialogue Has Ended . . .

❦ Don't use what your partner has told you about his thoughts or feelings to later incriminate or punish him. Such behavior would greatly inhibit his willingness to share his feelings with you in the future.

Communication should always have the goal of inviting the other person to get closer. If both of you can keep this in mind, you will prevent your dialogues from degenerating into a series of recriminations that will only create more distance between you. Often the best way to get closer to someone you love is by saying very little, keeping an open heart, and just listening.

The next part of this chapter will highlight three key relationship concerns, each of which can be improved with better communication between partners:

- ❦ feeling distant from your partner;
- ❦ feeling stuck in the same argument;
- ❦ holding different cultural ideas about the perfect marriage.

Once you identify the issues that apply to your relationship, you can try some of the suggestions and exercises offered.

FEELING DISTANT FROM YOUR PARTNER

By now you understand that good communication involves two basic skills: honestly and respectfully expressing how you feel, and attentively and respectfully listening to what your partner has to say. But how do you get started, if you and your partner have never known how to talk intimately with each other or if you used to be closer but have somehow drifted apart?

You might begin by saying something like, "I want to talk to you about something that's bothering me. I'd like you to listen to me, and I am not going to blame you or criticize you. I just need to tell you what I'm feeling." This kind of approach invites the other person to be receptive, because you are talking about how you feel rather than what the other person has done wrong. Since there is no accusation in your statement, your partner will not be pushed into becoming defensive.

It's also very important to begin by identifying your underlying feeling—whether it is pain or anger or sadness or irritability. This information will alert your partner to the reason you are bringing up a particular issue. Sometimes accurately acknowledging and stating how we feel is the most difficult aspect of open communication. Women often have a hard time admitting anger, for example, because it is a culturally unacceptable emotion for us. Similarly, many men can't admit to feeling sadness or hurt because these emotions tend to signify weakness in Latino cultures.

Approaching your partner with the need to talk on an intimate level, accurately identifying your feelings, and letting go of your old styles of communication can be quite difficult at first. But like any other change you want to make, the new way becomes easier the more you become accustomed to it. The first few times you approach your partner in this new way, you may feel that your words sound awkward or unnatural, but that awkwardness will subside as both of you become more experienced in this new closeness and honesty.

In order to help couples begin this unfamiliar way of communicating, I often suggest that they try the Expressing, Listening, and Repeating Exercise, which I have adapted from a technique called the Mirroring Technique, created by Dr. Harville Hendrix. This exercise basically accomplishes two purposes: it helps partners to articulate their feelings and issues more clearly, and it helps people become better listeners, more receptive to what their partner has to say.

This exercise is especially useful for Latino partners, because we tend to come from families in which often more than one person speaks at the same time. When two or more people are talking at once, it's difficult for either one to really listen and reflect on what the other is saying. You may hear the words, but you're not really listening. The Expressing, Listening, and Repeating Technique allows you to listen carefully and reflect on what your partner is telling you.

If you decide to try this exercise with your partner, reading through the examples first will give you a better idea of how it works.

❦ Exercise

THE EXPRESSING, LISTENING, AND REPEATING TECHNIQUE

This exercise gives both people an opportunity to:

- ❦ express their thoughts and feelings,
- ❦ be accurately heard by the other person,
- ❦ listen attentively to the other person,
- ❦ accurately hear what the other person has to say.

This exercise may seem tedious at first, but if you stick with it, you will be surprised how much you'll learn about yourself, your partner, and your process of communication. It is extremely important to be patient when practicing this exercise, especially when you are talking about feelings that are apt to be misinterpreted. So often when we listen to someone during an argument, we make false assumptions or draw inaccurate conclusions based on what we hear. This technique allows you to correct those false assumptions immediately, so that you are both dealing with the same accurate information. Only after you have both honestly expressed yourselves and been accurately heard can you begin to think about how to resolve your problem.

Here is how the exercise works. One person is the "communicator" and the other is the "listener."

Step 1. The *communicator makes a brief statement*, beginning with the word *I*, in which the listener is briefly told what the speaker is thinking or feeling.

Step 2. The *listener repeats* what the communicator has just said.

Step 3. The *communicator verifies* that what has been repeated was indeed the message that was communicated.

Step 4. If the message has been heard incorrectly, the *communicator corrects the listener's version* of the message. (This step is very important, since one of the main purposes of this technique is to make certain that the communicator's message is not misinterpreted by the listener.)

Step 5. The *listener restates* the message, until the communicator can verify that the message has been heard correctly.

Step 6. The *communicator may now choose to add to what she has already said*, so that the listener can understand more fully how she feels.

Step 7. Once the communicator is satisfied that she has said what she wanted to say and that the listener has accurately heard her, the *communicator and listener switch roles*.

Here is a sample of how The Expressing, Listening, and Repeating Technique can be used to deal with a fairly simple problem. In this case, the wife is upset because her husband always forgets her birthday. She takes on the role of communicator first.

COMMUNICATOR: When you forget my birthday, it makes me feel sad. (Step 1)

LISTENER: So you're saying it's my fault that you're sad, because I don't remember your birthday—right? (Step 2)

COMMUNICATOR: No, that's not what I said. I said that when you forget my birthday, I feel sad. (Step 4)

LISTENER: Okay. I hear you saying that when I forget your birthday, you feel sad. (Step 5)

COMMUNICATOR: Yes, that's what I said. (Step 3)

COMMUNICATOR: One of the ways I show you that I love you is to remember things like your birthday. So when you forget my birthday, it makes me feel that you don't love me. (Step 6)

LISTENER: So you're saying I don't love you as much as you love me. (Step 2)

COMMUNICATOR: No, that's not what I said. I said that when you forget my birthday, I *feel* that you don't love me. (Step 4)

LISTENER: So you're not saying I don't love you. You're saying that you *feel* unloved when I forget your birthday? (Step 5)

COMMUNICATOR: Yes, that's what I said. (Step 3)

Let's listen to the same couple as they switch roles. (Step 7) Notice that the communicator begins by expressing his feelings, and then briefly explains why he feels this way. It is always important that the message be as brief as possible, so that the listener can easily understand the message without forgetting pieces of it.

COMMUNICATOR: When you tell me that it makes you sad if I forget your birthday, I feel angry. Because I do love you. I just show it in different ways—like providing a good home for us. (Step 1)

LISTENER: I hear you saying that my message made you feel angry. And I also hear you saying that you love me, but you have a different way than I have of showing love. I can understand how my statement would therefore make you angry. (Step 2)

COMMUNICATOR: That's right. That's what I said, and that's how I feel. I appreciate your understanding how I feel. (Step 3)

Another important part of this technique, as exemplified by the listener's last sentence, is for the listener to *empathize* with the communicator by offering a statement like, "I can understand how you must feel." This kind of response helps both partners to identify with and feel supported by the other. When you can do so, even in the midst of a serious disagreement, you create a positive feeling between the two of you, which then makes you more willing to work together to come up with a solution.

And what might the solution be for the couple dealing with the issue of "olvido de cumpleaños"—forgetting a birthday? Since the wife initiated the discussion, she needs to take responsibility for her hurt feelings by suggesting a possible solution. She might choose one of the following statements that offer solutions to the problem.

❦ "I would like it if you wrote my birthday down on your calendar, so that you won't forget it. Celebrating my birthday with you means a lot to me."

❦ "I enjoy a special dinner or getting flowers or other romantic gifts on my birthday. If you did this, it would mean a lot to me."

❦ "I will make sure to remind you that my birthday is coming up, so that you won't forget. When we celebrate special days together, it makes me very happy."

In this exchange, the wife is not blaming her husband for the ways his past behavior has affected her. She has told him why she feels the way she does, and she is offering a solution, so that her feelings won't become hurt in the same way again.

FEELING STUCK: HAVING THE SAME ARGUMENT OVER AND OVER

Do you and your partner repeatedly argue over the same issues without ever arriving at a resolution? Many couples have told me that most of their quarrels boil down to the same underlying argument. Each time a quarrel breaks out, they becomes stuck in the recurring contest to prove that one is right and the other is wrong. They may make up temporarily, in order to live together peacefully, but the basic disagreement remains unresolved—and therefore reappears during their next quarrel.

If you'd like to be able to resolve the recurring arguments in your relationship, you may want to try a quite simple procedure. It involves asking for what you want and giving what you can give. You begin by telling each other four things: what you appreciate about each other, what you would like to request of each other, which requests you would like to fulfill for the other person, and which requests you cannot fulfill.

Beginning this process by telling your partner what you appreciate about him or her enables you to create a more respectful, loving atmosphere, so that you can go on to confront areas of ongoing disagreement and work out how you can each satisfy the other's requests.

We hear so much about "compromise" when it comes to relationships and marriage, but to some of us the word means never getting what you want. I believe that two people who are essentially compatible can both get most of what they want in a relationship if they are flexible enough and willing to give to the other person in return. If you and your partner can come to a discussion with open hearts and talk about those areas where each of you would be willing to give the other person what he or she wants, I think you will discover that you can both be happily satisfied.

If you would like to take your Asking and Giving discussion to a more formal level, you can try the following exercise.

❦ Exercise

ASKING FOR WHAT YOU WANT, GIVING WHAT YOU CAN GIVE

When you and your partner are feeling stuck, this exercise helps you to distinguish between those things you can change and those you cannot.

Here are the steps in this exercise.

1. Write out a list of ten qualities you appreciate in your partner; title this list, "What I Appreciate About You." Once you have written your lists, exchange them. As you read what your partner has written about you, pay attention to your feelings. Receive the appreciation of your partner and feel it with intensity.

2. Next, make a list of ten things you want to request of your partner; title this list, "My Requests." When you have both completed these lists, exchange them. When you receive your partner's list, read it very carefully; then take turns asking each other to explain anything on the other person's "Request List" that isn't clear.

3. Each of you will then make a list entitled "My Commitments." The list should include those items from your partner's "Request List" that you are definitely willing to do. Your commitments should represent those elements of your own behavior or attitude that you know you can change without difficulty.

4. The next list will be entitled, "My Good Intentions." This list should consist of those items from your partner's "Request List" that you are willing to do but that you need some time to accomplish. Make a second column next to each of these elements in which you write down how long you think it will take you to master them.

5. The next list will be entitled, "My Limitations." This list will enumerate those elements on your partner's "Request List" that you are definitely unable to do because they are either not within the realm of your own capabilities or they go against your values or wishes.

6. Now share with each other your "Commitments," "Intentions," and "Limitations" lists and talk about them. Discuss with your partner the possible difficulties that may arise in attempting to fulfill the other's requests, but at the same time, try to focus your energy on opening communication between the two of you. Concentrate on each other's willingness to make commitments and to put forth good intentions rather than on the frustration regarding each other's limitations.

This method of sharing your appreciation, your commitment to change, and your recognition of what you cannot change helps both of you to grow as individuals and as partners. As you explore together the possibilities for ways your relationship might improve, you will find yourselves becoming allies rather than adversaries.

HAVING DIFFERENT CULTURAL IDEAS ABOUT THE PERFECT MARRIAGE

Learning to respect our differences and communicate more honestly also involves reflecting on the cultural values we bring to our relationship. Acknowledging the ways your concept of "the perfect marriage" has been influenced by both your Latino background and the mainstream American culture in which we live, may help you understand the communication problems with your partner.

As you think about what it means to be a loving husband or

wife, and as you become more aware of the cultural beliefs that underlie your and your partner's picture of a good relationship, you will gain new insights into why you think the way you do. This new understanding can pave the way toward creative solutions that you and your spouse can both feel good about.

Think about what it is you really want from your marriage. What matters most to you? Does your relationship currently reflect any or most of these attributes? Where do you think you got your ideas about the ideal marriage? Would you characterize these ideas as more "Latino" or more "American"? Do these values come from your parents and grandparents, from your friends in the community, from the mainstream American culture, from your religious beliefs? Have these ideas changed over the years? Why did they change? And how would you like your marriage to conform more closely to these ideals?

Talk to your husband or your wife about these things and discover what your partner thinks about the ideal relationship. Where did her ideas come from? How realistic is his picture of the ideal marriage, and how realistic is yours? What can each of you do to make your marriage reflect your values? Which ideals are impractical or inappropriate to the two of you? Talking openly with your mate about the "Latino" and "American" aspects of what each of you perceives to be the "ideal marriage," presenting your "wishes" for ways you would each like the relationship to change, and discussing realistic compromises are much more productive than harboring resentments or making demands.

If you and your partner would like to explore your cultural attitudes about marriage in greater detail, you may want to try the exercise entitled "Our Intercultural Picture of the Perfect Marriage."

❦ Exercise

"OUR INTERCULTURAL PICTURE OF THE PERFECT MARRIAGE"

Doing this exercise together will not only help you to understand yourself and your partner better, but will also enable you to work out solutions you can both accept.

1. Write down three qualities that make up "the perfect marriage" from the Latino point of view and three qualities that make up "the perfect marriage" from the American point of view.
2. Next to each quality, describe where you learned about it (for example, from an uncle, a teacher, the media, the Church), why it is so important to you, and how this particular quality makes you feel.
3. Exchange the descriptions of these six qualities with your partner and give yourselves some time to read what the other has written.
4. Using the information from what you have both written, come up with "Listas de Deseos" (wish lists) that state ways you wish your partner might alter their culturally influenced behavior. Include how that change would make you feel.
5. Exchange wish lists and give yourselves time to read them.
6. Discuss your wish lists and decide which wishes you want to turn into goals. Goals are the specific behaviors you want to incorporate into your relationship.
7. If you disagree on which wishes should be turned into goals, be very clear about why you won't accept a particular quality that your partner wishes for. Just saying "No" because "I don't want to" is not enough. Offer your partner honest reasons why you find it hard to go along with one or another of

their wishes. If your partner really wants to introduce a particular quality into the relationship, be willing to hear what they have to say, to empathize, and to try to understand why this is so important. Suggest possible ways to compromise, so that each of you gets something you wish for.

8. Discuss with your partner what you are going to do to achieve the goals you've chosen together. Your discussion may include: leaving yourself notes around the house to remind you of your goals or visualizing the desired behaviors you have both agreed upon. (See Creating a Wish List Exercise that follows at the end of this chapter.)

The following is an example of how the Intercultural Picture of the Perfect Marriage Exercise works. A husband's "Latino Picture of a Perfect Marriage" might include the following:

Quality:

Having a wife who enjoys the preparation of special family meals.

Where I learned it:

From my Puerto Rican family—parents, aunts, uncles, grandparents.

Why this quality is so important to me:

I remember being at my Tía Blanca and Uncle Ray's house and looking forward to sitting down at their table. The act of preparing a meal was an act of love, because Tía Blanca put so much into it. Not just cooking, but giving something of herself. She took the time to prepare delicious and wholesome food and always presented it beautifully, with the table nicely set. Sharing a meal like that was like a gift she gave every day to my uncle and to her whole family. I want to experience that kind of thing in my relationship.

How this quality makes me feel:

It makes me feel special and loved.

This same husband's "American Picture of the Perfect Marriage" might begin this way:

Quality:

Having a wife who contributes to the family income.

Where I learned it:

My Tía Clara, and the American culture in general.

Why this quality is so important to me:

Although I take pride in providing for my family, I want to feel that I'm more than just a paycheck. Tía Clara went to work after the kids were in school, and that really helped out her family. But Tía Blanca never worked, which meant that Uncle Ray had to have two jobs. He was always tired, and he missed out on a lot that was going on with his own kids. I don't want that to happen to me. I want our family to have a good income, but I also want to spend time with my wife and children. If my wife worked too, we could share the responsibility and wouldn't have to worry about money.

How this quality makes me feel:

This quality would make me feel that my wife loves me for more than just my provider role. I would also feel secure in knowing my wife could support herself if I died.

The following is how the above husband might translate his Latino and American ideal marriage qualities into a wish list:

"I wish you were willing to find a job, so that I don't have to be the sole provider for the family. This would make me feel less stressed out and more loved."

"I wish you would cook a special meal for me once in a while, even though I understand you're busy with the children and many household chores. This would make me feel special and loved."

After this husband combines his wish list with his wife's, and they discuss which qualities are most important to them, they can decide which wishes they want to pursue as goals.

❦ *Visualization Exercise*
CREATING A WISH LIST

1. For behaviors that are distinctly "Latino," put on taped music from your country of origin; for "American" behaviors, choose appropriate music and play it softly while you do the visualization.
2. Close your eyes and do several minutes of deep breathing.
3. Focus on the first quality from your wish list. Feel it in your body, through your senses. Think about it in your mind. Let yourself fully enjoy the sensations and thoughts surround-

ing this quality, and experience the good feeling as you visualize how you will incorporate this quality into your relationship. Give yourself five minutes to fully enjoy this sensation, imagining yourself and your partner embodying this new attitude or taking on this new behavior. Notice your surroundings. Receive a warm feeling from this experience. (Don't think about how these behaviors might conflict with your present life or how others might perceive you. Just enjoy your experience of how it would feel to include these behaviors into your life.)

4. Write down your experience of this visualization exercise, then share what you've written with your partner.

5. Choose another quality from your wish list, and go through the visualization exercise again.

THE VALUE OF DISAGREEMENTS

When I was younger, before I married and before I became a psychologist, I used to think that a good relationship meant being with someone who was so similar to me that we would never have fights or disagreements. I envisioned the perfect relationship as one in which both people share the same values, ideas, desires. "Why," I used to ask myself when I was a teenager, "would couples stay together if they continued to have quarrels?" I told myself that I would never settle for anything less than "armonía" and togetherness when I married.

When we're teenagers, we tend to think that everything has to be perfect. But life teaches us differently. Now, when I look back at my early vision of the "perfect relationship," I smile to myself. Actually, I think it would be pretty boring to be in a marriage in which the two people agree on everything. There would be no incentive to learn from each other, to consider other ideas and

points of view, to question your own values, to see yourself differently in another person's eyes. None of these things is possible if
your partner always agrees with you.

Differences and disagreements with our spouse help us to explore aspects of ourselves that otherwise might remain unexam-
ined. They help us stretch our consciousness and expand our
sense of what is possible in love and in life. It is only by interacting with someone who embodies different characteristics that we
can evaluate our own qualities and discover new directions we
may want to take.

This is not to say that conflicts with those we love are necessarily welcome. Usually they are not. It is not always easy to work
through our disagreements, and serious conflicts often cause us a
lot of pain. But in the sense that they require us to look more
deeply at our own emotions and behavior, to reconsider our concepts of right and wrong, to figure out new ways to get along with
the person we've chosen as our mate, or even to finally break away
from an unhealthy relationship, conflicts can be viewed as very
beneficial.

It is amazing how the simple "act" of shifting your attitude or
changing your perspective can often create an enormous change
in your life. When we approach disagreements with a new openness to learning about ourselves and our partner, not only do we
find it easier to resolve our differences, we also find ourselves developing into more enlightened individuals.

HOW COMMUNICATION EXPANDS YOUR LIFE

Human relationships offer us the incomparable opportunity to enhance and expand our lives. When we're born, our mothers and
fathers give us love, encouraging us to love back and to decode
their loving expressions and words. We learn what language and

love are about, and we become both more knowledgeable and more loving. In this process of growth, our life expands.

When other relatives and friends care for us and show us attention, we further develop our ability to relate to people. We learn from them and expand our sense of who we are in relation to others. When we go to school, our classmates and teachers open our eyes to new worlds, new information, new ideas. Again, our consciousness and our life grow to encompass what we have learned from and about other people.

Just as traveling to a foreign country is a uniquely enriching experience, those of us who are immigrants, who permanently settle in a "foreign" country, can't help but broaden our perception of life. We're continually in the process of incorporating different viewpoints into our thinking and our behavior. We are exposed to new norms, new ideas, new rules, new choices—especially in this country, which includes so many ways of living and being. We learn to communicate and get along with people whose traditions are vastly different from our own. As we adapt, we enlarge the scope of our lives and expand who we are.

Adult intimate relationships offer us perhaps the greatest opportunity for personal growth. In the process of conveying to our partner how we feel, what we want, what we're afraid of; listening to his or her fears, needs, hopes; and learning to accept and respond to our differences—we develop aspects of ourselves that we might never have discovered on our own. It is in this sense that communication expands and enriches our life. By learning about our partner, and sharing ourselves with them, we become more than we were on our own: more expressive, more self-aware, more empathetic, more open-minded, more insightful, wiser.

Communication is about more than talking. Sometimes it doesn't even involve words. Ultimately, it is about the interchange between two souls. It is two beings bridging the distance between them by reaching toward each other with openness, compassion, and understanding.

In the next chapter, we will explore the uniquely intimate form of communication human sexuality affords us. And we will discover that the same qualities that are so necessary for healthy communication—empathy, understanding, self-awareness, open-mindedness—are integral to a healthy and fulfilling sexual life as well.

LATINO LOVERS
UNDER THE SÁBANAS

I **am** *still a young woman, but I feel like my body is dead. I don't feel any sexual excitement when my husband and I make love, and I have never experienced an orgasm. I thought sex with my husband would be so wonderful, but I am so disappointed, and I keep wondering what is wrong with me. I feel like an incomplete woman.*

—Mariana, age 28

M**ariana** *and I were passionate for each other before we married. We could hardly keep our hands off each other. She felt so much desire for me then. I don't know what happened. I want her to enjoy sex, but it doesn't seem that it is something she likes. I never imagined this would be what our married life together would be like.*

—Ramón, age 30

E xpressing your love sexually can be one of the most inti- mate ways to communicate with your partner. Sexuality is a language all its own, and it can bring passion, pleasure, com- fort, and a particular kind of understanding to your relation- ship. It allows you to share emotions with your partner that cannot be conveyed any other way.

But sex is also a form of communication that is frequently

misunderstood, and it can create conflicts for even the most well-intentioned couples. In my practice I hear from women who claim that they are incapable of enjoying sex. Others come to me complaining that their husbands demand sex all the time, regardless of the woman's desire. Husbands tell me that they don't understand why their wives don't want to have sex as much as they do. On the other hand, some men are confused and intimidated when women begin to take the initiative sexually, thereby taking on the "masculine" role.

Although we live in a time when openness about sexuality is becoming more common, in our private lives many of us still feel shy about discussing sexual issues with our partner. It is helpful to know that many people have similar difficulties and to realize that talking about them is the first step toward a more pleasurable sex life.

As Latinos, we bring to our sexual relationships a unique set of cultural values, and often these are at the root of certain conflicts in the bedroom. Sexual roles and taboos promulgated by both traditional Latin culture and the Catholic Church can't help but affect our attitudes and behavior when it comes to sex—and we'll be talking about this at greater length later on in this chapter.

Sexual dilemmas may also be a reflection of problems in your relationship that have either been ignored or inadequately addressed. If issues between the two of you go unresolved, they frequently wind up being fought over "under the sábanas," sometimes unconsciously. Unacknowledged anger or resentment, for example, can have a very harmful effect on your sex life. One of the goals of this chapter is to help you recognize the root of your sexual problems. Once you turn your attention to resolving trouble spots in the nonsexual part of your relationship, you pave the way for improvement in your sex life as well.

In this chapter, we are going to be very honest with one another. We're going to discuss intimate sexual matters, as well as strategies for overcoming the sexual and philosophical differences you and your partner may be experiencing. My hope is that, in hearing the stories of women and men like yourself, you will gain an understanding of your own sexuality, so that this part of your life can be a satisfying and joyful one.

MARIANA AND RAMÓN: REDISCOVERING THE PLEASURE OF SEX

The above brief excerpts from Mariana and Ramón's story leave us with a kind of mystery. What happened to Mariana's passion? She and her husband are two young people, deeply in love, who once felt mutual desire. Why are they now having problems expressing their love sexually?

Mariana was a virgin when she married. Her Catholic upbringing dictates that saving yourself for your husband is the proper and moral way to deal with your sexuality. Interestingly, the result of this belief was that in the two years prior to their marriage, Mariana and Ramón played around a lot sexually, never actually engaging in intercourse but exciting one another in a variety of physical ways. During these times, Mariana would become extremely aroused. At times, she even came close to orgasm. She envisioned that her actual sex life, once their wedding day was behind them, would be explosive. Both she and Ramón expected her to feel the same level of excitement, if not greater, during intercourse that she had felt during their two years of premarital sexual play.

The clue to Ramón and Mariana's sexual "mystery" lies in the physical experimentation they engaged in prior to their marriage. What had excited Mariana so intensely then was the fondling, touching, rubbing, and kissing that are distinct from actual sexual penetration. Once she and Ramón began to have sex, however, this kind of sexual "play" stopped. Ramón assumed that the sex act by itself would be more than enough to arouse Mariana as she had been aroused by their foreplay prior to marriage. He was wrong.

Women and men have very different sexual styles. Women usually require more time, more caressing, more fondling, before they can become aroused. The insertion of a penis into a woman's vagina is generally not enough to kindle her desire or to bring her to climax. Not only are most women's bodies calibrated for a slower sexual pace than men's, but often women like to be invited into a seductive, romantic atmosphere. A feeling of tenderness needs to be established before most woman can respond physically.

Unfortunately, both Ramón and Mariana were unaware of this process. Neither had received this kind of sexual information, either from parents or friends when they were young or from a professional once they were adults. Mariana felt so ashamed of being an "incomplete" woman, that as her sexual dissatisfaction grew, she unconsciously cut off whatever feelings of physical desire she might have had.

She also secretly began to resent Ramón, because she had trusted that he would "show her the way" sexually. She had assumed that, as the man, he would know just what to do to excite her and masterfully orchestrate their sex life.

One of the sexual issues Latinos have to deal with is that many of us believe that the man is the one who knows what is best, that he is the one who has all the sexual knowledge and experience. What many women don't realize is that a man's erotic experience is not necessarily vast, and even if it is, it may not be at all helpful to his understanding of the sexual needs of the woman he is presently with. Even if a man has had a lot of sexual relationships, every one is unique. Whatever happens between two people is a unique experience for both of them. So having "vast experience" doesn't really count. What you learn about the technical part of sexual intercourse doesn't constitute the art of making love,

which is a creative rapport two people develop between themselves.

Once we understand what it really means to make love with
someone, we know that what applies to one lover doesn't necessarily apply to another. There's no such thing as having "experience with women" or, for women, having "experience with men."
Sexual experience may give you an understanding of how your
own body responds, what it is that you like, and what it is that you
appreciate in someone else, but you still must learn, step by step,
about your present partner and how the two of you come together
sexually.

For anyone to assume that a particular position or technique is
foolproof is foolish. We women share a general physiology, but our
bodies respond differently; our personal psychological makeup
also dictates how we react to certain sexual activities. And the
same goes for men.

In the case of Mariana and Ramón, his previous sexual encounters do not equal a "degree in lovemaking," which would
somehow guarantee him automatic success in sexually satisfying
Mariana. Both of them need to learn about their own bodies, their
own emotions, their own sexuality, and what brings them pleasure. Then they can share that knowledge with one another. In
this way, together they can create a loving sexual connection.
These steps will be a learning experience for both of them that requires time and understanding and patience, and it can only be
pursued when both people trust and are committed to one another.

Developing a satisfying sexual life together doesn't happen
overnight; it's a process that unfolds within the day-to-day context of a loving relationship. Once Mariana and Ramón understand this, they will realize that Ramón's past experiences cannot
be used to magically transform Mariana into a sexually responsive
partner. The two of them must explore sex together, so that their
unique, shared sexuality can emerge naturally.

Another factor affecting Mariana and Ramón's sexual relationship is one that applies to a number of conservative Latino couples. Ramón's premarital sexual relationships were confined to
so-called one-night stands. This habit arose because of the very
taboo Mariana referred to in explaining why she remained a virgin until marriage: "Nice girls wait." In the eyes of many people in
our culture, therefore, the women who don't wait are worthy only
of fleeting encounters. But being with a woman one time only is
vastly different from pleasing one woman over a period of months
or years. A man like Ramón, who has been with a number of
women but has never sustained a long-term sexual relationship,
probably has very limited sexual knowledge. And, more important, being with a woman you don't respect or love is nothing like
making love with someone you love and to whom you have committed your life.

So let's see how Ramón and Mariana went about solving their
sexual difficulties. I helped Mariana to understand that her body
wasn't "dead," as she claimed; it was merely asleep, and she had
put it to sleep herself. All of us have the capacity for sexual pleasure, and if we don't experience it, it's often because we've anes-
thetized our body for one reason or another. Mariana had turned
off her sexuality because her shame at not being a "real" woman
and her disappointment with Ramón for not taking charge were
overwhelming. In turn, her lack of interest made Ramón feel inadequate and disappointed in himself; his own sense of shame at
not being able to arouse Mariana and make her enjoy their sexual
relationship only made matters worse.

Mariana's body had certainly been very "awake" when she and
Ramón were boyfriend and girlfriend, and what they both had to
do now was rediscover those feelings. Remembering the kind of
sexual play Mariana had responded to before marriage, they now
needed to go back to that sort of activity. Passionate kissing,
fondling, and caressing could be brought back into their physical
relationship.

I often suggest to women that they explore their own bodies, to discover all the areas that are arousing to them. I encouraged Mariana to experiment alone, maybe with some body lotion or oil, touching herself all over to find out what parts of her body are more sensitive than others and just to know how her own body feels. She might start far from the genitals and slowly move to the genital area.

I also like to suggest that women look at their genital area, because this part of our body is hidden from our eyes. One can use a mirror to see herself there. And she can also look at her entire body, not to see if she has more fat than she would like, or to compare herself to other women, but just to look at how nature has made her own body so unique. When she is by herself, she can look at herself, feel confident, feel fine about herself. It is so important for us to admire our own uniqueness and to love it. Learn to love what we've got, whatever that may be.

Before touching Ramón or letting him touch her, Mariana needed to admire and feel comfortable with her own body and to realize that it's hers. Because some women tend to feel that their body exists primarily to be given to their partner, it's important to establish that sense of ownership. A woman needs to own her body before she can fully share it with her companion.

As for Ramón, he needed to know that he was definitely capable of giving Mariana pleasure. Understanding that he was feeling frustrated at being unable to excite Mariana, I reminded him that he had given her immense pleasure before marriage and that he could do so again. Because men tend to evaluate themselves in terms of actions and their immediate results, Ramón had to be convinced that just because it wasn't happening at the moment didn't mean that he wouldn't be able to arouse Mariana once again.

I encouraged Ramón to reevaluate Mariana's needs, to go back in his mind and remember what it was that was so exciting to her before. He also had to understand that, for women, sexual motivation is not merely physical. In addition to touching and fondling, there are elements that precede foreplay—the loving gestures that happen even before a couple begins to touch.

Most women need to be in a romantic mood in order to disconnect from the everyday world and connect with their lovers. Preoccupied with so many concerns—our jobs, our kids, the laundry, the meals—we need time to detach from our day-to-day life, so that we can transfer all our energy to that intimate moment. Transforming into our sexual self requires creating a certain mood and romantic space. Most women appreciate it when a man gives them care, understanding, and affection; it inspires them to passionately join with that other soul who wants to interact sexually with them. If that kind of caring isn't demonstrated to a woman, it is usually very difficult for her just to have sex and derive pleasure from it.

Ramón thought that the only thing that was missing in his relationship with Mariana was sexual intercourse. He had already completed the "courting" part of the relationship before they married, and he assumed that Mariana knew how much he loved her and how deeply he felt for her. "Why do I have to perform that Latin lover role again and again, when she knows how much she excites me?" he asked me in all sincerity.

My answer was that, for Mariana as for many women, courting is a lifelong need. Even after marriage, most Latinas (and non-Latinas!) require that the romantic aspects of the "Latin lover" be present if they are to be fully aroused. The stereotypical boastful lover who counts his numerous conquests or judges his sexual success according to how long he can sustain sexual penetration usually holds little interest for women. But the romantic lover whose aim is to focus his full attention on the woman he loves, who appreciates her, and who takes the time to find out what takes her breath away—this kind of "Latin lover" will be rewarded with the reciprocal love of a passionate "Latina lover."

When a woman thinks about the ideal way of being loved, it is in terms of being lovingly seduced with words or other means of expressing, "Mi reina [my queen], there is no other woman like you in the world." A woman wants a man to make her feel, through all the things that come before sexual intercourse, that she is exquisitely loved. When a man makes his lover feel special, she will react by making him feel adored, and that's how mutual communication in bed begins: both partners enjoying making the other feel cherished, making the other one feel like mi rey or mi reina.

In addition to the emotional expressions of love that are so important, there are various physical techniques that are especially pleasing to women during lovemaking—massaging each other, playing with each other's bodies without sexual intercourse, touching all the places on each other's bodies except the genitals, so that desire has a chance to build, and talking in erotic terms (if that kind of talk is pleasing to both partners) are all effective means of pleasuring and exciting one another.

Ramón needed to understand that a woman often requires more time to become aroused than a man does and that gentle, tender foreplay is especially important to Mariana. For her part, Mariana needed to be much more specific about what gave her pleasure, showing Ramón what she liked instead of being vague and expecting him to read her mind about her preferences.

As Mariana and Ramón became more aware of the many dimensions that play a part in creating passion between them, Mariana's body began to awaken from its sexual slumber. And as a result, both are rediscovering the excitement and deepening the connection that initially brought them together.

JUAN AND LUPE: WHY DOES HE WANT SEX ALL THE TIME?

Probably the most common sexual problem I encounter in my practice is the situation in which a man wants sex more often than his wife does and pressures her to oblige him, regardless of her feelings or desire. Sometimes this conflict leads to quarrels that may not even be related to sex. In extreme cases, the "pressure" builds up, and sex can become forceful.

Fortunately, Juan and Lupe's situation didn't reach that point. Married seven years, with three children, they say that they rarely have arguments or serious conflicts. But the discrepancy in their sexual urges was a problem that had both of them constantly on edge. Here's what Lupe had to say about the difference in their sexual appetites.

> Juan wants to have sex at least once a day, if not more. For me, I usually feel like it only on the weekends, when I'm not so tired. But if I tell him I'm too tired, he gets upset and thinks I don't love him. It's just that when I get home from work, there's the children to take care of and the house to clean. I'm exhausted at night. Who has the energy for sex?

Men often desire sex more frequently than women and become resentful when their partner isn't available to them. But there's much more to Lupe's story than the scenario she describes. What she doesn't mention is that Juan brings to their marriage a set of very conservative Latino beliefs. He was raised to think that having sex as often as possible confirms a man's masculinity. For the most part, Latino men are taught, in a nonverbal way, that having frequent sex is what helps to define a male. For a married man, frequent sex becomes a requirement. How often you have sex is much more important than the quality of the experience. When I mentioned to Juan that, according to recent research, most couples have sex only once or twice a week, he was shocked!

Juan also clings to the notion that it is a wife's duty to fulfill her husband's sexual needs, regardless of her own. He was brought up with the belief that the way your wife shows you that she loves you is by having sex with you whenever you want. Sex is the way many

Latin men communicate love, and they assume that if a wife doesn't want to receive this love, she must be lacking in love for her husband. In Juan's mind, Lupe's lack of sexual desire was irrelevant. The fact that Lupe's sexual needs were overlooked by Juan was central to their dilemma.

This situation touches on the issue of female sexuality, a topic that was ignored in Latino families like Juan's. Even in mainstream American homes, a woman's sexual needs were generally not considered important until sexual mores in this country underwent fairly radical changes during the late 1960s and early 1970s. One of the offshoots of the women's movement was the belief that women ought to be able to enjoy sex as much as men, to assert their own sexuality, and to become more than simply the recipients of a man's desire.

But for many men like Juan, the belief remains that women don't have the same sexual appetite as men. "If a woman enjoys sex," so the thinking goes, "fine." If she doesn't, it's a part of her role as "pleaser" to please her man in this area.

And even those men who are aware of women's sexual needs tend to feel that a woman ought to be more flexible when she's "not in the mood" and understand that men need sex more often. There are many husbands who contend that their wives should have sex with them even when they don't particularly feel like it, as a way of showing their love and commitment.

Another factor that figures into Juan's desire for sex all the time actually has little to do with his sexual appetite. Frequent sexual activity is a way for Juan to allay his sense of insecurity concerning Lupe's new independent status as a working woman. Over the past several years, Lupe has gone from a stay-at-home housewife and mother to a secretary with a good job and a steady income. Although he finds it difficult to discuss this crucial change in their family dynamic, Juan's sexual compulsivity is a reflection of his urgent need to feel dominant over Lupe. Sex is an unconscious way to reassure himself that, even if his wife is establishing herself outside the home and earning as much as he is, he's still the man of the house. Feeling in competition with Lupe's stronger identity, his response is to assert his power sexually.

What about Lupe's side of the story? Although she talks about being too tired to want sex, what she doesn't say is that Juan feels that it is not his obligation to share the kinds of domestic duties she must attend to every evening after work. Like Juan, Lupe was also raised in a traditional Mexican family, in which women were expected to see to all the housework and child care. One of the ways a woman proves her love for her husband is to clean the house and take care of the children. Taking on these responsibilities while also holding down a full-time job was not a problem for Lupe, nor was attending to Juan's sexual needs. But his insistence that they have sex every day, whenever he wanted it, whether she was exhausted or not, finally made her snap.

Ever since she had taken the secretarial position, Lupe felt a greater sense of confidence in herself. And living part of her life in the working world she had the chance to become exposed to more mainstream values concerning men and women and the way they treat each other. She began to see that a woman has a right to expect a certain kind of treatment from her husband and that she has a right to say whether or not she wants to have sex. Lupe slowly began to acknowledge to herself that she resented Juan for his unwillingness to help out around the house, his insensitivity to her needs, and his unreasonable sexual demands.

Finally, she was willing to confront Juan with her dissatisfaction. Getting up the courage to talk to him about these issues was an entirely new role for Lupe. She had always believed that a wife should satisfy her husband emotionally and sexually as a sign of her love for him and that she should not complain even if she was "not in the mood." Speaking up for herself was indeed a significant change.

But Juan and Lupe's sexual relationship couldn't change for the better until certain fundamental aspects of their overall relation-

ship changed first. Most importantly, they needed to be more open
with each other and more understanding of each other's perspective. What Juan needed to do more than anything else was to
learn to listen to Lupe and understand her feelings. Once he could
do this, he might be able to relax some of the cultural expectations
that placed Lupe in the role of pleaser rather than partner. Juan
would have to learn that when a woman feels both respected and
nurtured, she is much more likely to feel a deepened intimacy toward her mate.

Like many other women whose husbands want sex more frequently than they do, Lupe was not only overburdened by household chores that made her too tired for sex, she was also bored at
the prospect of daily sex. She wanted sex to become more than
just another chore she had to perform each day. She wanted to
feel special to her husband, and she wanted him to take the time
to seduce her. Juan had to discover ways to make Lupe feel that
sex was more than a wifely duty. He had to make her feel loved
every day, as an invitation to intimacy, as a preliminary condition
for making love.

Lupe felt that Juan became romantic only in bed. That was the
only time he approached her tenderly. But the kisses and the hugs
he gave her had no real meaning for her, because they were always
given so that she would have sex with him. Instead, Juan's loving
approach needed to be a daily thing, included in other moments
and times of the day, so that Lupe could feel that Juan really loves
her. In this way, having sex could become a continuation of that
loving feeling of everyday life, not just an act that has no connection to Lupe's emotions.

I also suggested that Lupe and Juan work out a more equitable
way of dealing with the housework, so that Lupe would no longer
be carrying the entire burden by herself. Since both of them came
home from their jobs tired and worn out, it was only fair that they
share the chores and child care. I explained to Juan that this
change in his routine would be very beneficial to him. If he did his

share of the housework and parenting, Lupe would no longer harbor the resentment that was hurting their sex life. Rather, she would feel more loved and appreciated by him. Further, by becoming a more equal partner in the domestic life of his family, Juan would become more emotionally attached to his children and feel more connected to the activities of the household.

I explained to Juan that when a woman feels that her man is giving to her in a nonsexual way, she is much more likely to open up sexually than she will if she is seduced in purely sexual terms. By participating in the household chores and child care, or by listening to what Lupe has to say about how her day went, Juan will be creating a closeness between them that is a prerequisite for authentic intimacy. Lupe will doubtless respond by feeling more loving and more willing to engage in sex.

For her part, Lupe needed to understand Juan's feelings of inadequacy that stemmed from her new role outside the home. She had to find a way to let him know that her success at work didn't mean that she loved him any less or that he was in danger of losing her. Even when she didn't feel like having sex, she could be affectionate toward Juan and let him know that he is special to her.

In addition, Lupe could consider opening herself more to the pleasure of sex—not the experience of pleasing Juan, but pleasing herself. If she were willing to acknowledge that sex is sometimes an opportunity to relax, to feel good, to release herself from daily pressures, she might find herself enjoying it more. Even when she's not particularly "in the mood," she could approach lovemaking with a new openness, with the anticipation that she was about to experience something very pleasurable.

Lupe and Juan had to begin the challenging process of sexual reconciliation. They needed to bring their sexual wishes out into the open so that they could then infuse their sexual encounters with more intimacy. Juan was to tell Lupe what he wanted for their sexual relationship, and Lupe was to do the same. They agreed to do so without amending or criticizing the other's wish list. The object was for both of them to hear what the other person wanted and to experience being heard in turn.

Lupe had mentioned that when they had sex, it "always follows the same pattern," so I also suggested that they try a new approach. By giving their attention to the many little sensual acts of lovemaking that precede sexual climax, they could both enjoy their sexual encounter more fully and discover how pleasurable it can be to take your time. Enhancing the quality of their sexual experience would mean not only that Juan would focus less on how often they made love, but also that Lupe would actually look forward to sex as a rewarding experience instead of considering it a marital obligation.

❦ Exercise

SLOWING DOWN AND INTENSIFYING YOUR SEXUAL ENCOUNTER

Many couples wish that their sexual encounters could be more exciting and varied. Here is the "prescription" I gave Lupe and Juan, and I highly recommend it to any couple, especially those of you who feel that your sex life has become too mechanical, dull or routinized.

First of all, designate a specific time to enjoy this experience to the fullest—and make it your "special" time of the week. Choose a time when neither of you feels rushed or tired. Make a conscious decision to take the focus off the "climax" of your sexual encounter; instead, plan to make your lovemaking session last as long as possible.

Avoid becoming too aroused too quickly by not touching the genital areas at first, enjoying each moment rather than anticipating your orgasm, and building up very, very slowly. If the man feels that he is becoming excited almost to the point of orgasm, try doing something different to divert attention from climaxing. Slow yourselves down by dancing, bathing each other, talking to each other about how wonderful you each look or smell, stroking and playing with the nonerogenous parts of the other person's body. Explore each other's neck, back, arms, fingers, legs, ankles, face. Discover your shared sensuality using all five senses:

Hearing. Talk to each other, using exciting words; or listen to stimulating or exotic music.

Sight. Look at each other without speaking or touching; rediscover the uniqueness of the other person's face and body; and enjoy being watched.

Touch. Use your fingertips, the backs of your hands, and the palms of your hands to feel your partner's skin, bones, and hair. Use small, circular strokes. Experiment with feathers and other pleasing textures.

Smell. Burn aromatic candles or incense to intensify the sensual mood; or use scented oils to slowly massage each other. Smell each other's natural essence. Bathe each other using special fragrant soaps and shampoos.

Taste. Kiss, lick, and taste different parts of each other's body—especially parts you may have ignored before.

As you let yourself go and really enjoy all your senses, you'll find that a new sexual dimension opens up. Orgasm is no longer the goal, because you are focused on the moment-by-moment sensual pleasure you are giving and receiving. You let orgasm come only when you're ready to conclude this fascinating and pleasurable shared time together. Once you have experienced how varied and fulfilling this kind of lovemaking can be, having intercourse without such relaxed, creative exploration will seem incomplete.

On the other hand, we should not expect that sex will always be an intense, deep, or intimate experience. Just as we don't have exquisite feasts every day, every time we're to-gether sexually will not be an extraordinary or profound event. We have casual dinners, we have quick lunches, we have snacks; and in the same way, our sexual appetites vary with our moods and needs. All the levels of sex are welcome, including the "snacks" or "quickies." For men especially, the quickies are sometimes very important. So if a woman likes the prolonged gourmet dinners, and her husband likes the quick snacks, they can enjoy the snacks on some days and the lavish dinners on others.

What I want to emphasize is that once the two of you have experienced a richer sexuality, it will open up a new level of intimacy that will then improve all your subsequent lovemak-ing. And you will find that you don't need to have sex every day or more than once a day, as Juan had expected. Rather, you will come to intimately understand the striking difference between quality and quantity.

RAQUEL AND TONY: GIVING YOURSELF PERMISSION TO TOUCH

For many of us, knowledge of sexual matters is sketchy at best. We pick up a little information in sex-ed classes at school and from our parents, friends, and older siblings, but what we come away with is not always accurate or helpful. In addition, we are brought up with many cultural beliefs that result in confusion, misunderstandings, and disappointment when it comes to sexual pleasure.

We've already mentioned that many women are raised to think that their husbands will teach them everything they need to know about sex, that women are just supposed to lie back and let their husbands lead the way. Traditional Latino culture also sets forth the notion that a woman must look to her man for sexual fulfillment. He is responsible for arousing her, satisfying her, bringing her to climax. The possibility of self-pleasuring for women is rarely alluded to.

For Raquel and Tony, it was Raquel's discovery of self-pleasure that was central to liberating and enriching their sexual life together. Raquel talks about the problem that led to this discovery:

> We had been married about six or seven years, and I usually experienced sexual pleasure when we made love, but my sexual satisfaction was always dependent on whether Tony touched me in a certain place, my clitoris. I could only have an orgasm if he touched me there. Sometimes he would do it, but sometimes he wouldn't—and I would get angry inside of myself when he didn't. Because I told him that's what makes me have an orgasm very easily. But he wouldn't do it all of the time. I didn't always want to have to ask for something I had already told him I wanted. I felt inadequate and humiliated to have to ask over and over, like "Hey, do me this favor." I preferred to keep it to myself, but my resentment against him grew.

Raquel's problem became more complicated when, during one particular lovemaking session, she asked Tony to stroke her clitoris, and he responded by telling her to just touch herself. Raquel then felt even more humiliated, because she strongly believed that this was something Tony was supposed to do for her, and not anything she should do to herself. She had never approved of masturbating, and in fact, had never touched her own genitals, either as a teenager or as an adult. When she was a child, not only had she never touched herself, she had never looked at herself or noticed the sexual parts of her body. Now she not only felt that Tony's suggestion was a terrible rejection, she also believed that what he was suggesting was somehow immoral.

Certainly, part of Raquel's bias against masturbation has its roots in her Catholic upbringing. The Catholic Church has always condemned masturbation and is responsible for striking fear into many a young boy's heart with its warnings against the practice. Such cautionary advice and reprimands after the fact were traditionally aimed only at boys, since the Church could not even acknowledge that girls might engage in such an act.

In fact, until fairly recently, even those who considered themselves open-minded with regard to sexual matters thought that masturbation was appropriate only for boys and men. Female masturbation was pretty much assumed to be a contradiction in terms. The implication was that males engage in masturbation because their sexual drive is so much stronger than a woman's. A woman would have no need to touch herself, and if she did, there must be something wrong with her; perhaps she was "oversexed." Of course studies now verify that women also have strong sexual drives, and that these drives are definitely present to varying degrees in adolescent girls and women of all ages.

What the erroneous perceptions and moral prohibitions surrounding masturbation added up to for Raquel were fear of and aversion to the idea of touching and pleasuring herself. There was something very distasteful about Tony's suggestion, and she was not going to do it.

Then an interesting thing happened. Raquel had held a part-time job as a teacher's aide but found a better position working for the local government. She started earning a higher salary; just as important, her new job made her feel much more self-confident and self-reliant. She came out of her shell socially and made a number of new friends, with whom she felt comfortable talking and sharing her feelings.

Little by little, Raquel's new energy and openness translated into her willingness to be more sexually experimental. She gave herself permission to touch herself, to excite herself during both foreplay and intercourse. She discovered that not only was she enjoying sex much more, but so was Tony. He found it very exciting to watch Raquel stimulating herself and deriving more pleasure from their sexual encounters. So Raquel's act of self-stimulation became a way for both of them to become more aroused. Tony and Raquel are now enjoying a much more diverse and satisfying sex life because Raquel was open-minded enough to alter her preconceptions about what "should" and "shouldn't" happen under the sábanas.

JORGE AND VILMA: WHO CONDUCTS THE ORCHESTRA? WHO PLAYS THE MUSIC?

I have received many calls on my radio talk show from listeners who are almost too embarrassed to ask the question. But the fact that they were motivated enough to make the call means that their problem is one that definitely needs to be addressed. In Jorge's case, he had a hard time coming out with just exactly what was bothering him.

JORGE: My wife and I don't talk about these things but I know from previous experiences that . . . well, and I've heard my friends discuss it, and I've seen enough movies to know that . . . actually, it probably isn't that big of a deal, but I think our sex life would be a lot better if . . .

ME: It's okay to ask me, Jorge. We are here to talk openly. I am a professional woman, and I hear things like this all the time. It's part of my job.

JORGE: It's just that . . . she only wants to make love in one way . . . I mean . . .

ME: And what position is that?

JORGE: You know, the usual one.

ME: With you on top?

JORGE: Yes. And I know that this is not the only way to do it, that you can do it in many other ways. But I think she's afraid. I've tried to get her to trade places with me, but she doesn't seem to want to. It's probably not that big of a deal, is it?

ME: It must be, or you wouldn't have called.

Many women share the reluctance of Jorge's wife, Vilma, to make love in any manner other than the "receiving" position. This fear or uneasiness comes from sexual inexperience and insecurity. For so long, women have been taught to be sexually passive that even in this day and age, such conditioning persists. Vilma probably feels at a loss being on top of Jorge, or sitting on him, because she has fears of being inadequate, of not knowing exactly what to do, of being incapable of giving him any pleasure if she is "in charge."

As Jorge and I talked further, it became clear that, indeed, Vilma admitted to feeling much more comfortable sticking to one position, because this way she knew Jorge would take the lead. She had also told him that sex was not as important to her as it was to him. "So, how can I be in charge?" she had asked. My professional experience and intuition told me that it wasn't a question of sex being less important to Vilma; rather, she didn't feel confident about changing the sexual pattern that had been established between her and Jorge. Here's how the call proceeded.

ME: I want you first of all to focus on communication, talking and sharing with each other. And then—

JORGE (interrupting): But I don't see how talking is going to help! That's not what this is all about.

ME: You want to become more intimate, right? And for Vilma to feel more relaxed and creative in bed?

JORGE: Yes.

ME: Then I want you to do the following exercise, which will help you to understand each other better. I want you to tell Vilma what you experience when you're on top. How enjoyable is that for you, and what exactly do you feel? Then, I want Vilma to describe to you how it feels for her to be on the bottom, what she senses and what that is about. Perhaps you will say something like, "Being on top means I can move however I want to. I can direct our sexual experience, like conducting the orchestra. I can set the pace, and create the kind of music I want to hear." And Vilma might respond, "Being on the bottom makes me feel loved, treasured, adored. I feel stimulated knowing that I am the inspiration for your sexual creativity, for creating that vibrant music." When the two of you have this conversation, when you share with each other how your sexual roles make you feel, it will be an invitation to the other to switch roles. Then you can start experimenting with one being the conductor and the other being the inspiration, or perhaps both of you being both parts simultaneously. Next, you can come up with new parts, new sounds, new movements, freeing yourselves from any particular role. Because there are no limits to your sexual creativity once you are open to the possibilities. Are you willing to try this experiment, Jorge?

JORGE: It will be difficult, the talking part.

ME: Well, just see if you can do it. . . . And call me back to let me know how your relationship is going. Okay?

Jorge did call me back several months later. And guess what? The "talking part" was very successful. As they started to share with each other how they felt in bed, he and Vilma felt closer to each other and more relaxed about trying different positions and roles. Vilma was relieved to learn that Jorge also felt insecure at times, that he also doubted his sexual competence. She was not the only one! Ironically, although Jorge had always tried to show her that he was in control and sexually sure of himself, his honesty and openness were what finally made Vilma more willing to experiment sexually.

After Jorge phoned that day, I reminded my listeners of something that his and Vilma's story brings up: whatever you do within your own four bedroom walls is absolutely acceptable. You can do whatever you want, as long as both of you are willing and comfortable. Knowing that there are no taboos, no set role one partner or the other must always play in bed, both of you can open your minds to anything you want to include in your sexual "orchestra."

One of the keys to a satisfying sex life is openness. There is no specific position or series of positions that will guarantee the ultimate erotic experience. The important thing is that, as you both allow yourselves to be more open with each other, you will feel increasingly free to experiment with different positions and different styles in bed. Discovering your own sexual frontiers and inviting each other to be as uninhibited and creative as you like will not only intensify your sexual intimacy, it will also enhance your lives and your relationship outside the bedroom.

❦ A Word About Erotic Films and Literature

Some couples who want new ideas of what to do sexually turn to erotic films for unexplored possibilities. If this activity is something that sounds appropriate for you, remember that pornography is usually designed for men, and the images portrayed in these films don't necessarily suggest the "right way" to have sex. Pornography is not an example of what sex is supposed to be, because there's no way a movie can capture the level of intimacy you are experiencing. But viewing such films may excite you and your lover and stimulate your imagination. You may, for example, be inspired to come up with new, unusual positions or with creative environments in which to make love.

It is very important to remember that pornography or erotic films are not for everyone. If they are unacceptable to one or the other of you, they should not be included in your shared sexual activity. It is never appropriate to force your partner to do anything that he or she finds distasteful. The religious beliefs of some people prohibit the viewing of such films, and others find this type of material derogatory to women. I would like to mention, however, that there are some pornographic films that do not exploit women. There are also movies that are more subtly erotic ("soft porn"), and women usually find these more arousing than overt pornography. Interestingly, more women are now producing and directing pornographic films, introducing erotic elements that are more appealing to women. *The Wise Woman's Guide to Erotic Videos*, by Angela Cohen and Sarah Gardner Fox, is an excellent guide to nonsexist porn and soft-porn titles.

Reading erotic literature to each other can also be an interesting way to begin a lovemaking session. Books leave more to the imagination than films do, an attribute that many find much more exciting. Some of the world's most esteemed writers have written erotic poetry, short stories, and novels. *Twenty Love Poems and a Song of Despair* by Pablo Neruda is one of my favorite collections of love poetry, and many of these poems are elegantly sensuous and erotic. Lonnie Barbach's *Erotic Pleasures: Women Write Erotica* and *Erotic Interludes* are two tantalizing, women-friendly literary collections.

TERESA'S FANTASIES: AS OUR LIVES CHANGE, SO DO OUR SEXUAL DAYDREAMS

Unless we repress them, all of us have sexual fantasies. Those who repress their fantasies do so because, for one reason or another, they cannot accept the sexual thoughts or images that originate in their own "uncensored" minds. Some believe, for example, that entertaining fantasies about a man or woman other than their partner is the same as actually being unfaithful, and therefore they feel the need to strongly reject these fantasies in order to comply with their sense of morality.

But it is natural to have sexual fantasies. They may occur at different times to different people: during sexual inactivity, during masturbation, or during sex itself. It's important to understand that our fantasies may or may not bear any resemblance to our actual desires. We may fantasize that we are making love in an unusual setting or with an unlikely partner, but such imaginary events don't mean that we actually want to engage in the behavior.

Fantasizing about sexual encounters provides mental stimulation to our sexual yearnings, and the "meaning" of our fantasies is often difficult to discern. Sometimes the content of our fantasies may disturb us. Such was the case for Teresa.

She told me that in order to achieve orgasm, she had to fantasize that she was being raped or touched against her will. The circumstances varied slightly, but the common theme was that, without her consent, a stranger was forcing her to become aroused. This is how Teresa described her recurring fantasies:

> One fantasy always starts out that someone is forcing me to have sex, and it is not really what I want. This kind of rape is not a violent rape, it's not a rape where I am in pain, but a stranger grabs me and in some way imposes himself on me, and I let myself be raped. There's usually the feeling that this man can't help himself, that I have turned him on so much that he's gone crazy almost. And this excites me. Then I experience the pleasure of sex, even though it's with this stranger and I didn't ask for it.
>
> Another fantasy is of being touched in different situations where

I didn't solicit it. For example, I'll be trying on clothes in a changing room, and a male salesperson comes into the room and touches me, and I begin to enjoy it.

What is the meaning behind Teresa's fantasies? Is she secretly wishing to be taken by force or to be raped? Actually, her mental scenarios have nothing to do with a masochistic desire for violence or abuse. It is not uncommon for women to have violent sexual fantasies; these are completely unrelated to the disturbing flashbacks (not fantasies!) experienced by women who have been actual victims of sexual abuse. Violent fantasies simply allow non-victims like Teresa, who may have repressed or ambivalent feelings about sex, to experience pleasure without feeling guilty.

Teresa was raised with the idea that the only thing men want from women is sex. She learned from both her mother and her grandmother that sex is not enjoyable for women; it is a duty you have to perform as a wife. Her mother and grandmother didn't exactly come out and say these precise words, but as a little girl, Teresa got the sense that sexuality was degrading to women.

Even though Teresa enjoyed sex with her husband, and felt very differently from her mother and grandmother, in her mind, in some ways, sex was still not acceptable. Because when she was growing up, it was implied that men are more interested in sex than women, as an adult, in order to give herself permission to experience pleasure, Teresa had to fantasize situations in which she didn't ask for it. Before she had sex with her husband, she needed to conjure up these fantasies in order to allow herself to become aroused.

Teresa wanted to know if there was any way she could continue to enjoy sex without having to imagine situations of being molested or overpowered, because it bothered her that she had to resort to these fantasies. First of all, I told her that she should not feel guilty about the fantasies. Many women imagine such scenarios, and fantasizing about having sex with someone who wasn't her husband, or having sex in different places, with details that were very exciting to her, was perfectly normal. She need not feel ashamed, because she knew she wasn't going to act on those fantasies; they were merely a device to excite herself.

If she wanted to do away with the fantasies, she could work on two different aspects of this issue. First, I asked her to refocus her mind during sex. Instead of imagining the various scenarios that allowed her to become aroused, she would try instead to concentrate on the ways her body responds and where she experiences pleasure. She would take deep breaths, and refocus on her own body every time these other images came to her mind. In this way, Teresa would be giving herself permission to experience pleasure, and the fantasies would become less and less necessary.

The other part of my advice was for Teresa to begin to acknowledge herself as a deserving, competent, spirited woman. She had come to this country with a high-school education and initially had to work at a menial job in a factory. She then decided to continue her education and enrolled in night and weekend classes at the community college. Her hard work paid off, and she got a better job, a nicer house, a more satisfying life. I encouraged Teresa to think about these accomplishments and to give herself credit for the spirit and self-confidence she had shown. Just as she could enjoy the fruits of her labor, she could also learn to enjoy sex without feeling guilty about it.

At the same time, she would work on feeling more accepting of her husband. In contrast to what her mother and grandmother had foretold, Teresa was married to someone who was with her for more reasons than sex. He was committed to her in many other ways. I asked her to make a list of all the ways her husband was there for her in their shared daily life. And she was to reflect on how these ways demonstrated her husband's love for her.

Teresa had to work quite a lot on eradicating her shame and on feeling worthy of sexual pleasure. As she began feeling more self-loving, more confident, more whole as a person, she found that

she didn't need to fantasize that some imagined stranger was forcing her to have sex. She learned not only that her body could respond through her own or her husband's physical stimulation, but
also that it was permissible to be a sexual person. It was all right
to let go of the degrading image of sex that had been instilled in
her as a girl. She could, instead, take pleasure in sex by genuinely
welcoming and embracing the sexual part of herself.

THE SENSUAL DIMENSION

Throughout this chapter, we have seen that our sexual experience
is a kind of mirror reflecting many other aspects of our relationships and our life. Our sex life reveals how well we're getting along
with our partner, whether or not there are problems we may be
avoiding or feelings we are holding back. Sex can communicate to
our lover the desire to get closer or the longing to be cherished,
even when we are unable to state these things verbally. How we
express ourselves sexually is also a reflection of how we were
raised: our cultural values, our fears, our beliefs about what is right
and wrong. The mirror of sexuality can even reflect aspects of our
daily struggles at work and the positive strides we may be making
toward our personal goals. The freedom or joy or delight we may
feel in our everyday life is physically conveyed to our partner when
we make love—as is the anxiety or disappointment we may be experiencing.

By sexually communicating who we are and what we're feeling,
lovemaking can bring us closer to the one we have chosen to love.
It also gives balance to our lives by providing both energy and re-
laxation. But sex is more than a physical release of feelings and a
mode of communication.

Sexuality adds to our lives a sensual dimension that we can
never quite define or explain. There is something both mysterious
and spiritual about two people coming together in this way, and

for this reason, sex deserves to be both treasured and respected. Honoring the sexual part of ourselves means appreciating the delicate connection between our bodies and our inner spirit and treating ourselves and our partner with love and care. Confronting those issues that stand in the way of a loving sexual life with our mate is the first step toward enjoying this uniquely meaningful and delightful part of our lives.

TAKING IT OUT
ON EACH OTHER

W**hen** *Joseph started having problems at work and was afraid he might lose his job, he began to act very different at home. He wouldn't talk to me, he started drinking a lot, and then he found every excuse to fight with me. I felt sorry for him, because I knew they were making things rough for him on the job. But I didn't know how much longer I could stand to be around him. He was so full of anger.*

—*Barbara, age 27*

I**t** *was very hard for me to defend myself at work. I let a lot slide off my back because I didn't want to get into any hassles. I need the job, and it took me a long time to get where I am. But there was a long period there when, unfortunately, Barbara was the one who took the heat.*

—*Joseph, age 32*

Ideally, marriage ought to be a comfort to us whenever we go through hard times. Most of us feel that we can depend on our spouse to provide the needed relief from our outside burdens and troubles. When the world gets us down, we look forward to coming home and receiving the compassion and love that will ease our emotional pain.

But when trouble strikes, those who are in need of such

comfort aren't always straightforward about what's upsetting them and instead make things even more difficult for themselves and those closest to them. In such instances, partners may react to outside stresses by taking it out on those at home—often in a violent or abusive way.

While all couples are challenged by life's inevitable obstacles, Latino couples often experience the added stresses of prejudice, the language barrier, economic hardship, and American customs that clash with our own cultural values. Frequently, these pressures play a part in provoking serious family problems, including infidelity, alcoholism, drug use, domestic violence, and child neglect. This is not to say that all Latinos face such problems or that our culture alone attracts them. Every ethnic and economic group is vulnerable to these troubling behaviors.

In this chapter we will look at what happens when family members displace their anger and disappointment by taking out their frustration on those they love rather than confronting difficult situations head-on. You may not be dealing with any of these problems in your own family; but if you are, or if you know of someone who is, you can refer to the end of this chapter for important statistics and information on where to get help.

JOSEPH AND BARBARA:
RACISM AT WORK, ALCOHOLISM AT HOME

The incident that precipitated Joseph and Barbara's crisis was a theft at the warehouse where Joseph works. Unfortunately, prejudice among both management and Joseph's fellow workers meant that, as one of the few Latinos in the company, Joseph was singled out as the suspect. A loyal employee for more than ten years, he was falsely accused of stealing company property and was subjected to a humiliating internal investigation. Coworkers who had known Joseph for years began hurling such racial slurs as "thieving wetback" and "dirty Mexican." Joseph remained subdued and reserved. Keeping his job was more important to him than retaliating against those who wanted to demean him.

Unfortunately, because we Latinos are often subjected to this kind of prejudice, we feel that we must prove to others that the stereotypes about us are wrong. We feel that we must constantly show ourselves to be even better students, workers, or professionals than everyone else. This sense of having to prove himself was part of what motivated Joseph's reserved behavior. He felt that if he defended himself against the false allegations, he would lose the dignified image he had always tried to maintain. So he bided his time, hoping that eventually the real culprit would be apprehended.

But each day was a trial. Joseph had to withstand the taunts, complete his work as usual, and somehow manage to get through the day knowing that his honor was being questioned and that his job and family's security were in serious jeopardy. He succeeded in keeping the lid on until he got home. Then, his anger would begin to tear him—and Barbara—apart. Barbara describes his mood on those evenings after Joseph returned from work.

> I knew something was wrong, but I didn't know what. Joseph would walk in and grab a beer and not even talk to me. When I tried to ask him what was wrong, he snapped back that it was nothing, and why didn't I just leave him alone—that I was always hassling him about something. Or if I asked him if he wanted to hold the baby or play with our three-year-old daughter, he would start arguing for no reason at all, saying that I expected him to work all day and then be a baby-sitter at night. He never treated me like this before, and I was really scared that he was changing into someone I didn't recognize. I tried to be understanding, but he shut me out completely.

Barbara finally found out from a woman whose husband worked with Joseph what was happening at Joseph's workplace.

When she tried to bring up the subject with Joseph, however, he lashed out at her verbally, calling her a "chismosa," a gossip, insisting that he did not want to talk about it, and that he resented her talking about him with her friend behind his back. In Joseph's mind, the conversation between the two women tainted his role as head of the family with a sense of distrust.

Meanwhile, he was drinking more and more, which of course, caused his angry outbursts to escalate. As the turmoil at work ate him up inside, he released the rage by fiercely criticizing Barbara for almost everything she did. Barbara recalls how Joseph's words stung her almost as much as physical abuse.

> It was like nothing I did was right. I would be with the children all day, trying my best to take care of them and do all the cleaning and cooking. But Joseph always found fault with something. He accused me of spoiling the baby because I picked him up when he cried, but he would get so upset hearing the baby cry—what was I supposed to do? And he complained about my cooking, telling me I wasn't nearly the cook his mother had been.
>
> We pretty much stopped making love, and if I tried to approach him, even just to kiss him, he put me down or told me I wasn't attractive any more since I'd had the kids. That I didn't even bother to fix myself up and look attractive. Joseph's personality had become so unpredictable that I really didn't know what I was going to do. It was so hard for me because I knew if I tried to defend myself, he would become even more upset. It was like constantly being on edge from the minute he got home to the time he left the next morning.

This is how Joseph remembers that difficult period in both of their lives.

> I know the drinking was getting out of hand, but I just wanted to come home and forget about everything that was going on at

work. I wanted to blank it all out. And alcohol seemed like the easiest way to go. I didn't realize how it would make me get even angrier. What I wanted was for Barbara to just leave me alone and wait until the whole thing blew over.

Like Joseph, many Latino men and women are caught in a similar bind when faced with discrimination, mistreatment, or limited opportunities in the workplace. Having achieved a certain degree of success, they're reluctant to rock the boat. But they're also unable to bury their feelings of indignation and outrage. So those feelings erupt, and the wrong people end up being the target.

Why was Joseph so adamant about not discussing his job crisis with his wife? Why couldn't he be honest with her about how angry he felt at being falsely accused? Wouldn't she have understood how humiliating it was to have a crime pinned on him simply because he is Mexican-American? The answers to these questions lie not only in Joseph's reserved personality, but also in the cultural beliefs underlying his behavior.

Latino men have a particularly hard time discussing anything negative about their work situation, for a number of reasons. First of all, pride is a critical issue. Regardless of the type of work they do, our men take pride in it and want to be known for doing a good job. This attitude brings honor to them and to their family. A man cannot feel that he is a man if his honor is in question. Also, many women and men look upon the man as the family provider, so a man's very identity is tied up in this role.

Another reason Joseph couldn't confide in Barbara is that Latino men are expected to solve problems by themselves. Bringing home your problems and looking to your wife for sympathy or answers connote a certain weakness. Depending on a woman, even for moral support, is not considered proper masculine behavior.

Thus, Joseph believed that telling Barbara about the racist allegations would have filled her with serious doubts about their economic security, his moral standing, and their own relationship.

Because his self-image is so intrinsically connected to his role as family provider, divulging the truth would have been a terrible blow to Joseph's pride.

Furthermore, Latino men tend to think of the company they work for as another kind of family, toward which they feel a strong sense of identification and loyalty. Joseph's altercation at work implied more to him than just the possibility of facing unemployment. His integrity was being questioned by those with whom he felt a very meaningful bond. To admit to Barbara that this bond was in danger of being broken would, in Joseph's mind, have exacerbated the problem, not helped to solve it.

From Joseph's perspective, it was simply too risky to talk about all these issues with Barbara. At stake was his very identity as a man, not just his reputation and income. He figured that it was better to dull his senses with alcohol and hide his problem until it was resolved. But the use of alcohol doesn't work that way; it doesn't minimize your problems, it amplifies them.

Joseph was eventually cleared of the charges at work when the actual thief was caught. The coworkers who had made the discriminatory comments apologized to him, and although Joseph understandably still resents those who falsely accused him, the job situation returned to normal for him. Reclaiming his marriage didn't come about as easily.

Joseph is not the type of man who knows how to talk to a woman about his emotions or to apologize for hurting her feelings. And to make matters worse, although the ordeal at work was over, he still drank heavily when he got home each night. It was a routine he had fallen into when he was under stress, and it became harder and harder to break.

When Barbara came to me for individual counseling, I told her that before she could work matters out with Joseph, he would have to agree to attend AA meetings to address his alcohol problem, and she needed to go to Al-Anon meetings for partners of alcoholics. Until Joseph stopped drinking, the possibility of communicating with him was nil. Alcohol changes your personality, cuts off your thoughts and feelings, and makes it impossible to honestly open yourself up to someone else.

Initially, Joseph reacted angrily to Barbara's suggestion of AA, and he even denied that he had a drinking problem. But after the crisis at work had been resolved, Joseph began to feel better about himself and could acknowledge that he had perhaps been treating Barbara badly. He finally agreed to attend the meetings.

What is great about AA for Latinos is that by joining, you become part of a group that functions like a family. Members not only give each other the moral support that is needed to deal with this difficult problem, they also form a community and create a sense of belonging that is so often missing in people's lives, especially Latinos who may feel cut off from their culture. Because so many Latinos, especially men, are reluctant to share their problems with strangers, it is important to have access to this kind of organization, which makes people feel welcome and works to combat the stigma attached to asking for help. AA has become more and more acceptable to our community, and many AA meetings are now held in Spanish in Latino communities nationwide.

Attending AA and Al-Anon meetings allowed Joseph and Barbara the opportunity to be with people like themselves, who understood what they were going through. The other members of Joseph's group, all of them Latinos, understood the anger he felt at being the target of prejudice. But they also got him to realize that turning to alcohol and taking out his anger on Barbara was not the solution. Barbara's fellow Al-Anon members gave her support by understanding how difficult it is to live with an alcoholic, but they also made her acknowledge that her continual criticism of Joseph helped neither of them.

One of the most important things both of them learned from AA was that talking to each other was essential. This realization sounds so obvious, but each of them admitted that honestly communicating their feelings to each other, without becoming defensive or blaming the other person, had never been easy. Listening to others in the group meetings, and hearing other people talk honestly about their lives, taught Barbara and Joseph that communication is a two-way street: one person must respectfully listen while the other talks, and the one who talks must be sincere and respectful as well.

As Joseph worked on maintaining his sobriety, and as they both began the process of talking and listening to each other in a more open and respectful way, Barbara and Joseph's marriage improved. Joseph came to understand that, although projecting a dignified image at work was very important, even more important was his sense of inner dignity. As he learned to talk with Barbara about what was going on at work and at home, he also learned to speak up on the job—and to stand up for himself whenever his integrity was called into question.

DORA AND RAFAEL: LIFE'S PRESSURES AND THE SPIRAL OF VIOLENCE

I never wanted to harm my children, but they were getting so out of control. I don't know how it happened to me that I went from being a happily married woman with a good job to losing my husband and my job . . . and now having these problems with my kids. I thought I was finally living a successful life, and then it all collapsed.

—Dora, age 38

Before Dora and I split up, she was always pushing me to be more, to do more. She didn't realize that I felt stuck but that I was trying to get myself to another level. Then I met Maureen, and I knew that here was a person who really believed in me, whereas Dora didn't.

—Rafael, age 40

Dora and Rafael's story is a sad example of how economic and personal pressures can lead to an escalating series of serious problems—in this case, infidelity, spousal abuse, and finally child abuse.

Dora was a successful career woman with five children. She and Rafael had been married for fifteen years when their marital difficulties began. Rafael had reached a point in his career where he felt that it was time to move on, but he could not find another job and was stuck in his old one. Although well qualified for the job he'd held since he and Dora married, he had obtained it in the context of an affirmative-action program, and thus others at work regarded him as a "token Latino." Rafael always felt humiliated by this situation, and in some way he had bought into this negative view of himself. He also felt humiliated by Dora's success and by her constant reminders that he wasn't living up to his potential.

Then he met Maureen, who viewed him in an entirely different light. She thought that Rafael was fantastic, intelligent, handsome, accomplished. Rafael had had previous extramarital affairs, but they had never been more than short, superficial, purely sexual relationships. With Maureen, however, he felt the boost to his self-esteem that was so lacking both at work and in his relationship with Dora. The new relationship with Maureen made him want to escape Dora all the more. Dora was too aware of his insecurities and berated his inability to better his life. Rafael's impatience with Dora's demands finally gave way to violence. Dora explains:

Rafael had been verbally abusive before, he had pounded the wall and slammed doors, but he had never hit me. Somehow, when it happened, though, I wasn't surprised. Because he has a terrible temper. I told him I wouldn't put up with it, but he kept at me verbally until it would get worse and worse and he would shove me against a wall or hit me in the face. Finally he hurt me really badly, and this time I called the police.

Rafael was booked for domestic violence and forbidden to see his children for a certain period of time. But Dora's difficulties did not end. Because of all the emotional problems she had had with Rafael, she was performing poorly at work. Her job requires her to focus her mental abilities, and she couldn't concentrate under so much duress.

She finally had to take time off for disability. She was now left with the total responsibility for her children, her income had decreased considerably, and she had become very anxious and very insecure about herself, her job, and her future. That's when she started hitting her children, which she had never done before.

> I was at the lowest point in my life ever. And the kids were so out of control. I know they were affected by all our troubles, but some days, I just didn't know what to do to get them to calm down. They would be screaming and fighting with each other. I didn't really think that much about it at the time, but I was getting more and more out of control, too. I would slap them when their behavior got out of hand, thinking this would help to discipline them. And when one slap didn't do it, I started hitting them more. Rafael had always been the one to raise his voice with them, and that always seemed to keep them in line. But once he was gone, I was at a loss to get them to behave.

The cycle of violence begun by Rafael's abuse of Dora sadly continued with Dora's abuse of her children. As statistics and studies continually show, those who abuse have almost always been victims of abuse themselves. And Rafael and Dora were no exception. Rafael had been exposed to domestic abuse as a child, having witnessed his father hitting his mother. While he vowed that he would never behave in the same way toward his own wife, he was unable to control his bad temper and ultimately followed in his father's footsteps.

Dora had never been abused as a child, but Rafael's violent behavior toward her, and her own escalating problems, combined to push her over the edge. She didn't mean to harm her children; she just wanted to discipline them. But by using inappropriate physical punishment, she was not only hurting her children at that moment, she was also potentially harming their future well-being by teaching them that physical violence is an acceptable way to resolve conflicts.

While some people believe that physical punishment of children is a necessary disciplinary measure, it is my confirmed belief that violent behavior only creates more violent behavior. And hitting a child is a violent act. With all the pressures of life, many parents need to have quick control over their children, and they therefore resort to physical punishment. But taking the time to join your children, to listen to what is bothering them, to talk to them and explain to them about your morals and values—all these are well worth the expenditure of minutes. There is no way that hitting or slapping children can take the place of talking to them and getting them to understand right and wrong.

Fortunately, in Dora's case, social services intervened early enough so that she and her children could get the help they needed to work out their problems and get back to being the kind of family they used to be. Dora was grateful to the agency for giving her a chance to talk to people who could teach her about better ways to respond to her children during this time of crisis.

Rafael was also required by the court to attend classes on domestic violence, to learn to cope with his temper in a manner that will not harm others.

SEÑOR X—AN EXTREME CASE

Domestic violence can be perpetrated on a number of different levels. As with Rafael, it may start out as emotional abuse and escalate to physical violence. Or a person might lose control and destroy property within the home but never actually hit another person. Still, when a high level of unresolved anger is present, the threat of physical violence is always there.

The worst scenario I encountered in my professional life was one reported to me by an anonymous man who called in to my radio show. He was in his twenties and began by saying, "I have something to confess that I have never told anybody." He went on to tell about his terrifying childhood and the events that followed.

My father used to beat up my mother, and that made me very, very angry. So I would go out into the streets, and I'd look for cats and dogs, and I would kill them, pretending that they were my father. I knew that the only way to prevent my father from continuing to beat up my mother was to kill him. So I fantasized about killing him for a long time, while actually killing cats and dogs and other animals in the streets in Mexico.

At one point, I was present when my father was beating up my mother, and she was screaming and bleeding, and I decided that this would be the last time my father would do this. So I killed him. I killed him and buried him, and no one ever found out.

Although haunted by what he had done, the caller had kept this tragedy to himself until he called me on my radio show that day. No one who knew his father was even aware that the man was dead. Everyone assumed that he had simply gone off with another woman, since he was a habitual womanizer in addition to being a wife beater.

The case of Señor X is an extreme example of the effects of domestic abuse, but it is not at all unusual for me to come across children in my practice who fantasize about killing their father when they see him physically or emotionally abusing their mother. "I'm going to kill him when I grow up!"—that's what these youngsters, most of them boys, say.

We all have a sense of fierce loyalty toward our mothers, who gave us life. And as Latinos, we place our mothers in a very prominent position. We adore them, we would give up our lives for them. So the most difficult thing to endure is watching them being treated violently.

And what is the message passed on to the children who witness this kind of violence? That the one who is physically stronger can take advantage of anybody else. Thus, like Señor X, male children harbor the fantasy that "When I grow up and get physically stronger, I'm going to kill him." Of course, very, very few actually fulfill that fantasy. But they often go on to abuse the women with whom they become involved, having no other model for relating to women than the one they learned from their fathers. Or they vow to be everything their fathers weren't, bending over backward to control their anger and violent tendencies. In either case, they're emotionally scarred by the domestic violence they've witnessed.

Daughters of abusive fathers grow up feeling inferior, powerless, and resigned to accepting abuse or being abandoned. Very often they become involved with men who are abusive, in an unconscious attempt to reform the abusers and right the wrongs that were committed against their mothers.

Women are often inclined to make peace, even in the most dire of circumstances. Some think that if they tolerate or ignore violence, it will subside or even go away altogether. Some think that it is better to put up with physical or emotional abuse and to continue to have a father for their children than to risk having no husband and no father figure. But we have to really think about the kind of man we want in our life and the kind of father we want for our kids. It is very important to have a husband and a father in the family, but abusing a wife or a child is not being a husband or a father. It is being someone who takes advantage of the situation because he is physically stronger.

Violence or humiliation of any kind should not be tolerated. If

victims remain silent when they're degraded or abused, that si-
lence is understood by the perpetrator as acceptance and an invitation to continue the violence. Humiliation and abuse are the
extreme opposites of respect. Since the first rule in any type of af-
filiation between people is respect for the other person, abuse has
no place in any marriage, any family, any relationship.

THE STORY OF LUCY:
WHEN ECONOMIC ABUSE CAUSES CHILD NEGLECT

There is another kind of abuse that many people put up with in
order to survive: economic abuse. As in the following case, this
type of mistreatment too often results in children's paying the
price for their parent's job-related hardships.

I heard Lucy's story from a colleague in San Diego. Lucy is a
single mother and a full-time clerical worker with three young
children. She is grateful for her job and works hard to provide for
her family. When the company she works for began increasing her
work load without giving her any increase in pay, Lucy, being a
conscientious employee, went along with the new demands.

What Lucy didn't realize at first was that these requirements
went beyond what an employer has the right to enforce. Her company's officials were taking unfair advantage of her because they
knew that she was unlikely to challenge them. Since jobs at her
level are so hard to come by, the employers were confident that
Lucy and others in her position would comply.

Such treatment can definitely be labeled abuse, but it took
Lucy several weeks before she acknowledged the toll the situation
was taking on her family. She got home too late to prepare dinner
for her children, and she could not afford to have the baby-sitter
stay past four o'clock. So for several hours, Lucy's eleven-year-old
daughter, Briana, was in charge of the younger two. The young girl
made sandwiches for the others, gave them baths, and changed

the baby's diapers. Although Lucy alerted a neighbor that Briana was alone and told her daughter to call the neighbor if there was any problem, the girl was nevertheless expected to fill a role that was not appropriate for an eleven-year-old.

In her effort not to "make waves," Lucy tried to rationalize her situation. She said that her heavier work load was only temporary, until the company could afford to hire another person, that she didn't really mind putting in the extra hours, and that Briana was doing fine in her new job as "assistant to Mami." Lucy came from a Latin-American culture in which women are taught to go along with authority figures, be they fathers or husbands or bosses. Again, as with so many Latinas, the role of "pleaser" had been instilled in Lucy from a very early age.

But what my colleague told Lucy was that it was unfair to expect Briana to take her place. Children cannot properly raise each other, even though this practice exists in our native countries and is increasingly evident here in the United States. Children benefit from the attention and guidance of older siblings, but they need to be supervised and cared for by adults.

It was not right for Briana and Lucy to pay the price for Lucy's employer's unfair labor practices. Lucy needed to confront her employer about the increased work load and lack of additional pay. It was suggested that she talk to management about the impact of her work situation on her family's well-being. Perhaps her employers could provide an extra stipend, so that Lucy could hire a baby-sitter, or arrange for more flexible hours, so that she didn't have to leave her children alone. If those suggestions didn't have an effect, she could consider consulting an attorney who specializes in labor practices, and if it was legally advisable, the lawyer might file a complaint with the appropriate labor board. One way or another, the situation had to be resolved, so that Lucy's children were assured of receiving the care they required.

Lucy was very frightened at the idea of standing up for herself in this way. It took a number of meetings, first with my colleague and then with Lucy's coworkers, for Lucy to gain the courage to take action. But eventually she did. She and her fellow employees were able to persuade the National Labor Relations Board to help resolve their problems. Just as important, Lucy learned the crucial importance of protecting her children and valuing herself as a deserving person and employee.

ARE WE PREJUDICED AGAINST OUR OWN?

The Ramirez Family: Showing Favoritism Toward Lighter-Skinned Children

There is a particular way in which we "take it out on each other" that is especially humiliating to have to admit. It has to do with an ingrained prejudice we have learned from the culture at large and, sadly, too often employ against our own people and even our own family members. The prejudice to which I am referring concerns skin color. Al Ramirez tells how this sensitive issue affects his family.

> We have three beautiful children. Luisa is the oldest, Alejandro is the middle boy, and Juan Carlos is the youngest. Luisa and Juan Carlos are dark-skinned like my wife, and Alejandro is light like me. I love all my kids the same and would never think of favoring one over the other, especially based on anything so meaningless as physical appearance. But I honestly think that my wife has always favored Alejandro because of his lighter skin.
>
> Maybe I'm more sensitive about this because, as a light-skinned Mexican-American, I remember feeling ashamed of being treated better than the other Mexican kids when I was growing up. The Anglo teachers would often mistake me for white—until they learned my last name—and, even when they knew I was Mexican,

they somehow made this assumption that I was smarter because of my lighter skin. It hurts me to think that my wife, Mary, has the same kind of bias when it comes to our children, but I notice how she seems to think Alejandro is special and puts him on a pedestal.

If we are honest with each other, don't most of us have similar stories about prejudice within our own families? We tend to sweep such truths under the rug, because they reveal our self-deprecation and lack of pride in who we are. We don't like to admit that, with this kind of cruel and senseless favoritism, we are using the same psychological weapon to harm our children, our brothers and sisters, as those who have oppressed Latino people—and all people of color—throughout history.

A desire to identify with the mainstream United States culture, with those of European ancestry, with the successful people at the top is usually what is behind our self-deprecating attitude toward our brownness. But valuing lighter skin and the European concept of beauty didn't begin with *People* magazine or with *Baywatch*; it's been with us for centuries.

In terms of our own Latino history, the notion that lighter-skinned people are more deserving of respect and adulation began when the Spaniards conquered the Indians. The indigenous people of America looked up to their lighter-skinned conquerors for essentially one reason: the Europeans were successful in overcoming them. The Indians were in awe of the white men who were able to wrest the power from them. Generation after generation, our ancestors learned the bad lesson of admiring those who had power over us, those who imposed their culture and religion on us. We learned to emulate the way they behaved and the way they looked. And we also learned to look down on the Indian in us, the brownness in us.

For generations, it has been very common for mestizo families to place a premium on their lighter-skinned offspring. This preference arises from the fact that parents and grandparents know how much easier it is for lighter-skinned people to fit in and to succeed in a predominantly white culture. They have learned firsthand that you are much more likely to be given the opportunity to progress if you are white. Brown-skinned or black people, on the other hand, are generally looked down upon and held back. Since a successful son or daughter reflects well upon the entire family, having a light-skinned child is felt to be a blessing.

What makes this prejudice within the family even more tragic is that we do the same kind of damage to our children on a personal level as the outside world does to them on an institutional level: we dole out unfair advantages based solely on physical appearance. And since children who feel more validated by their parents will have a better chance of succeeding in life, parents who favor their lighter-skinned children are setting in motion a self-fulfilling prophecy: those lighter-skinned children are more likely to succeed because their parents instill in them belief in themselves. And the darker-skinned children, lacking in that positive reinforcement, will have an uphill battle.

As for the Ramirez family, Mary Ramirez had been treated differently when she was a child because she has dark skin. Why would she, as a mother, show favoritism to the child who has the lightest skin? Wouldn't she have been particularly sensitive about this inequity, given that she had been a target of such prejudice herself?

Mary grew silent when I first asked her; then she quietly explained.

> My brothers and sisters used to call me "negra" or "india" or "chocolate cookie" when we were little. I know now that they didn't mean any harm, but it hurt my feelings terribly at the time. I would yell names back at them, but one day I just couldn't take it

anymore, and I remember running inside the house to my abuela and crying in her lap. She tried to soothe my hurt feelings, telling me I was just as good as anyone else. But I always felt I wasn't quite as good or quite as beautiful.

When Al brought up this whole thing about Alejandro, I was shocked. It may be true that I have a special feeling for him, but I never ever associated it with his skin color. It's that Alejandro has certain qualities that I identify with. I would never want my other children to feel the kind of inferiority I felt.

Discrimination and prejudice have taken their toll on all of us. Although we have made impressive strides over the last several decades, we continue to struggle against racist attitudes in our schools and workplaces, in our neighborhoods, in our government, and sometimes even in our own homes. What was fortunate in the case of the Ramirez family was that Al had the courage to confront Mary with his gut feelings and that Mary was able to respond openly.

Although she contended that her "special feelings" for Alejandro were primarily based on the artistic interests they share, Mary confessed that she may have unconsciously felt that Alejandro was unique and more worthy because of his "more Anglo" appearance. It was an attitude she had learned from her own family but one she is now committed to eradicating. Interestingly, her children are helping her in this process.

My kids are fortunate in that they attend a public school where the teachers are very dedicated to cultural diversity and give the students an understanding of their cultural background. So my children have been educating me about the Mayan and Aztec and Inca cultures, how developed they were long before the Spaniards arrived. I am so proud that they are learning to value who they are and where they come from. I wish I had received this kind of instruction when I was growing up.

Rudy: An Afro-Latino's Struggle with Racism

Many clients, friends, and talk-show guests who are Afro-Latinos have talked to me about the ways racism has personally affected them. Frequently, they tell me that they are not accepted by either African-Americans, because they are Latino, or by Latinos, because they are dark. They are thus left in a kind of limbo, questioning their identity and feeling uncertain about where they belong.

How tragic that we demonstrate the same kind of racial bias against one another that we condemn in those who attempt to hold us down! What will it take for us to fully embrace all our cultural familia, regardless of our differences?

Rudy is a Puerto Rican–American living in Chicago who has struggled with the color issue all his life. He recalls a particular experience in the seventh grade that not only hurt him on a very personal level but also foreshadowed the prejudice he would have to deal with for years to come.

I liked a girl named Carmen, who was a very fair-skinned Puerto Rican girl. At the time, I was making money cleaning shoes and cleaning windows, so I bought her a box of handkerchiefs as a gift. I knew she liked me too, but she couldn't accept my present to her. And it was because she didn't want to get involved with someone who was black. I felt so rejected, and at that point, I became even more self-conscious about my own color.

I shied away from girls for a while after that. But the color issue didn't go away. I remember one time I was going to participate in a quinceañera but was told that my cousin would take my place instead. Of course, he was lighter than me. My family didn't say so in so many words, but I guess they didn't want to have a dark-skinned guy as an usher.

When I got a little older, I decided to date only African-American girls. I needed to be accepted as I was and to stop feeling ashamed of who I was. It wasn't until I was twenty-one that I started dating Puerto Ricans again. Having to deal with this kind of prejudice has made me stronger, though. I would tell myself, "They may not like me, but I'm going to get ahead anyway." And I did. I don't earn a huge income, but the kind of work I do helps open the doors for others who might not otherwise get the chances everyone is entitled to.

RESPECTING OURSELVES AND OUR FAMILIES

Whether it's acknowledging and combating racism in our own family or getting help with a problem of spousal abuse or excessive drinking, we do ourselves and our children the greatest favor when we make an effort to change an offensive pattern in our lives. It may be easy to justify destructive or abusive behavior by pointing to the many hardships and indignities we're forced to put up with as Latinos in this culture. But this explanation doesn't improve our situation, and it certainly doesn't help our children to build a better life for themselves.

When we have the courage to face difficult problems and do something about them, we're giving our children a legitimate reason to respect us. And we're developing the self-respect that each of us deserves to feel. Changing the ways we handle the severe stresses in our lives is never simple. It is a day-by-day process, entailing small successes and occasional defeats. If you're struggling with one of the issues we've been discussing in this chapter, be patient with yourself. Every day that you work toward creating a healthier life for yourself and your family, you demonstrate your strength and your love. And that's something you can be proud of!

Facts and Resources on Abuse
ALCOHOLISM

Some Facts About Latinos and Alcohol

❦ Acculturation has a dramatic effect on drinking patterns. One study showed that:

> 75 percent of Mexican immigrant women abstained from alcohol, as compared to 38 percent of third-generation Mexican-American women who abstained.

> 36 percent of women in the general United States population abstain.

❦ Another study revealed that:

> First-generation United States–born Hispanic men drink more frequently and more heavily than do foreign-born Hispanic men.

❦ A study of alcohol-related mortality in California showed that blacks and Hispanics had higher rates of mortality from alcoholic cirrhosis than did whites or Asian-Americans.

❦ Hispanics are less likely to have health insurance and more likely to be below the poverty level than whites—factors that may decrease their access to alcoholism treatment. (Source: *Alcohol Alert*, National Institute on Alcohol Abuse and Alcoholism, January, 1994)

❦ Alcoholics Anonymous reports that there are more than 400 Spanish-speaking AA groups throughout the country, 200 of which are in Los Angeles.

Alcoholism: Getting Help

Alcoholics Anonymous, Al-Anon, and Alateen are listed in most telephone directories. Call for meeting schedules and literature or to talk to a member.

DRUG ABUSE

Drug Abuse and the Latino Community

According to the 1993 National Household Survey on Drug Abuse, Hispanics have higher substance-abuse rates for illicit drug use than do non-Hispanic whites. A total of 6.2 percent of the Hispanic population uses illicit drugs (not including alcohol or cigarettes), as compared to 5.5 percent of the "white" population and 6.8 percent of the "black" population.

Drug abuse follows the same pattern of addiction as does alcohol abuse in that it is a progressive disease, with no possibility for a "cure" until addicts get help from a recovery program. In my experience, adults usually take drugs to find solace from difficult lives and to gain a sense of belonging somewhere (we will discuss teenage drug use in the following chapter). Drug abusers usually feel desperate, lonely, or uprooted from a life where they once belonged. I have never seen drug abuse in people who were focused on their lives, who had a strong goal and knew where they were going. Without the stability provided by a good job and a supportive social and family structure, many people are tempted to turn to the drug community for relief. Of course they don't find relief, and their problems escalate—their habit demands that they find money to support it, they often turn to crime, marriages fall apart, children suffer.

Drug Abuse: Getting Help

If you or anyone in your family needs help to combat a drug problem, contact your local branch of Narcotics Anonymous (the phone number can be found in your yellow pages) or the National Alcohol and Drug Abuse Hot Line: 800-252-6465.

CHILD ABUSE

Child Abuse: Getting Help

As Dora's story illustrated, child abuse can sometimes take place in families that once were happy and loving. Regardless of the circumstances, however, if you know or even suspect that a child in your family is the victim of abuse, contact a group that can help. The following is relevant information for those who need help with this problem.

National Child Abuse Hotline referral number: 1–800–422–4453
In Los Angeles: 800–540–4000
In Florida: 800–96–ABUSE

Tips for Parents from the National Committee to Prevent Child Abuse:

❦ When you feel everyday pressures building up, take a break. Even a phone chat with a friend can be helpful.

❦ When you feel tempted to lash out at your child, *stop*. Count to ten. Get hold of yourself before you take hold of your child.

❦ Don't use hurtful words; remember, children believe what their parents tell them.

❦ Encourage children every chance you get.

❦ Share your children's triumphs and disappointments.

❦ When a child misbehaves, criticize the behavior, not the child.

❦ Take an interest in all your child's activities, especially school work.

❦ Teach your child that using violence is not the way to settle disputes.

Child Abuse: Some Facts

❦ Approximately 3 million cases of child abuse and neglect are reported annually. This represents 15 out of every 1,000 children in the United States. (Source: American Academy of Pediatrics)

❦ Researchers estimate that 40–60 percent of child victims of physical abuse have also witnessed the abuse of their mother by her male partner on one or more occasions. (Source: *Journal of Independent Social Work*, 1990:4)

❦ The Children's Defense Fund reports that nearly 800 Latino babies are abused or neglected every day in the United States. (Source: Children's Defense Fund press release, May 1996)

DOMESTIC VIOLENCE

The Signs of Spousal Abuse

There are different levels of spousal abuse, as well as different forms. There is physical abuse and there is emotional abuse, and both can be devastating. While there are many more instances of male-perpetrated than of female-perpetrated physical spousal abuse, neither is excusable. If your spouse or partner exhibits any of the following behaviors, I suggest that you get help—from a counselor, an abuse hotline, or in extreme cases, the police.

1. Does your spouse slap, hit, or punch you? Even if he or she apologizes or feels guilty later or promises that "it will never happen again," abuse of this kind should never be tolerated.
2. Does your spouse force you to have sex, even when you don't want to?
3. Does your spouse use anger as a means of controlling you? Does she or he intimidate you by screaming or throwing things or threatening to hurt you?

4. Does your spouse demand that you go out with no one else and excuse this behavior by calling it *love?*
5. Is your spouse so possessive and jealous that you are never free to have your own friends or social life? Are you falsely accused of infidelity?
6. Does your spouse consistently put you down, call you derogatory names, belittle you, or criticize you? Does your spouse consistently ignore your opinion, calling your remarks "dumb, stupid, crazy"?
7. Does your spouse become furious when you do not obey—or for no reason at all?
8. Does your spouse threaten suicide if you ever try to leave?

Domestic Violence: Getting Help

Domestic violence is a dangerous situation that needs to be addressed as soon as you realize that you or a family member is in trouble. The volunteers and staff who work for emergency hotlines and battered women's shelters can offer crucial advice to those whose safety is being threatened. There are also groups for perpetrators of domestic violence who want to stop this behavior. Please take advantage of the expertise available through such groups. Your life or that of someone you love may depend on it.

The page listing community services in your telephone book will usually include the number for the battered women's hot line or the battered women's shelter nearest you. If not, you can call the Domestic Abuse Hotline (National Coalition Against Domestic Violence) at 1–800–799–7233, and you will be referred to a local number. The Domestic Abuse Hotline can also refer you to a batterers' program or group near you.

HELPING OUR CHILDREN
TO VALUE THEMSELVES

W**hen** I married my husband, an Anglo, we never thought the difference in our backgrounds would be a problem. But it comes out in little things—which sometimes turn out to be big things. Like how I relate to his son from a previous marriage, who is part of our family. The boy is only four years old and needs a sense of discipline. But my husband overindulges him. To me, this isn't being a good father. This little boy needs to know that his father and mother are in charge, not him. Yet my husband accuses me of being too hard on my stepson and not asking him how he feels about things. In Mexican families, you show your love by doing the right thing for your kids, not asking them how they feel.

—Liliana, age 30, mother of two

I**f** I had spoken to my parents the way our kids talk to us sometimes, I would have been whipped good. We knew our parents loved us, but we also knew we had to respect them, because they are our parents. My father had a special place in the front closet where he kept the belt, and we all knew he would use it if we misbehaved. I don't believe in hitting my kids, but I think things have swung too far over in the other direction.

—Rick, age 40, father of three

D**r.** *Nogales, you must help me to get my daughter back. She has fallen in with the wrong crowd, and I don't know what to do. She's a very intelligent, sweet girl, but she always feels sorry for the underdog. Recently I found out she has been hanging around with gang members, troublemakers. She said she didn't tell me about her life because she didn't think I would approve and didn't feel comfortable talking to me. When one boy she thought she was in love with rejected her, she tried to commit suicide. I had no idea my daughter would try such a thing. How did I lose touch with her, when I care about her so much?*

—Esmeralda, age 37, a single mother

In previous chapters, we explored various issues that can cause conflicts in a relationship. Parenting is another area over which many couples disagree. This is because every mother and father—as well as every grandparent, every pediatrician, every child psychologist, and every "expert"—seems to have their own theory about what is best for a child. Even when both parents try to do the right thing for their son or daughter, their difference of opinion about how to raise the children can contribute to a lot of family tension.

Clashes between Latino and American values are often at the core of our parenting dilemmas. We argue with our spouses, as well as with ourselves, about whether, as parents, we should be more progressive or more authoritarian. Should we follow the rules laid down by mainstream American "experts" about child-rearing, or are we better off following in our parents' and grandparents' footsteps? Should we give our daughters the same kind of encouragement and advice we give to our sons—or is Latino culture correct in making greater distinctions between the sexes? Is American culture—with its emphasis on consumerism and "doing your own thing"—to blame for enticing our children down the wrong path? Is the strength of Latino families enough to prevent children from making wrong choices?

Regardless of our philosophical differences, we're all involved in the struggle to prevent our children from being lured by drugs and gangs, dropping out of school, or becoming parents before they've finished growing up. We also want to develop the parenting skills that will help us help our daughters and sons to become confident, happy, and capable people. We strive to teach our children not only how to live according to the beliefs most valued by our culture but also how to believe in themselves, so that they can truly enjoy the life they have been given.

In this chapter we'll listen to both concerned parents and their children as they grapple with a variety of issues commonly faced by Latino families:

❧ deciding on appropriate discipline for young children;

❧ balancing a child's respect for parental authority with a parent's respect for a child's feelings;

❧ overcoming the lack of communication between parents and teenagers;

❧ preventing teenage pregnancy;

❧ dealing with the threat of gangs, teen suicide, and alcohol and drug use;

❧ motivating girls and boys to develop their potential;

❧ teaching children of all ages to combat prejudice and develop tolerance;

❧ helping children to value who they are and the culture of which they are a part.

This important chapter will examine each of these parenting challenges, and I will offer you the advice and insight I have derived as both a psychologist and a mother.

LILIANA, DAVID, JOSH, AND MARA:
HOW MUCH DISCIPLINE DO YOUNG CHILDREN NEED?

*David refuses to set a bedtime for Josh. He lets him lie on the
floor watching television until he gets tired and falls asleep. I'll
come into the living room at ten thirty or eleven to nurse the baby,
and little Josh will be all curled up in his clothes, sleeping. No
pajamas, no teeth brushed, no bed!! I don't see how David can
allow this. To me this isn't being a good father.*

—Liliana

Liliana and David's story relates to the issue of discipline, but it
has more to do with David's behavior than with Josh's. Liliana
claims that her husband doesn't take charge of her stepson Josh's
daily routine, that he allows the four-year-old boy to do basically
what he wants when he wants. Because Josh is a fairly quiet child,
Liliana has no real behavior problems with him. But she and
David differ greatly on how the boy should be treated. They also
have a new baby in the family, and both are concerned that the
patterns they establish with Josh will affect how they decide to
raise Mara.

Liliana is a Mexican-American from Albuquerque. She told me
that she was raised by loving parents who believed in rules. She
and her brothers and sisters knew what their chores were, were
aware that they had to do homework before they could go out and
play, and always started getting ready for bed at nine o'clock because that was bedtime. These were some of the basic rules the
children never questioned—and if they strayed from them, there
were consequences.

Liliana believes that her family's way of life was a healthy one
and wants to continue it with Josh and Mara. The bedtime problem she refers to is symbolic of how her background and philosophy differ from David's. His parents, non-Latinos also from

Albuquerque, had certain rules as well, but they were much less strictly enforced. There was not as much structure to everyday life in his family as there was in Liliana's. David believes that his children should be more like equal partners in the family rather than being subjugated to "a bunch of arbitrary rules." He says, "If Josh is comfortable falling asleep in the living room, I don't see why that should be a problem." David wishes that Liliana could "be more sensitive to Josh's feelings instead of simply laying down the law."

Knowing how your children feel is important, but such sensitivity doesn't mean that you indulge them and neglect to set limits. Perhaps allowing Josh to fall asleep on the floor in the living room isn't the worst thing in the world, but such a relaxed attitude about bedtime does have its downside. Children need to learn early on to calm themselves down and fall asleep on their own, without the aid of a television set or a parent who remains in the room until the child falls asleep. Otherwise, they may always be dependent on an outside source to become relaxed.

Even more important, every child needs a sense of structure, a comfortable routine. Children derive a feeling of security from knowing that certain things always happen at certain times. While many of us dread the familiar cry of kids who do not want to go to bed at night, children actually feel much more comfortable knowing that there are appropriate rules and that their parents are in charge of enforcing them.

As parents, we have to be flexible enough to know when a certain limit is appropriate and when it isn't. Knowing how your child feels is part of this flexibility. Many of us come from families where there was a rigid sense of right and wrong. Yet right and wrong are dependent, not only on what happens, but also on how the child is feeling and on the child's developmental stage.

How did Josh feel about bedtime? "I like to watch TV with my dad, and then he carries me to my bed, and I don't even know." In talking to Josh, I felt that he was apprehensive about falling asleep alone and being in the dark. Being with his dad and becoming so tired in front of the television set that he never remembered falling asleep was a way for Josh to deal with his fears.

It was also easier for David, his father, to follow this routine than to begin the more disciplined process of establishing a bed-time, seeing to it that Josh had his bath and brushed his teeth, reading to Josh in bed, and then saying goodnight. I convinced David to try the new routine for Josh's sake and also for Mara's. Not all rules are arbitrary, and Josh and his baby sister will ulti-mately benefit from the lovingly imposed structure in their lives.

As for Liliana's becoming more sensitive to Josh's feelings, David did have a point. Although Josh had lived with Liliana and David for most of his life, understandably he didn't feel as close to Liliana as he did to his father. And Mara's arrival may have made him feel even more estranged from his stepmother. I encouraged Liliana to take a little more time to get to know Josh, to involve him in the care of the new baby, and to spend time with him alone—just the two of them. Knowing more about the kind of person Josh is will help Liliana make the right decisions about how best to raise him.

I also discussed with Liliana the fact that often in blended fam-ilies—those involving second marriages and children from the previous marriage—subtle struggles are going on. For example, she may have unknowingly felt that she was competing with Josh for David's love and attention. This feeling may have influenced her strong need to impose discipline on her stepson and prevented her from growing closer to him. Becoming aware of this situation, Liliana could now consciously take steps to improve her relation-ship with Josh, a change that, in turn, will enhance her relation-ship with her husband and strengthen the family as a whole.

RICK'S FAMILY: RESPECT FOR PARENTS, RESPECT FOR CHILDREN

Rick and his wife, Donna, are first-generation Cuban-Americans from Miami. Rick is a bank manager, and Donna teaches in a high school. They live in a nice neighborhood with their three children; Daniel is twelve, Tomas is nine, and Rona is seven. They describe their family life as happy and "fairly typical," but Rick is especially concerned about how differently his children behave from the way he remembers his own childhood. He worries that they haven't learned to respect his and Donna's authority.

> There are times when my kids talk back to us as if we weren't their parents. I remember treating all the adults in my family with respect. I loved my father, but I was also afraid of him, and I think that kept me and my brothers in line. I may not have liked some of his decisions, I may have been angry that he didn't allow us to do certain things, but I didn't voice that anger. I knew my father had the last word.
>
> Not my kids. They get into this debate with us every time we tell them they can't do something. I think Donna is partially responsible, because she thinks they have a right to their opinion. As far as I'm concerned, what we decide is not open for discussion—and that's that.

What does it mean to be an authority figure to your children? Do you exercise authority by inspiring fear in someone else, so that the person will respect you? Fear makes children understand that they're not supposed to do something, but it doesn't help them to understand why. The problem is that when another situation arises that seems different, the child may repeat the same mistake, because the reasoning behind the prohibition has not been made explicit.

We cannot train a child to do or not do something through fear. The behavior of twelve- or nine- or seven-year-old children who talk back to their parents may be stopped by slapping them or raising your voice or refusing to "debate the issue," but you won't stop the motivation behind their behavior, and it will come out in another way.

We have to teach our children in ways that our own parents may not have used. Perhaps they disciplined us by just making the decision for us, so that we wouldn't bother them anymore. Maybe if there were many children in the family, there was not enough time to explain "why" to each one. Certainly, most of our parents didn't have access to the information about child development that today's parents do. The question is: as mothers and fathers of the 1990s, how can we teach our naturally curious children—who are trying to learn more about their environment by "testing" their will against ours—the "right" way to behave? How can we help them to learn to make the right decisions themselves?

Let's look at Rick and Donna's children's behavior ("talking back disrespectfully to their parents") and see if we can understand it more clearly. As with all negative behavior, parents need to find out why their children are acting this way.

❦ Are the children angry or upset simply at not getting their own way?

❦ If so, why can't they tolerate not getting what they want?

❦ Is it because the children generally *do* get their own way?

❦ Whose fault is that?

❦ Could they be upset about something else that's going on in the family that isn't being discussed? What might that be?

❦ Are Rick and Donna explaining to their children the reasons why certain decisions are made?

❦ If so, do the children understand these reasons?

❦ Do Rick and Donna treat each other and their children with respect, so that the children learn what respect is all about?

❦ Are the children learning disrespectful behavior from their friends, or from television?

❦ Do Rick and Donna properly monitor who their children play with and what television programs they watch?

Children need to know that their parents are the ones who make the "final decisions," and they need to respect their parents' authority. However, we also need to respect our children. We need to respect their feelings, their interests, their individuality. And we need to remember that part of their "job" as children, part of the task of growing up, is to test us as parents. They have to try to see how far they can get in exercising their own will, so that we will do our job and let them know when they've reached their limit.

Giving our children enough room to experiment with being in control of themselves, while exercising enough parental control so that they know what's right and wrong, is a tough job. But that's what we signed on for when we became parents. Somewhere down the line, perhaps when we least expect it, we'll notice how well our children have learned to make good decisions on their own. And we will feel immensely rewarded.

A NOTE ABOUT "SWINGING TOO FAR IN THE OTHER DIRECTION"

I know what Rick is referring to when he says that sometimes parents "swing too far in the other direction" when it comes to disciplining their children. Latino families traditionally adhere to a more authoritarian way of raising their children, but some adults, who were treated too harshly as children, try to behave in the exact opposite manner with their own kids. Such parents vow never to be too hard on their children. They want to allow their kids to be "free" in ways they were never permitted to be.

It is obvious to most of us that there must be a balance. I so often see parents who don't give their kids any boundaries for proper behavior. I'll walk into a waiting room, for example, and see children running wild, making a mess, screaming loudly—and their parents aren't doing a thing about it. These parents may have been badly treated or physically punished as children, and now they are reluctant to control their children at all.

Of course, this is not good for the children (or very pleasant for those who must be around them). They will never learn to control themselves unless their parents teach them what proper behavior is. If children aren't taught these lessons when they're young, they will have a very difficult time interacting with other children—and with other people throughout their lives.

ESMERALDA AND ELENA: WHY DON'T TEENAGERS AND PARENTS COMMUNICATE?

When I first talked to Esmeralda, her daughter Elena was in crisis. Although she was, fortunately, rescued in time to thwart her attempted suicide, this fifteen-year-old girl was at a dangerous crossroads in her life. Esmeralda told me that she had never anticipated that her daughter's life would come to such a point. She had had such bright dreams for herself and her children.

> When I came here from El Salvador as a single mother, I wanted to get an education and better myself. That was my dream, and I had no doubt I could make it happen. But life here was very different from what I had imagined. I had to work very hard to support my children. For years I cleaned houses—the only kind of work I could get. After about ten years, I eventually got hired to do clerical work—a big step up! Now I am finally taking some college classes, which I'm very proud of. And my older daughter is in college, doing well.

But this problem with Elena has upset me so much. I feel that I don't know her. That we have strayed so far from each other.

It's never easy being a single parent, charged with the responsibility of being both father and mother to your children. Although Esmeralda had taught her daughters the proper values and set a positive example for them by working hard and striving for a better life, she didn't always have time to find out what was going on in her younger daughter's life. Working, going to college at night, and taking care of the home are enough to stretch any woman's schedule to the breaking point. But Esmeralda's estrangement from Elena wasn't merely a question of time. Even when they were in the house together, mother and daughter didn't often talk about things that really mattered. Why not?

Actually, Esmeralda didn't think there was anything wrong with the way she and Elena related to one another. When I asked her what took place when the two were together, she said:

We talk about what we're going to make for dinner, whose turn it is to do the laundry, or how much noise the neighbors made last night. We joke about a television program or something that happened in the neighborhood. We get along fine. We don't have fights or anything. I thought we had a very good relationship.

It was more a question of what wasn't taking place between Esmeralda and Elena. They didn't share their feelings or their problems. They didn't know what it was to open up to each other. Esmeralda told me that it was only after her daughter's attempted suicide that Elena admitted that she didn't feel she could come to her mother and talk about her problems. She thought Esmeralda would not understand what was going on in her life. Perhaps she was right.

Open communication between parents and children was not something Esmeralda had learned from her own mother and father. Her parents had cared for her, seen to her needs, loved her, disciplined her. But talking over worries or problems wasn't part of the family routine. It didn't seem necessary. As in many of our native countries, child rearing was something the entire extended family participated in. The children in Esmeralda's extended family generally followed the established patterns set forth by all their elders, not merely the parents. Esmeralda always had a favorite aunt she could turn to, or a cousin who was a few years older, after whom she would model her behavior. And all the adults watched out for all the kids. There was never any fear that children weren't being given enough attention or love or discipline.

There was another aspect of Esmeralda's childhood that was very different from her daughter's. In El Salvador there was not the array of choices that exists in our diverse American culture, so making decisions was never as difficult for Esmeralda as it is for Elena. Esmeralda behaved the way her parents and grandparents and aunts and uncles expected her to, and she socialized with those whose background and values were identical to her own.

What I told Esmeralda is that, because of all these differences in the way children grow up here in the United States, it is very important for Latino parents to cultivate a more active parenting role. Esmeralda needs to become more comfortable in discussing matters with Elena, so that Elena will receive the necessary guidance to help her distinguish between the many positive and negative choices that face her. This kind of direct communication and guidance may not have been necessary in El Salvador, but it is essential in this country.

One of the reasons Elena fell in with the wrong crowd was that she was seeking approval and identity through her friends. She was trying to discover who she was and stake out a place for herself among her peers by playing the "rescuer" to the "bad boy" in the group. But when he rejected her, Elena's new identity, the one she had created separate from her mother, crumbled.

She attempted suicide because she didn't feel that Esmeralda loved her for who she really was, and she didn't find love in the boy who rejected her. So she drew the conclusion that no one loved her and that therefore life was not worth living. She would have liked to have turned to her mother for comfort, but she couldn't, because Esmeralda still expected her to conform to the image of the good little girl. Elena wore the mask of the obedient daughter at home, but she was someone entirely different when she was with her friends. In essence, she was living a double life. She was confused but not articulate enough to talk about her confusion.

Elena is a loving, caring individual, but she is in the midst of defining who she wants to be, and in this very normal process, she unfortunately became involved with troublemakers. With the proper support from her mother, she will most likely be able to find out what she wants from her life and avoid the kind of desperation that led to her attempted suicide.

Esmeralda and Elena are communicating much better today. Whereas before Esmeralda was overly authoritative and demanding with Elena, today she still sets limits but is also taking the time to learn who her daughter really is, to find out how she thinks and feels, to respect her individuality.

Mother and daughter must talk to each other about their differences and accept each other for the unique people they are. Elena needs to learn to ask her mother, "What do you mean when you want me to behave this way or that? What are the values behind that particular rule you're setting forth?" It is important that she understand the reasoning behind her mother's guidelines.

The experience of nearly losing her daughter taught Esmeralda that there is a dark side to the "American Dream." Our children are exposed to influences here that those of us who are immigrants never had to worry about in our native countries. Not only do gangs and drugs and teenage pregnancy threaten our daughters and sons, but certain attitudes and values prevalent here also pose serious problems. American teenagers don't seem to respect authority or their elders to the degree that most of us are accustomed to. Rebelling against your parents is usually viewed as the "cool" thing to do. And while much of this rebellious behavior is harmless, it can steer many young people in the wrong direction.

Hopefully, Esmeralda and Elena will be able to overcome such obstacles. They love one another, and if they can build on that love and work together to strengthen their communication, Esmeralda's fears about her daughter's well-being will be greatly alleviated.

The Threat of Teenage Suicide

Like Esmeralda, most Latino parents are so concerned about the dangers of drugs, alcohol, teen sex, and *pandillas*—gangs— that they overlook an even bigger threat: teenage suicide. The statistics are sobering. According to new figures compiled by the Centers for Disease Control, the suicide rate rose 120 percent for ten- to fourteen-year-olds between 1980 and 1993, and almost 30 percent for fifteen- to nineteen-year-olds. In 1993, 315 youngsters in the younger group and 1,884 in the older teen group committed suicide. Perhaps even more alarming, a 1993 study of 16,000 high-school students, conducted by the Centers for Disease Control, found that 1 in 12 youths admitted to a suicide attempt in the previous year.

The stories behind the statistics are tragic, because it seems to us, as adults, that there is no valid reason for young people to take their own lives. However, like Elena, many teens begin to romanticize the idea of suicide when they feel that they have nowhere to turn, when they feel that they are unloved and unaccepted by their parents or their peers or both. Teenagers' feelings go very deep; what to us may seem like minor problems (losing a boyfriend, being criticized by a parent) are crushing and insurmountable blows to them.

Parents are usually unaware that teenagers view suicide as a viable solution to their problems. While sometimes the goal of attempted suicide is to gain attention, to cry out for help, the attempt too often is successful, and a young life is lost. And when drugs are in the picture, suicide becomes an even greater threat.

There are no simple answers to preventing teenage suicides, but making certain that the lines of communication are open between you and your child, letting your children know that you are there to listen to their problems and to give them the support and love they need, will go a long way toward preventing the kind of isolation that can result in this tragic loss.

"I THOUGHT BECAUSE I WAS IN LOVE, I WASN'T GOING TO GET PREGNANT"—THE STORY OF JESSICA

I belonged to this gang, dressing up as a chola. After school I'd invite these kids to come to my house while my parents were at work. There'd be about ten of us, listening to the radio really loud, drinking some beers, and making a mess out of the house.

My eight-year-old brother told me these people were not good for me because they were involved with drugs. Then I started to be concerned when he said to me, "You're smoking marijuana, so I want to do it too." That's what made me think I should stop. But I didn't want to get rid of my friends, because it made me part of the neighborhood.

—Jessica, age 13

As a little girl, Jessica was "delightful to be with," say her parents. She was always well behaved, got good grades in elementary school, dressed nicely, never gave her parents anything to worry about. But they are worried about her now. At the age of thirteen, she is attracted to the gang life, she already has experience with drugs, she wants to drop out of school, and she has just had an abortion.

The forces that have driven Jessica to make the choices she has are similar to those that motivate many teenagers, including many of our Latino teens: peer pressure, alienation from parents, lack of direction, and a perceived lack of opportunity.

Jessica is at an age when belonging to a group and feeling accepted by her peers is of the utmost importance. This need to belong is exacerbated by her feeling of alienation from her parents. In fact, there are some valid reasons why Jessica feels that her parents don't accept her for who she is. Here is how she describes her mother's and father's lack of acceptance of her.

> My mom is always comparing me to all the other girls in our family and to all her friends' daughters. Why can't I be like them? They are achieving this, and wearing their hair like that . . . or getting some award in school or something. And my father talks about my cousins, and how they know what they want already, that they are going into the army, or have a big interest in sports. They don't want me to dress the way I want, they compare me to everyone else, and they won't let me do what I want.

As is often the case with teenagers, Jessica's parents' criticism of her made her want to do the exact opposite of what they wished her to do. She told me she wanted to be "the opposite of what my mom wants." When I asked her why, she said, "I don't know." But as our conversation continued, Jessica realized that she was upset at her mother for not listening to her, for not talking to her—the way her friends did. When I asked her to tell me more about her friends, I found out that their ability to be there for her diminished as soon as drugs entered the picture.

> The new friends I started hanging around with seemed like they really cared for me. They were like my family, the kind of family I

*always wanted. I used to feel like I wasn't wanted, because of the
way my life treated me. People who belonged to the pandilla were
close to me, they helped me out. When I had problems, I could talk
to them. They listened to me and knew what I was talking about.
But after they got to know me, they started changing. Instead of
listening, they would say, "Just smoke this [marijuana] and get it
out of your head."*

Meanwhile, Jessica became involved with Antonio. She actually met him on the phone, through a friend, and their conversations led Jessica to feel that he cared about her. Antonio didn't
belong to the neighborhood, but he was a "cholo" too. Because
the neighborhood cholos didn't like him, they approached him
and told him that they would come after him if they found him in
their neighborhood. That was a threat to his life, and Jessica was
very scared, because she had seen a friend get hit in a drive-by
shooting. The possibility of losing Antonio, and his apparent willingness to risk his life for her, made Jessica fall even more deeply
in love with him.

On one of the afternoons when they were together, she became
pregnant. What was a devastating experience for her parents was
initially a happy one for Jessica. She tells it this way:

*Antonio and I went together to the doctor. When the doctor told
me I was pregnant, I started crying, but Antonio told me, "Don't
cry, you should be happy, like me." We were both very happy, and
we wanted to take care of the baby together and stay together.
Why was I so happy? Because I was going to have something that
was mine, for the first time.*

When Jessica told her parents that she was going to have a
baby, they were extremely upset and disappointed in her. She told
them that it had not been her intention to get pregnant but that

she loved Antonio very much. Explaining to me how the "mistake" of pregnancy had come about, Jessica said, "I thought because I was in love, I wasn't going to get pregnant. This was an act of love, not an act of having a baby."

Much to Jessica's horror, her parents insisted that she have an abortion. In fact, they threatened her: if she didn't have the abortion, they would send her to Mexico and see that her boyfriend went to jail. Jessica had no choice.

Jessica's parents tried to explain to their daughter that a baby would destroy her chances of finishing high school, going to college, and having a career. Not only that, but the baby would suffer because it wouldn't have mature parents. Making babies may seem like just a physiological process, they told her, but raising and nurturing a child requires life experiences and abilities that a thirteen-year-old girl and a sixteen-year-old boy have not yet developed.

A host of questions arise concerning Jessica's story—and so many others like hers. Why do parents wait until after an unplanned teenage pregnancy to discuss sex with their children? Why do so many of us seem to avoid the truth about what's going on in our children's lives? And why do our young women feel that early sex and premature motherhood are the only ways to feel validated and loved?

In my conversations with teenagers, I have found that twenty-five years after the sexual revolution in this country, some very astounding myths about sex and pregnancy are still circulating among young people. For example:

—If it's your first time, you won't get pregnant . . . because your hymen acts as a barrier, like a diaphragm.
—If the boy is in control, he will make sure you don't become pregnant. Just leave it to him.
—All of my friends are already having sex, and none of them has gotten pregnant, so why would I?

Although statistics show that 50 percent of American females and 55 percent of American males aged fifteen to nineteen have had intercourse at least once, what I hear from teenagers is that many of them start having sex even earlier. It's a fact that a million teens a year become pregnant, and a third of them have abortions. Every day in the United States, 302 Latino babies are born to teenage mothers. And yet, parents often think that the way to prevent teenage pregnancy is to not talk about it.

If you don't talk to your children about sex, they will most certainly talk about it with their friends and make decisions based upon the kinds of reasoning listed above. So what should we be telling our children about sex? Are the scientific facts about how a woman gets pregnant, and a warning to abstain from sex until you marry, enough?

I hear a lot of Latino parents tell their daughters, "You have to respect yourself" and "What would our relatives say if you got pregnant?" But these arguments for remaining a virgin are usually ineffective, because teenage girls care less what their relatives are going to say than whether their boyfriends will stay with them. And they're often persuaded to have sex out of fear of losing their boyfriends to girls who will if they won't. Boys, on the other hand, feel pressured to prove their masculinity and maintain their competitive standing with their peers. And having sex, or "scoring," is seen as the way to do that.

I think we must bring more to our parent-child conversations about sex than physiological facts or threats about dishonoring the family or fears about AIDS and other sexually transmitted diseases. We must acknowledge the psychological needs of our teenage daughters and sons as well as the physiological changes taking place in their bodies. Young people need friendship, love, and emotional connection to their peers, just as adults do. We should communicate to our children that we understand their wish to be close to a boyfriend or girlfriend. Our kids need honest, realistic, and sensitive answers to such questions as "Why shouldn't I have sex with someone I love or feel close to?"

Every parent must answer this and similar questions according to their own values and beliefs. As you discuss with your children what sex between two people represents, and what the appropriate age might be to begin to have sex, let them know that you understand their emotional and physical needs. Also, make them aware that their teen years are a time to make lots of friends, to socialize and have fun, to study and prepare for a career they will enjoy, and to discover who they are. When early motherhood or fatherhood disturbs this process of forming their identity, it can be very confusing and very damaging.

In Latino families, although it's not always spoken about, boys are often given much greater sexual freedom, because they're not the ones who get pregnant and often don't participate in taking care of the child that may result. Parents need to begin to make a son aware that if he gets a girl pregnant, he becomes "pregnant" as well. Both he and the girl will be in the process of having a child, and the responsibility for that child should be shared.

Still, cautioning boys about their responsibility for pregnancy and warning them about sexually transmitted diseases is not enough. Parents must foster a boy's—and a girl's—sense of responsibility in general, beginning when the child is very young. Then, when issues pertaining to sex arise, teenagers will already have the experience of making responsible decisions, and their choices regarding sex will hopefully reflect the sensible behavior they have been practicing all along.

I would like to add that talking to a boy about sex is not only the father's job, as many believe. A mother can talk to her son about sex as well, emphasizing the issues of responsibility and respect for women. Children—especially Latino children—respect their mothers, and boys can learn from their mothers that every woman deserves respect. Acting responsibly with regard to sex involves treating a woman with the same kind of respect you would want for your sister or your mother.

HOW CAN WE MOTIVATE OUR CHILDREN?

At thirteen, Jessica is already saying that she doesn't want to complete high school, because she's not interested in an education. "What for?" she asks, since she just wants to have a big family. Her mother has five children, and that's what Jessica says she wants for herself. When I ask her, "What if your husband dies or leaves, how will you support your five children?" she answers, "I'll marry someone else."

Unfortunately, Jessica hasn't come into contact with any inspiring role models—Latinas who have established fulfilling careers outside the home. And these encounters are so important if she is to gain a sense of her own possibilities. Latinas have only recently begun to make tremendous academic and economic strides in this country, and those of us who have been fortunate enough to have reached our goals need to take it upon ourselves to inspire the children in our communities. When Latino parents and extended family members send the message—either verbal or unspoken—that girls ought to stay close to home and remain in the traditional role of mother and wife, a girl's own vision for her future narrows.

Girls are not the only ones in the Latino community who are lacking in motivation. I recently participated in a program in East Los Angeles which brought Latino professionals into the high schools to talk to the students about potential careers. Many bright students had high aspirations, and it was a pleasure to see this enthusiasm in our young people. But I also heard a lot of defeatism.

I heard one fifteen-year-old boy say, "Why should I consider going into a career? I know there's nothing more for me after high school. I'll just go and find whatever kind of work I can. But a career? I know that's not for me. I know they don't want me over there at the university. I know that this is the end."

Those words were devastating for me to hear, because they projected the very limited image this boy has of himself, of what he can do with his life. Where does this negative image come from? Again, it comes from the lack of positive role models available to our children; but it also comes from teachers who don't take the time to inspire our kids, from negative images on TV and in the movies—which repeatedly portray Latino youth as gangsters or lawbreakers—and from politicians and others who demean our people by stereotyping us as lacking in initiative and drive.

But we must also take at least partial responsibility for our children's negative self-image. As parents, we must make an effort to instill hope and courage and determination in our kids, to inspire them with a sense of enthusiasm for what they can do with their lives. True, we have an uphill battle, being Latinos in a society that grants privileges to those who are already at the top and plants obstacles in the path of those without status or money. But the opportunities are there for those who are prepared to grasp them.

How can a parent begin to inspire someone like this fifteen-year-old boy, who sees no future beyond a minimum wage job, or like Jessica, who cannot see any possibility for herself other than early motherhood? I often use myself as an example and talk on a one-to-one basis with a young person. This is so much more effective than a "lecture," in which you tell young people that they have to finish school because in the future they'll have to have a career, because they'll need to support a family, and so forth. Children and teens don't see themselves in terms of the future . . . but they can be motivated to search their minds for things that they like. When you engage in a give-and-take conversation and speak honestly about yourself instead of focusing totally on them, you encourage young people to open up and think about their life in a new way. For example, I'll begin by saying something like this:

> *I don't know how people can handle it, spending eight or ten hours at work at something they hate. It must be so hard. I'm so pleased with my life, that I can spend my time doing a job I really like. I'm so thankful for that, and I really hope that you'll be able to work at a job that you enjoy.*

If you're unable to tell your children how much you enjoy your work, talk about why you don't enjoy your work and how you want things to be different for them. How you want them to discover what makes them happy and fulfilled. Also, give them an example of people they know who are happy in their work. Then ask them about themselves. The conversation with your child or teenager might go something like this:

PARENT: What do you enjoy, what are you interested in?

CHILD: I don't know. Nothing.

PARENT: Well, tell me how you like to spend your free time, when you're not with your friends.

CHILD: I guess I like to draw. But just for fun, nothing serious.

PARENT: It's great that you like to draw. Sometimes, things that are just for fun turn out to be what people do for their careers.

CHILD: But all I do is doodle in class or draw crazy pictures in my room.

PARENT: Did you know that if you develop that skill, you could become a graphic artist and work in the advertising business? Or you could draw professional cartoons for an animation company.

Or you could even become an architect, if you want to invest more time. Maybe you could think about taking more art classes in school, or signing up for some special classes this summer.

It doesn't take much effort on our part to stimulate a young person's interest in self-development. We need to show children that we care about what happens to them, that we care about what makes them happy and what causes them anxiety, and that we're willing to listen to their thoughts and their ideas. We need to make sure that they have access to positive role models and that they can envision exciting possibilities for what they can do as adults. The earlier we begin, the better chance they have to start creating the life they want for themselves and the future we wish for them.

DO LATINO TEENAGERS VALUE THEIR EDUCATIONS?

Statistics show that Latinos in general are becoming better educated. In 1994, the percentage of Latinos with a high-school diploma was 60 percent for the twenty-five- to thirty-four-year-old age group, compared to 49 percent for Latinos over the age of thirty-five. About 37 percent of older Latinos had less than a ninth-grade education, compared to 21 percent for the younger Latinos. But do our young people appreciate the value of education?

A 1996 study by Professor Marcelo Suarez-Orozco of the Harvard University Graduate School of Education revealed that Mexican immigrant teenagers value school more than either second-generation Mexican-Americans or Whites.* Here are the responses of each group to two statements:

*Terminology used in the study.

"To me, school is the most important thing."

	YES	NO
Mexican Immigrant	84%	16%
Mexican-American	55%	45%
White	40%	60%

"Doing my homework is more important than helping my friends."

	YES	NO
Mexican Immigrant	68%	32%
Mexican-American	36%	64%
White	20%	80%

The study's findings show that immigrant youngsters attending middle and high schools near San Diego, California, seem to like school more and have greater respect for such authority figures as principals than do classmates of European descent and second-generation Mexican-Americans. The study reveals that the more acculturated teenagers become, the more school is viewed as "not cool." (Source: *Los Angeles Times*, February 22, 1996)

I believe that this study demonstrates that children who come from places where the educational opportunities are more limited appreciate school to a much greater extent. And parents who are new arrivals in this country reinforce the importance and value of education. On the other hand, children born in the United States place a priority on dating, socializing, being with their friends. It's a question of priorities. You invest your time in whatever you consider valuable. Immigrants really push themselves to excel, and often we lose that drive when we take our opportunities for granted. As parents, we need to make sure that we instill in our children a sense of excitement about education and an appreciation for how valuable it is.

Another study, involving tenth and twelfth graders and conducted by the Rand Corporation's Center for Research on Immigration Policy, found that Latinos' educational goals decline significantly the longer they live in the United States. The study's authors speculated that this "aspiration gap" between Latino immigrants and Latinos born in the United States may be related to Latinos' overall lack of economic progress, causing both adults and their children to be pessimistic about their economic future once they're aware of the limited status of most Latinos. (Source: *Los Angeles Times*, July 3, 1996)

What I believe the study reveals is that some of our children aren't motivated to continue their education and to strive for a job or career that is better than their parents' because they feel that their chances for success are slim. Although language skills, cultural differences, discrimination, and educational opportunities are obstacles to many of our youngsters, we must fight the kind of pessimism that can hold our kids back. Their success depends on our involvement and encouragement.

RACISM HITS HOME

There is a particular parenting issue that is especially relevant to our Latino community and that my husband and I just recently had to confront with one of our daughters. The issue is racism aimed at your child. I will share with you the incident that occurred in our family.

Our ten-year-old daughter, Gabriela, went to school one day dressed as the native American character Pocahontas, in celebration of Early California Missions Day at her school. Unfortunately, she confused the dates and showed up in costume on the wrong day—becoming the target of some teasing by the other kids. She was very embarrassed and broke down in tears in front of my husband, Alex, when he came to take her home to change her clothes. Gaby's embarrassment and her father's relaxed, comforting attitude about the costume mix-up caused her to open up to Alex and tell him about some other incidents that had upset her, which she hadn't mentioned to us before. A boy had been taunting her with the words "Mexican, Mexican, Mexican!" in a very derogatory, demeaning fashion. This teasing had been going on for a couple of months.

Gabriela is a very bright little girl, who is always considerate of others. Alex and I have tried to raise her in an atmosphere of justice, tolerance, and wholesomeness. The boy's behavior had made her feel terrible, but she had not brought it to our attention—even though she's usually very open with us—until the incident with the costume opened the floodgates of her emotions. I believe that, up to this point, she thought she could handle the situation on her own, that it didn't really bother her. But it obviously had.

Alex met with the principal who told him, "If it is happening, it is a reflection of what is happening in that young man's home, because these are not the values we teach in this school." And Alex responded, "Yes, I'm sure. Nevertheless, the behavior has to be confronted. If we let it go, it becomes acceptable behavior, and then the kids' perception is that this kind of bigotry is tolerated."

So the teacher called in the boy and his parents. Gabriela was to come in as well. We explained to Gabriela before she went into the principal's office that the boy would probably deny having done what he did and that she would have to tell the truth regardless of what he said. Of course the boy denied having teased Gabriela in a demeaning way. Gabriela was upset and started crying, but to her credit, she confronted the boy very directly, stating the facts and nothing more. "No. You are not telling the truth. You've said the same thing to me many times, including yesterday, and there were others who heard you, not just me." The boy had no recourse but to admit his behavior.

The point of this story is that bigotry has to be confronted, and taunts of the kind this boy was making must be shown to the other children to be negative, not clever or funny or acceptable. Children have to learn as early as possible that insulting others because they are different is completely unacceptable.

Gaby felt proud that she had stood up for what was right. She felt supported by us and by the principal, but she felt proud that she had spoken the truth. I'm sure this won't be the last time she has to face racist comments. But the next time she has to confront them, it will be easier for her because she has the experience of speaking out.

Although children should be taught that prejudice is usually the result of ignorance, this explanation doesn't mean that they—or any of us—have to tolerate discrimination. By speaking out against prejudice, we help to empower ourselves and to enlighten others.

TEACHING TOLERANCE TO OUR CHILDREN

Because we live in the diverse culture of the United States, teaching our children to be tolerant of those who are different becomes an important challenge. Within our cities and communities we come into contact with those of different ethnic backgrounds, religious faith, political and philosophical orientation, customs, lifestyle, ages, and gender. With so much diversity, it is crucial to respect the backgrounds and choices of other people and to demand that others respect ours as well.

If we keep silent when someone says something derogatory about us or any other group, we are, in a way, going along with what they're saying. We Latinos tend to be acquiescent, and when we're criticized, often we don't say anything because we don't want to provoke an argument. We may ignore a negative remark in the hopes that the sentiment behind it will go away. But eradicating prejudice doesn't work that way. When we keep silent, we allow ignorance and intolerance and racism to continue.

Respect and tolerance are essential ingredients in the evolution of humankind. Recognizing both the differences and similarities that define us can help us realize our potential as individuals and as a society. The best way to transform our society into a more tolerant one is to begin with our children.

When are children old enough to understand the issues of prejudice and tolerance? Usually when they begin preschool or kindergarten and begin to notice the individual differences among people—height, weight, hair, facial features, skin color, religions, and languages—any kind of differences. With young children, the discussion would involve talking about how we are all different. There are no two people who are the same, even twins. Even if the appearance of two people is similar, there are always differences in the way they act, the way they feel, their special talents. And that is what is so beautiful about life—that all human beings are similar and different at the same time. There is no reason to feel better or worse about being different, because we are all unique.

Here are a few suggestions for helping your children become more tolerant:

1. Get to know those who are different. Learn from them about their religion, customs, social conditions, political or philosophical views, age, and gender.
2. Read books and watch movies that portray and explain different cultures in an authentic way. (See the "Suggested Reading List For Children—Diversity/Tolerance" at the end of this chapter.)
3. Speak out against negative stereotypes of Latinos and any other group, since no stereotype can possibly reflect a universal truth.
4. Do not accept ethnic jokes, because they help maintain stereotypes and perpetuate intolerance.
5. Confront those who, out of ignorance, make ethnic slurs

against Latinos or anyone else. When someone offends you in this way, ask them, "What do you mean?" Those four words are very powerful in confronting any message of racism, prejudice, or intolerance.

6. As mentioned earlier, confront any prejudice that may exist within your own family. Ending favoritism based on skin color or ethnicity begins in your own home.

7. Be proud of who you are and where you come from, so that your children can also value their cultural background.

Regarding this last point, I feel that too often we tell our children to be proud of their background but we don't tell them exactly *what* they should be proud of. If we want our kids to know their heritage and to satisfy their curiosity about what they can take pride in, we have to become more knowledgeable about our heritage ourselves. We have to be aware of our history in order to develop a feeling of authentic pride in our ancestors' accomplishments. If we don't, we risk passing on to our children an empty pride, which tends to breed an attitude of "We're better than them."

There is so much to learn about our history and our culture—about the Mayans, the Aztecs, the Incas, for example, and the contributions each of those important civilizations made to humankind. Exploring the culture and contributions of contemporary Latinos is also crucial. Finding books about our heritage, and sharing them with our children, is an invaluable investment in their sense of identity and pride. We can read about the indigenous American cultures, about African cultures, about our Spanish and other European ancestors, and we can also read the biographies of such important Hispanics as Cesar Chavez, Bert Corona, Ruben Salazar, and Rigoberta Menchú. (See Suggested Reading Lists for Children and Adults at the end of this chapter.)

My friend Henry Barbosa is a wonderful example of someone

who feels authentic pride in his cultural background. He is proud that during the 1920s his grandfather was involved in the populist Cristero revolution against the Mexican government, which was persecuting the Catholic Church at that time. For him, being Mexican is about being Catholic and about being connected to the history of Mexico, to the music, the food, the dance. He admires the Mexican people's warmth, their commitment to family, their respect for the elderly. Henry has a lovely way of expressing what is so unique and promising about being Mexican.

> We represent the clashing of the New World and Europe, the unwitting blend of such sophisticated cultures as the Aztecs and Mayans with the imperialistic Spaniards. They clashed, they fought, but they also mixed—and the mestizo were created. To me, it's like a rebirth of humanity, a second chance. A new mix of people, which blends the best of the two parts.

WHAT A PARENT GIVES A CHILD

A parent's responsibilities can sometimes seem endless. Just when we've completed one hurdle, another one stands before us. As soon as you think your life has become easier because your infant has learned to sleep through the night, you're chasing after a six-month-old who wants to crawl around searching for things to put in her mouth. And no sooner has your toddler "graduated" from toilet training than you must teach him to "use his words" when he's angry instead of hitting the other preschoolers. As much as we give of ourselves when our children are growing up, they reward us in countless ways—with their smiles, their curiosity, their individuality, their love.

And our constant love for them is ultimately the greatest gift we can give our children. We demonstrate that love by making them feel secure, challenging them to try new things on their own, teaching them the thousands of skills and life lessons they'll have learned by the time they leave us. Being a loving parent means helping a child develop into a confident, capable, loving individual—someone who values who he or she is and where he or she comes from.

In the next chapter we're going to take a closer look at the personal environment each of us comes from. Learning more about our family history, our personal roots, can help us to understand why we feel and behave the way we do; and this understanding can contribute to a healthier, more rewarding relationship with our children and our partner.

Suggested Readings

For Children—Diversity/Tolerance

All the Colors of the Earth, by Sheila Hamanaka
Children come in all the colors of the earth, in every shade of you and me. With soaring text and majestic art, this book celebrates the dazzling diversity of children—laughing, loving, and glowing with life. (Ages 3–8)

The Big Book for Peace
This special book was created by more than thirty of the best-loved authors and illustrators of children's books. Filled with stories, pictures, poems, and even a song, it is a book about many kinds of peace—peace among people of different lands, next-door neighbors, people of different races, and family members. (Ages 6 and up)

We're All Special, by Arlene Maguire
Using rhyming text and delightful illustration, this book shows that we come in all different colors and sizes, that we enjoy different things, and that we are all unique and special. Helps kids accept others and love themselves. (Ages 3–8)

Who Belongs Here? An American Story, by Margy Burns Knight
This award-winning book about immigration, racism, and tolerance
　helps children consider some of the most challenging issues of our
　time. (Ages 8–13)

For Children and Young Adults: Latino Culture and Values

Cesar Chavez: Union Leader, by Bruce W. Conord
The Desert Is My Mother/El Desierto es mi Madre, by Pat Mora
Firefly Summer, by Pura Belpre
Fitting In, by Anilu Bernardo
The Girl from Playa Blanca, by Ofelia Dumas Lachtman
Pepita Talks Twice/Pepita Habla Dos Veces, by Ofelia Dumas Lachtman
The Secret of Two Brothers, by Irene Beltran Hernandez
Walking Stars, by Victor Villaseñor
. . . *Y No Se Lo Trago la Tierra*, by Tomas Rivera

For Adults: Latino History and Culture

Anything but Mexican, by Rodolfo Acuña
The House of the Spirits, by Isabel Allende
Bless Me, Ultima, by Rudolfo Anaya
Border Correspondent: Selected Writings, 1955–1970, by Ruben Salazar,
　edited by María T. Garcia
Days of Obligation: An Argument with My Mexican Father, by Richard
　Rodriguez
Decade of Betrayal: Mexican Repatriation in the 1930s, by Francisco E.
　Balderrama and Raymond Rodriguez
Distant Neighbors: A Portrait of the Mexicans, Alan Riding
Gringa Latina: A Woman of Two Worlds, by Gabriella de Ferrari
Growing Up Chicana/O, edited by Tiffany Ana Lopez
Handbook of Hispanic Cultures in the United States, edited by Nicolas
　Kanellos and Claudio Esteva Fabregat
The Hispanic Condition: Reflections on Culture and Identity in America, by
　Ilan Stavans
I, Rigoberta Menchú: An Indian Woman in Guatemala, by Rigoberta
　Menchú and Elisabeth Burgos-Debray

The Latin Deli: Telling the Lives of Barrio Women, by Judith Ortiz Cofer

Latina: Women's Voices from the Borderlands, edited by Lillian Castillo-Speed

Latinos: A Biography of the People, by Earl Shorris

Lydia Mendoza: A Family Autobiography, by Lydia Mendoza, Chris Strachwitz, and James Nicolopulos

A Matter of Pride and Other Stories, by Nicholasa Mohr

Muy Macho: Latino Men Confront Their Manhood, edited by Ray Gonzalez

No Longer Voiceless, by Luis Leal

North from Mexico: The Spanish-Speaking People of the United States, by Carey MacWilliams and Matt S. Meier

The Other Side: Notes from the New L.A., Mexico City, and Beyond, by Ruben Martinez

Silent Dancing: A Partial Remembrance of a Puerto Rican Childhood, by Judith Ortiz Cofer

Stolen Continents: The "New World" Through Indian Eyes, by Ronald Wright

The Way It Was and Other Writings, edited and introduced by Jesus Colon, Edna Acosta-Belen, and Virginia Sanchez Korrol

When I Was Puerto Rican, by Esmeralda Santiago

With His Pistol in His Hand: A Border Ballad and Its Hero, by Americo Paredes

WHAT OUR FAMILY HISTORY TEACHES US

I loved my father, but I was never able to forgive him for how deeply he hurt my mother. He was a womanizer, always having affairs and not even attempting to hide that fact from my mother. This was back in Venezuela. When I moved here to begin a new life, I told myself I would have a completely different marriage from my parents'. I was going to avoid those problems that caused me and my mother so much pain. I never would have thought that the problems I have with Anita could be traced to what went on in my family.

—Javier, age 34

I'm so different from my mother. She was raised with the typical values of my grandparents, who came from Mexico when they were young. My mom was very subservient to my father, which always made me angry in a way, because I grew up in the 1980s and I consider myself to be more "Americanized" and a pretty strong feminist. I have a career, I believe a woman should have the same opportunities as men, and that in a relationship men and women ought to be equal. Still, I was unaware how much my family history has affected my own relationship. My father ruled our family, he was the strong one. And I guess that made such an impression on me that if a man doesn't have a certain kind of strength, it's a problem for me.

—Cynthia, age 23

Sometimes the relationship problems that are the hardest to confront and deal with are those that have their roots in our family history. Many of the difficulties we face in our relationships with boyfriends or esposos, novias or wives, are closely linked to the ways we were treated as children, the kind of relationship our parents had with one another, and the family values we were taught. Since the importance of family is so central to Latino culture, the influence of our family background on our relationships is bound to be very strong.

Often the lessons we learn and the messages we receive from our parents, grandparents, and others who help raise us are unintentional. Children pick up on what is going on around them, even if the behavior is not acknowledged and the feelings are not articulated verbally. As adults, many people unconsciously repeat undesirable behaviors they witnessed as children as a way of maintaining a familiar environment.

Throughout this book, we've noticed the connection between how people were raised and the kind of relationships they have with their mate and their children. In this chapter, we will take a closer look at the ways behavioral patterns filter down through generations and how we can uncover the family origins of our current relationship difficulties. I believe that all of us have the ability to improve our lives if we can learn to honestly confront who we are and understand the various influences that helped shape us. Exploring the reasons why our parents may have acted the way they did, including the uniquely Latino aspects of their attitudes and conduct, can contribute to a deeper understanding of our own behavior and how we tend to relate to our partner.

By looking back on our childhood, we can become both more objective and more accepting toward our parents and relatives—even if they didn't always do the right thing. Instead of feeling "stuck" in the past, we can try to gain a new awareness of it. With a clearer picture of what went on when we were growing up, we'll be better prepared as adults to make the healthiest decisions concerning our partner, our children, and ourselves.

Later in the chapter, we'll also discuss the importance of sharing your family history with your spouse, novio, or novia. When you and your mate become more aware of the significant events in the other person's family, you can gain new insight into how your relationship as a couple has been influenced by the past. And this understanding can help bring you closer.

JAVIER AND ANITA: THE LEGACY OF INFIDELITY

Javier met Anita in high school, in Venezuela, when they were both fourteen. After dating for seven years, Javier came to the United States with the intention of establishing a better life for himself and the family he wanted to have with Anita. She stayed behind, pursuing a career as a medical technician, and waiting to join Javier when the time was right. For four years they wrote letters back and forth in which they shared their dreams for the promising future that lay ahead of them.

Javier adored Anita and vowed to himself he would never cause her the kind of pain his father had caused his mother. A womanizer throughout Javier's formative years, Javier's father never bothered to hide his infidelity, and in fact he often bragged to his teenage son about his conquests. As he looked forward to his marriage to Anita, Javier envisioned himself as the kind of loving, faithful husband his father was never able to be. What he didn't envision was the way in which his parents' unhappy relationship would unintentionally play a part in Javier's own behavior. Here's how Javier tells the story:

> I came to Los Angeles when I was twenty-one to find work. During the time I was alone, before Anita arrived, I got heavily into smoking marijuana. Looking back, I don't know how this habit escalated to the degree that it did. Drugs are frowned on where

Anita and I come from, but here it was just part of the scene. And I guess I was lonely and needed the companionship the drug culture afforded me.

When Anita got here, she was very upset to find out this was going on. She would cry and beg me to stop, but I would just leave the house and go on with my drugs. The arguing somehow made me want to do more drugs. It got to the point where I would spend days away from our home, so that I could continue smoking dope and also so that I could avoid Anita's criticism.

After several years of her crying and pleading with me to stop taking drugs, and after years of her threats that she would leave, Anita found someone else. That was devastating for me. A real blow. After all the pain I went through with my father's betrayal of my mother, and now to think my wife was doing this to me!

On the brink of divorce, Anita and Javier decided to consult me. During our first session, Javier repeatedly spoke of how devoted he was to Anita, how much he loved her, how hard he was working to make a good life for them, and how terribly hurt he was at Anita's betrayal. It wasn't until after our second or third meeting that Javier realized how absent he had been from the relationship. Instead of creating the close, loving relationship with his wife that he had wanted his father to have with his mother, Javier was repeating the pattern of abandonment his father had begun.

Rather than rejecting Anita by having affairs with other women, however, Javier had abandoned her by becoming involved with drugs. Becoming part of the drug scene was a way of distancing himself from his marriage, a pattern he had learned from his father. I told Javier that perhaps his behavior had actually been an unconscious attempt to provoke Anita to leave him, since this was also an aspect of the behavior that he had learned from his father.

After our fourth session, Javier and Anita agreed that they would try to rebuild their relationship. Javier was committed to saving his marriage and promised to get help for his drug habit.

And Anita acknowledged that an affair was not the way to solve problems in her marriage. One of the most important lessons Javier learned, as he began to face the unhappiness between him and Anita, was how influential his parents' relationship continued to be in his adult life, even when he thought he had left his past behind.

> *I finally realized that I was having an affair with drugs . . . just like my father had affairs with women. And I was using drugs to push my wife away, like my father pushed my mother away by seeing other women. The last thing I ever wanted to do was become like my father in that way. In fact, I moved thousands of miles away to get rid of the pain my father brought to our family. But I never really dealt with the pain until Anita had the affair. Then the horrible feeling of betrayal came back to me, and I had to look at my past and understand how I was repeating my father's mistakes.*

As much as we may desire to escape or bury our past, we cannot do so because it is part of our inner reality. It will continue to shape our behavior and our emotions unless we confront it and deal with it. Only by looking at what happened in our family when we were children, and understanding the impact our family history has had on us, can we begin to gain control of our own lives. Rather than unknowingly being controlled by our past, we can become liberated by our knowledge of it.

CYNTHIA: "WHY AM I BORED WITH A NICE GUY?"

Like Javier, Cynthia was influenced by her parents' relationship in a way she was unaware of at first. Her parents had struggled so that Cynthia and her sisters could go to college and achieve the kind of success that wasn't possible back in Mexico. Cynthia did extremely well in high school, was given a scholarship to a major university, and landed an excellent job in advertising when she graduated. At the age of twenty-three, she seemed to have every-thing in place.

Through work, Cynthia met someone she described as "too good to be true"—handsome, bright, kind, and respectful of her desire to pursue her career. They were engaged to be married when Cynthia came to see me, very unhappy. "Why am I feeling so depressed," she wanted to know, "when I have everything I al-ways wanted?"

She told me that she felt there was something missing in her re-lationship with her fiancé, Robert. She was bored with him and was considering calling off the marriage. When I questioned her about Robert, she explained that they had many things in com-mon and that she was physically attracted to him, but that he was almost "too nice"; their relationship lacked a certain kind of ex-citement that she couldn't quite define.

When we talked about Cynthia's past, I learned that she came from a family in which men were clearly more powerful than women. Cynthia's father was a very strong figure, a fact that left Cynthia with mixed feelings. She looked up to him, and even respected his strength to a certain degree. But his emotional and verbal abuse of her mother and the way he governed the family with a sense of macho superiority infuriated Cynthia. He was always telling Cynthia's mother that she was stupid or a fool or worthless, calling her names like "tonta," and accusing her of completely imagined wrongdoings. Even when he was not particularly violent, he constantly undermined whatever Cynthia's mom said, making fun of her, teasing her in a disre-spectful way.

Her mother had tried in little ways to become more assertive and independent, but she was never able to overcome Cynthia's father's domination. She was expected to remain subservient and to defer to her husband, and over the years she basically did just that. She always had to be on guard against his taunts and abuses, was made to feel guilty when the house wasn't kept spotless or the children were misbehaving, and was constantly "put in her place" by such statements of her husband's as, "I make the money in this house, and what I say goes." Cynthia told herself when she was a young girl that she did not want to lead the kind of life her mother had. Instead, she wanted to go to college and pursue her dreams.

After a number of sessions, in which we discussed what Cynthia was actually feeling when she said that she was "bored" with Robert, she came to an interesting realization. She wasn't really bored; rather, Cynthia was extremely uncomfortable with Robert's kindness and respectfulness. His treatment of her was so unfamiliar, given her family background, that it made her very uneasy. Rather than recognize this sensation for what it was, Cynthia had convinced herself that something was "missing" from the relationship. What was absent was the drama of an unhappy marriage. Robert was giving Cynthia peace of mind—a quality quite different from anything she had known as a child. She had witnessed constant conflict between her parents, and this "excitement" was what she sensed was missing in her peaceful, equal partnership with Robert.

As Cynthia began to understand how her parents' relationship had influenced her emotional response to Robert, she realized that she did not want their type of "excitement" to be part of her life. She wanted her own kind of marriage, in which both partners could love and support and nurture one another and yet be free to develop themselves as individuals. She wanted to give her relationship with Robert another chance.

"UNFINISHED BUSINESS"
BETWEEN YOU AND YOUR PARENTS

Are there certain troubling issues you have wanted to discuss with your parents but have never raised for fear of negative repercussions or hurting their feelings? Have these issues continued to affect your life as an adult? If so, this "unfinished business" should be addressed, so that your past doesn't continue to control you. When your energies are so consumed by what went on earlier in your life, you cannot give yourself fully to the present, and your interactions with others suffer. Overreacting or being defensive, for example, are usually signs that we have not dealt adequately with our past conflicts.

Sometimes it is necessary for us to confront our parents when our relationships with them have been painful or harmful. By doing so, we can come to understand what went wrong, so that this issue no longer plagues us. Only then can we move ahead and create a new reality for ourselves, one that transcends our old, unhealthy patterns.

If your parents are willing to have a conversation with you, and if they appear to be understanding about the issues that may have caused harm or pain in the past, such a dialogue can be a very healing experience. Such conversations can enable you to express how you feel, explore what went on in your childhood or young adulthood from your point of view and theirs, and talk about how you want your relationship with them to change. We'll discuss how to go about having such a conversation later in the chapter, after you've had a chance to prepare for such a dialogue by considering an "imaginary conversation," which we will address in the following section.

Even if the conversation with your parent ends with your feeling uneasy, or not listened to, or with unresolved issues, having the dialogue is still important for you from the aspect of learning to accept your parents as they are. By acknowledging and accepting that your parents are unwilling to change or to see things from your viewpoint, you can finally let go of "wishing they were different." This realization will free up your energy, so that you can focus on living your life rather than being preoccupied with changing things you cannot change.

Having conversations with relatives of your parents' generation, such as your aunts or uncles, can also help you deal with troubling family issues from your past. Often we are missing pieces of our own family history, matters we were never aware of or told about. These are the places where an uncle or aunt can fill in the gaps in our awareness, so that we can have a broader understanding of why our parents might have felt or behaved a certain way. Such conversations with family members can be very helpful and enlightening, providing new insights into the way the members of our family related to one another.

HAVING AN "IMAGINARY CONVERSATION" WITH YOUR PARENT

If you're not comfortable confronting your parents directly, or if your parents are deceased, seriously ill, or in some way emotionally unable to face significant family problems, there are several options available to you for expressing how you feel toward them and learning more about their perspective as well. These options can also be used to prepare yourself for an actual conversation with a parent. The goal is to get your own feelings out and at the same time try to put yourself in your parents' shoes and "listen" to what they have to say in response to your expressed feelings.

You can accomplish this end by having an "imaginary conversation" with a parent. Write down your feelings and your parent's response to those feelings in the form of a conversation or "script" between you and your parent. Start out by stating as clearly as you can what you feel the problem between you is. Then write down what you imagine your parent might say in response. Go back and forth between your point of view and your parent's until you feel that you have a better understanding of what each of you feels and why. You'll be amazed at how much you're likely to learn about your relationship by completing this simple activity. By putting your feelings down on paper and then placing yourself in the role of your parent, you will access many thoughts and emotions that you may not have been fully aware of.

❦ Exercise

AN IMAGINARY CONVERSATION WITH YOUR PARENT

This exercise entails focusing on one issue that caused a problem in your relationship with your parent, then talking to your parent as if your parent were present, and finally responding to yourself as if you were your parent.

Here's how the exercise works.

1. Place two chairs so that they face each other. Sit down in one and picture your parent seated in the other.
2. Open the conversation by telling your parent what happened in your relationship (be sure to focus on one issue only), how that particular behavior made you feel when you were a child, and how it has affected you as an adult.
3. Next, sit in your parent's chair, take a deep breath, and take the part of your parent. First, acknowledge what was just said by simply stating, "I have heard what you just said." Take another deep breath and try to respond as your parent might. Put yourself in your parent's shoes. Be as insightful

and honest as you can, concentrating on being your parent, feeling him or her within you.

4. Then go back to your original chair, take a deep breath, and acknowledge what was said by your "father" or "mother," summarizing what they just said to you.

5. Continue this back-and-forth process, sticking to the one issue, until the issue becomes clearer and you are able to reach a conclusion or resolution.

Having an imaginary conversation with your parent gives you the opportunity to express your emotions in a safe way, without actually hurting anyone. I have found the exercise to be very helpful to my clients and talk-show guests. Let's use Cynthia as an example and see what she gained from having an imaginary dialogue with her parents.

Cynthia always wanted to ask her mother why she didn't stand up to her father, why she put up with his behavior all those years. And she wanted to ask her father why he criticized her mother so often, when her mother had tried so hard to please him. My instructions to Cynthia were to ask these questions, to respond in the way she thought her parents might respond, and then to continue conversing with the parent until she felt that she had learned something from the dialogue.

Here are the imaginary conversations, first between Cynthia and her mother and then between Cynthia and her father.

Imaginary Conversation #1: Cynthia and Her Mother

CYNTHIA: Mami, Dad treated you so badly! Why didn't you ever stand up for yourself?

MOTHER: I was born in a different generation, m'ija. Women didn't talk back to their husbands then. We were raised to respect the

man of the house. Your father was the one who made the rules,
and I had to respect that.

CYNTHIA: But how could you live with a man who constantly criticized you and put you down?

MOTHER: Because, even with all that, I think he loved me in the
way that he could. And I continued to love him, even though
I wanted more for myself. I hoped that one day you would have
the kind of life I wanted, and that would make me happy.

CYNTHIA: And are you happy for me, Mami? Sometimes your eyes
look so sad, it makes me want to cry.

MOTHER: I am very happy for you, m'ija. Very happy.

CYNTHIA: But what about being happy for yourself?

MOTHER: You know, m'ija, your father is not as bad as you may
think. He's better than his own father was. Years ago, I asked
my mother-in-law the exact same things about your abuelo that
you are asking me. He really was what I would consider a bad
man. But she told me what I am telling you—"He loves me. We
have a family together, and we have to learn how to live together." In my day, if a woman divorced her husband, or if she
decided she wanted a career for herself, she was looked down
on by the entire community. So I had to accept the way things
were. And I take pride in holding our family together. Great
pride. I could have been a woman like you, if the times had
been different. But at least I can take pride in having raised a
strong woman like you.

During this "conversation," Cynthia remembered what her
mother had told her about her grandmother and grandfather, and
she came to the conclusion that her mother believed that her own
marriage was somewhat better. Cynthia realized that a pattern was
repeated from generation to generation, but that each time there
was some improvement.

Not everything is as static as we think it is. Changes occur, though sometimes in small increments. Cynthia's realization that her mother's life was a bit better than her mother-in-law's had been, and that her mother took such great pride in having held the family together and having raised her to be strong, allowed Cynthia to become more accepting of the way things were in her family.

Imaginary Conversation #2: Cynthia and Her Father

CYNTHIA: How could you have treated Mami the way you did . . . when she loved you so much?

FATHER: M'ija, I didn't treat your mom so badly. I provided for her, she had everything she needed. She was able to stay home and be with her children, as she wished to do. She was able to take care of her own mother, when her sisters and brothers were not able to do that. I provided well for my family.

CYNTHIA: I acknowledge that you were a good provider for my mom and for us. But that's not all there is to being a good husband! You really made Mami unhappy during all those years.

FATHER: Oh, m'ija, don't say that. I didn't make her unhappy. We had a good, happy life between us. Look, she didn't have to worry about the things you have to worry about these days . . . about working, and being preoccupied with keeping your job because you have to survive. She didn't have all those worries that you have now.

CYNTHIA: I understand that, Dad. But you diminished and belittled her. You didn't give her the respect and dignity that she deserves. She was a very good mother and wife.

FATHER: I know that. And that's why I have to say that I realize maybe I was not always right. But I'm just a human being. I was raised with very clear ideas about what it meant to be a man. I learned those ideas from my father, but I was not as harsh as he was. My own father used to hit my mother. And he hit me, too.

And I learned then that I would never do that to my own family. Una buena paliza—a good beating—made its impact in terms of teaching me what not to do. I never hit your mother or you kids. I tried to do the best I could for all of you. And always keep in mind, m'ija, that I love your mother.

CYNTHIA: I understand your feelings, Dad. And I know you loved Mami and me and my brothers and sisters. I just want you to know that I am planning to marry a man—and he's a Latino, too—who will never treat me the way you treated Mom. We respect each other, and we have an understanding between us that is completely different from what you and Mom had.

FATHER: I'm happy for you, m'ija. I'm glad that you found someone who respects you and loves you. That is what I worked for in my own life. Even though you have told me you resent so many things about me, I'm glad you turned out the way you have. I love you.

Each imaginary conversation ended with Cynthia in tears. She realized many things from these "inner dialogues" between herself and her parents: that her parents had faults, that they also had strengths, that they were different from her, but that they were proud of her and loved her. She also realized that, with all their problems, they loved each other. Her parents' relationship was not one Cynthia would ever want to emulate, but she is learning to take from her past the lessons she can use for her own life. And to accept the contradictions, as painful as they might be.

Are there areas in your own life where you need to confront your parents or other family members? Are there statements you've always wanted to make to them, or questions you've been meaning to ask? Are you angry at members of your family for things that happened when you were a child? Do you feel sad about something that happened between you that you never had the opportunity to talk about?

Imaginary conversations—either written down or acted out

through the Imaginary Conversation with Your Parent Exercise—
are an excellent way to get in touch with the unresolved issues between yourself and a family member. They are safe, because you
don't have to actually talk to the person, thereby risking a rift in
the relationship. But you will be amazed at how cleansing it is to
express these thoughts and feelings, to bring your emotions to the
forefront. Imaginary conversations enable you to learn a lot about
yourself, your family, and the feelings you have for the people who
are partly responsible for shaping who you are. And this new
knowledge and understanding will undoubtedly clarify certain key
issues between you and your husband, wife, or partner.

PREPARING FOR AN ACTUAL CONVERSATION
WITH YOUR PARENT

If you choose to have an actual conversation with your parent in
which you bring up difficult issues from your past, having "re-
hearsed" that conversation by writing or acting it out will be a
great advantage. Be aware, however, that in a real conversation,
your father or mother is likely to react defensively to what you say,
especially if you approach them with anger and accusations. You
cannot hope to come to an understanding about difficult past issues with your parents unless you feel that you can approach the
conversation calmly, without blaming or criticizing. There are several ways to develop this attitude.

You can prepare by carefully considering what you want to say,
making sure that your issue is stated in terms of how you felt then
and how you feel now. You want to concentrate on using such
I/me statements as, "This is what I was feeling at that time. This
is the impact my past is having on my life now." Accusing your
parent with statements like, "You did this and this and this to
me . . ." will only threaten them and undermine your ability to
reach an understanding.

Your conversation should end with a statement concerning what it is you want from your parent now. You may want to simply have your parent hear what you have to say, or you may want an apology for some serious wrongdoing, or you may want to work with your parent to create a better relationship.

And remember, deal with only one parent at a time. If you try to talk to both parents at once, you run the risk of one apologizing for the other or rationalizing on the other's behalf. You want to have a one-to-one conversation, in which both of you stay focused on your honest feelings.

To ensure that the conversation you eventually have with your parent does not begin with accusations, start by saying something like:

> There are things that I want to discuss with you that happened when I was a child. I would like for you to be able to listen to me, and I will listen to you, too. I need to learn more about how you and I related to each other, so that I can better understand not only our relationship but also my present relationship (with my wife, husband, partner.) So if you feel that you are ready to have this conversation, I would like that.

If your parent reacts angrily to this invitation, or if you feel that you cannot approach him or her without anger and accusations, then it is not the right time to talk to each other about these things.

If your parent agrees to a dialogue, and the two of you are able to calmly discuss the issue you have chosen, you may each come away with insights that can enable you to eventually let go of your guilt, anger, or resentment. You and your parent will also have an opportunity to apologize to each other, if that course of action is warranted.

If the issues you're dealing with are very serious—such as physical abuse or incest—a conversation between the two of you may not be enough. In such cases, family therapy with a professional counselor is a good idea.

RAÚL AND HIS MOTHER: AN UNHEALTHY ALLIANCE

Children have a basic need for their parents' love and approval. In healthy families, these are given to them unconditionally—with no strings attached. In unhealthy families, children must fulfill certain needs their parents have in order to receive the love or approval or safety they require. Such a situation is very unfortunate, because children should never be responsible for their parents' well-being or happiness. When parents blame their children for their own frustrations, or place an emotional burden on the children by requiring them to play such inappropriate roles as pleaser or caretaker, this behavior can have serious consequences.

Raúl's case illustrates what can happen when a parent assigns a child the inappropriate role of substitute spouse. Raúl's mother resented her husband because he was a workaholic who never had time for her or their children. He had difficulties communicating with his wife, rarely spent time with her, and never invited her to discuss feelings or problems with him. When she confronted him about these issues, he responded that he worked hard, so that the family could live well. In his own mind, he believed that he was fulfilling his role of husband and father.

Unfortunately, Raúl, the oldest son, was chosen to fill the void in Raúl's mother's life. When Raúl was as young as eight, his mother began discussing with him her frustrations over her husband's coldness and lack of attention. At this early age, Raúl became his mother's confidant and companion. Rather than reconciling her differences with her husband, she gave up on him and instead established a substitute "couple" relationship with her son. Raúl learned early on that his mother required an emotional connection to him, and in order to feel the love he naturally needed from her, he had to satisfy her needs.

As Raúl grew older, he wanted to spend more time with friends, but his mother became jealous of his relationships with other people. Because he was so emotionally tied to her, Raúl could acutely sense how left out his mother felt when he spent time with anyone else. She made him feel guilty, and he resented her for it, but neither of them confronted each other with their feelings.

Eventually, Raúl left home, went to college, and began his career. As an adult, he still keeps in close touch with his mother, telephoning her at least every other day and seeing her at least once a week. But his resentment has not gone away. Only now, in addition to resenting the closeness he feels compelled to maintain with his mother, he also resents any woman who wants to get close to him. He feels uncomfortable when girlfriends indicate that they want the relationship to grow "more serious," and he often retaliates by making hurtful or sarcastic remarks. As long as sex and superficial companionship are all a woman wants, he feels comfortable; but if she wants more, he automatically rejects her.

Because Raúl was forced into an unhealthy alliance with his mother, filling in for a father who was emotionally absent, he is now paying a great price. At thirty-three, he thinks about his bachelor lifestyle and senses that something is missing. But he cannot seem to get close to a woman without feeling deeply threatened. "I just don't think I will ever want to get married or have children," he told me recently. "From what I've seen of marriage, it's not really about love."

Sadly, Raúl's negative feelings about marriage aren't only a reflection of his parents' distant relationship; they also reveal his own experience with his mother—which was less about love than about obligation. And this sense of dread has carried over to his feelings about women in general. If Raúl is ever to overcome his inability to get close to someone, he will have to make a commitment to face his past honestly and to deal with his resentments. Until he does so, he is likely to remain stuck in the very history he wants so desperately to escape.

ACKNOWLEDGING THE NEGATIVE, APPRECIATING THE POSITIVE

One of the ways we can begin to deal with our feelings about the past, so that we don't remain stuck there, is to expand our perspective concerning what happened to us as children. The broader a picture we're able to draw in our minds of what our childhood was like, and why it looked that way, the greater our understanding of our psychological roots. We need to get to the point where we can acknowledge both the good and the bad, so that our mental family portrait is as representative of the truth as possible.

For example, if Raúl could objectively look back at his parents' behavior, how might he assess what they did right and what they did wrong? Was his mother totally to blame for creating an unhealthy alliance between them? Or did his father's coldness also figure into his mother's need to get too close to Raúl? Was his father's coldness the result of indifference, or was it due to his inability to express his feelings? And was this inability something Raúl's father inherited from his own father, as well as being related to the tendency of Latino men to hide their emotions?

What about the positive aspects of Raúl's upbringing? Both his parents always stressed the importance of an education, and that emphasis meant that Raúl never doubted that he would go to college. His father's strong work ethic influenced Raúl in his committment to performing well and striving to do his best. And his mother, for all her neediness, demonstrated her love for her son in countless ways.

When you think about how you were brought up, and what

your parents brought to your childhood experience of what life was all about, what comes to mind? In what ways did your parents prepare you to become a healthy, loving, competent adult? In what ways did they consciously or unconsciouly hold you back, hurt you, undermine your confidence? For some people, child-hood memories are so painful that it's difficult for them to identify any positive traits or feelings connected with their parents. Others find it hard to be objective about a time in their life that is so fraught with emotions, both good and bad.

The following simple writing exercise is something you might choose to try. It can help you sort through the positive and neg-ative memories, so that you can more honestly view your own past. You may find, after writing down your thoughts, that you will come away with a more balanced account of your family history.

❦ Exercise
ASSESSING NEGATIVE AND POSITIVE FAMILY TRAITS

Make two lists, one consisting of the negative ways your parent or parents treated you and the other stating their pos-itive attributes or the positive ways in which they treated you as a child.

For Example:

"I *acknowledge* . . .

. . . that you were critical of my efforts in school, and never encouraged me to go on to college;

. . . that you didn't want me to surpass your own achieve-ments;

. . . that you never took the time to find out what I was in-terested in;

. . . that you didn't tell me that you loved me.

"I *appreciate* . . .

. . . how much time you spent taking care of me and my
brothers and sisters, cooking for us, sewing our clothes,
caring for us when we were sick;

. . . your love of music, and how you passed it on to me;

. . . your sense of humor, even when times were hard;

. . . that you loved me, even though you never expressed it.

Note: You may prefer to do this exercise in the form of a letter. Write a letter (which will not be sent) to your parent or
parents, telling them what you want to acknowledge as negative experiences from your childhood, as well as what you
have come to appreciate about them as parents.

CAN WE CHANGE THE FAMILY PATTERNS WE'VE INHERITED?

It's often difficult to discern how much of our behavior has been
inherited from our parents or other family members. It can also be
hard to change the parts of ourselves that have been negatively influenced by our family history, since these traits were acquired at
such an early age.

As children, we received numerous nonverbal messages and acquired specific thought patterns and values that we may not even
be aware of as adults. For example, having witnessed how our
mother treated our father we might later incorporate those behaviors into our own demeanor with our lover or spouse, without
being conscious of what we are doing. If we can learn to objectively observe these patterns in ourselves, we can then consciously
choose to accept this behavior or to change it.

We cannot do so when we are children, because children don't
have the ability to be objective about their parents' conduct, nor
can they make conscious decisions about the best way to react to
their parents' actions. Children's response to their parents' treat-

ment is based largely on their need for the parents' love and support. Children unconsciously develop ways of adapting to their mother's and father's behavior, so that they can feel safer.

Our task as adults is to become more aware of how our inner conflicts and outward behavior came about and to take steps to change what we are dissatisfied with in ourselves. We cannot change our past nor can we change our parents, but we can change ourselves. Learning about why our parents behaved as they did and accepting our past allows us to make the desired changes in ourselves and move on with our lives. We can begin this process by finding out about our parents' backgrounds.

The reason perfect parents do not exist is that all mothers and fathers carry their own imperfect childhood with them throughout their parenting experience. Our parents may have lived through very difficult situations with their own parents. They may have been exposed to abuses, to a lack of love, even to traumas, and all these circumstances were beyond their control.

All children need to be nurtured with love, attention, compassion. They need to have their feelings respected, to feel valued, to receive guidance, to learn limits to their behavior, to learn to respect other people, to be given appropriate responsibilities, and to be taught good moral values. When children receive this kind of care, they naturally develop a sense of self-worth that enables them to face the world with curiosity, intuition, creativity, and love. They grow into people who can adapt to life, develop their potential, and have loving relationships.

If our parents didn't receive the proper nurturing or guidance as children, they don't usually know how to give such nurturing and guidance as parents. We may feel very angry at our parents for failing to love us or guide us in the way we would have liked, in the way that would have made it easier for us to develop into the kind of person we want to be. Acknowledging that anger and expressing it is fine. (See above, the Imaginary Conversation with Your Parent Exercise.) But holding on to the anger and resentment inhibits our ability to grow and change. Understanding what our parents went through, and having compassion for them, is much more healing. Once we're able to experience these feelings, we can move on and begin building the kind of life we want for ourselves.

If you feel that you are ready to forgive your parents for their shortcomings or negative behavior, you may want to try the exercise entitled Visualization Exercise: Forgiving Our Parents, which follows. The exercise is designed to help you forgive your parents for whatever they may have done, consciously or unconsciouly, to hurt you or impede your growth when you were a child. It can help you to see the value in moving beyond the past, beyond blame, beyond the need to look to others for approval.

Once we can forgive our parents for not meeting all of our needs when we were children, we can begin to fulfill some of those needs for ourselves. But let me add that it is not always possible to forgive a parent—especially if they hurt us in a very serious way, such as subjecting us to incest or other physical abuse. Some people's parents are very unhealthy, and their actions cannot be forgiven so easily. Do not feel that you should push yourself to forgive if you are not ready to do so.

❦ *Visualization Exercise*
FORGIVING OUR PARENTS

This exercise will put you in a more relaxed frame of mind, so that you feel comfortable and safe about confronting your own issues regarding your parents. The exercise is something you do within your own mind, with no pressures from outside. Nobody is telling you what you should think or how you should feel. You can do this exercise at your own pace, in your own way, so that you feel relaxed. Because you won't be under pressure, you'll gain the momentum to become more tolerant, more open, more in charge of the situation, and as involved with your parents as you choose to be.

1. Put some calming instrumental music (or a tape of the sounds of the ocean, the wind, birds, and the like) on a tape recorder.

2. Over this soundtrack, tape your own voice giving the instructions for this visualization exercise. Speak slowly and softly.

3. Find a place at home or outside, somewhere where you feel relaxed and comfortable and where you know you won't be interrupted. Close your eyes, and play the tape of your own voice reading the following:

"I feel totally relaxed, very comfortable (on this couch, underneath this tree).

"I take a deep breath. This breath goes into my abdomen, passes through my diaphragm. When I exhale, I let go of all my tensions, all my preoccupations, all my thoughts of the day.

"I take another deep breath. Which invites me to be with myself. And to feel good.

"When I exhale, everything that is not related to myself leaves. Any preoccupation leaves.

"And I keep inhaling, inviting me to be with myself. Exhaling, leaving anything that doesn't belong to myself. (I give myself some time . . . about two minutes or so . . . to go through this relaxing process of deep breathing.)

"I see within myself the images of my mother and my father. Both together. I let these images come to me. I choose one of them—my mother or father. I am going to have an encounter with him or her.

"I see mi mamá. I see her in front of me. My mind brings my mother into the present. She's standing here. She's looking at me. She gets close to me. I allow my feelings to come forward as we look into each other's eyes.

"I see my mother as I remember her. I feel for her. Many memories come into my mind. Good memories, bad memories. Things from the past. I let them come. I don't fight them. I don't resent them. We look into each other's eyes, and the need to talk arises. I feel that I need to talk to her and to tell her how much I needed her when I was a child. We keep looking into each other's eyes. I express this need with my eyes.

"We understand each other, just by looking into each other's eyes. Mom is looking very firmly into my eyes, as she never has before. She seems to understand what I mean. I feel very comfortable, because she is understanding me, she is listening. So I can express even further what I have to say. I take my time. And I tell her everything that is on my mind, just by looking in her eyes.

"Mom is still standing here, after listening to everything I have to say. Then she shows me the palms of her hands. I try to understand what she's trying to say. Why is she doing this? Many other times in my life I tried to understand her and couldn't. This also seems to be hard to understand.

"I look again at her palms. They are empty. There is nothing in the palms of her hands. Suddenly I understand that the emptiness symbolizes what she couldn't give me when I was a child. What she couldn't offer me then.

"I look again into her eyes, into her face, and I see a sadness. And I understand the emptiness that she is expressing with her hands. I understand what she couldn't give me when I was little.

"I look again into her hands. They continue to be open, as if she was attempting to give me what I am asking for. But her hands are still empty. Mom keeps showing me her hands, trying to say something else. As if showing me her hands is her attempt to give me what I'm asking for.

"Then I see a white light that comes from the palms of her

hands. And this light becomes more and more intense. It's a light that comes from her hands like a ray of energy. It reaches me. And I feel that light. And I feel the light is love. The love that couldn't come to me in other ways. But now, I understand it is there. And it has always been there.

"This light, this white energy, is full of life. It's around me, and inside of me, filling me with love. Love that, in some way, I knew was always there. But I could never see it or feel it. It is a love that allows me to forgive my mother for all that she couldn't give me when I was a child. It is a love that allows me to finally be myself.

"This love allows me to become an adult. It allows me to define myself. It allows me to forgive myself for my imperfections. To be happy. To be strong. To live in peace and harmony. To have a productive life. A wise life. It's a love that allows me to be honest in my relationships. It is a love that allows me to accept myself, even with the difficulties I had in my childhood.

"This light, this love allows me to realize how much I went through in the past. But it lets me be myself. With my own feelings, my own history. It allows me to accept my past as it was, without making it the present.

"This light allows me to leave my past in the past, without letting it control my present. And this light now gives me the power to change. To have my own feelings. To feel powerful. And to trust myself.

"And I enjoy this moment. And I enjoy this encounter that I am having with myself. It gives me such a feeling of wellness that I feel I can be generous with myself. I can accept that sometimes I may need help. And I will ask for help.

"I can be at peace with those who have harmed me. I can continue with my life. And they can, too. I can remember the difficult times in my life, but without the intensity of the emotions of that time. Because that intensity is no longer there, I can let go of the resentment and the negative feelings that once consumed all my energy.

"Now, I have all that energy to use for my own well-being. It's mine. I'm free. I can live my life and do what I always wanted to do. I can have that internal peace I've always searched for. That white light is still inside of me. I see it. I feel it. I sense it. I can even smell it.

"Slowly, slowly, my mother leaves. I let her go. But I keep that white light inside of me. It's the light of my being. The light that will stay with me for the rest of my days. The light from the one I can go to when I have doubts, insecurities. The light that will guide me. It's my own internal light.

"Now, I will end this exercise, keeping that light inside myself. I will never lose it. It's mine.

"Now, I will count from five to one. On the number one, I will keep this light for myself. Five. Four. Three. Two. One."

ASKING YOUR PARTNER ABOUT HIS OR HER FAMILY HISTORY

Just as we can discover more about ourselves by exploring our own family history, we can learn more about our partner by finding out what his or her childhood was like. The more we understand what life was like for our partner growing up, the better prepared we will be to have a relationship with him or her.

Many friends have told me that when they were first dating their future husband or wife, they spent a lot of time talking about their pasts, what it was like growing up in their respective families. This was a way for them to discover what they had in common, and certainly it is one of the best ways to begin to get to know someone. A person's willingness to share with you his memories, fears, doubts, joys and sadness relating to his family history means they are allowing you into his life. When a person confides in this way it means that he trusts you enough to tell you about moments and events that were crucial in his development, that may have entailed a great struggle, or that caused him pain.

It's never too late to begin this process of sharing your past with someone you trust. Everyone goes about this process in their own way and at their own pace. Perhaps you have been dating some-one for a while, or you may even have been married for a few years, and still you haven't talked very openly about your family background. Some people may find it threatening to reveal un-pleasant or upsetting things about their past. It's never appropri-ate to force someone to talk about events that make him or her feel uncomfortable. But the more partners can be open with each other, and the more forthcoming they are about their family his-tories, the closer they are likely to become.

¡SOCORRO!
WE NEED HELP!

I'm the type of person who keeps my personal life to myself. I don't need to broadcast to the world what's going on in my family. I take pride in the fact that I can handle whatever problems come up in my life, whether it's something with my husband or difficulties with my children. If it gets really bad, I know I can always find comfort in God and going to church. This time was different, though. Every night, I prayed things would get better, and I told myself I could endure it. But I found out I couldn't endure it alone. If it hadn't been for the support group I finally joined, I don't know what would have happened.

—Rosanna, age 38

It's true my wife and I were having lots of problems, but when she wanted us to see a psychologist, to me that seemed like showing someone else our dirty laundry. In our culture, people don't talk about their personal problems to a stranger. Maybe you would privately ask your parents or an uncle or your priest about a marriage problem. But psychologists? No way. Only people who are considered locos would need to go to one of those. Overcoming that prejudice was not easy for me at first.

—José, age 42

In the course of this book, we have discussed a range of personal and family problems—from difficulties communicating with a partner to sexual concerns to parenting dilemmas. And in the previous chapter, we saw how finding out more about our family history can help us to understand and resolve problematic areas in our relationships. But what if we find that we can't come up with solutions on our own? What if we feel that we need additional help in sorting out conflicts in our family, relationship, or marriage?

Although the average American takes marriage counseling, therapy, support groups, and twelve-step programs pretty much for granted these days, many Latinos are reticent when it comes to seeking outside help for their personal problems. Why are so many of us reluctant to seek professional help or to get the assistance we need to overcome our family conflicts?

The answer lies in the fact that, in our culture, we tend to deal with our problems in other ways. Therapy and self-help groups are not the norm in most of our countries of origin. The role of counselor or confidant is usually filled by an extended family member, a member of the clergy (in most Latino families, a Catholic priest), a curandero, or the family doctor. Whatever difficulty a person may be going through, emotional support is close by and intrinsic to normal life. Talking with someone you trust and know well is a very informal process, much less threatening than seeing a professional therapist or joining a group of strangers in a formal meeting.

Even those of us who are second- and third-generation often consider seeking help from traditional sources as part of our experience and orientation. Before we explore some important new options for getting help which are available to all of us, let's take a look at the number of ways Latinos have traditionally received emotional support.

TRADITIONAL SOURCES OF EMOTIONAL SUPPORT

The Family Doctor

The typical family medical doctor in Latin countries knows you very well, comes to your home, talks to you, talks to your spouse and children, and really listens to your personal concerns—in addition to dealing with your medical condition. This opportunity to talk and be listened to by someone who cares is, in itself, excellent therapy. And those of you who have experienced this kind of attention and concern know how valuable it can be.

But such a relationship rarely exists in doctors' offices in the United States. Here, because of the time constraints imposed by our managed-care health system, doctors barely have time to make a diagnosis and write out a prescription. There is little time to establish rapport, to ask about your family and your children, much less to form an actual relationship.

A highly respected pediatrician friend of mine in Orange County, California, Dr. Alberto Gedissman, has often told me how frustrated he is by the fact that he doesn't have more time to spend with his patients. "I know that when I take the time to talk to parents about their child's behavior or developmental problems, or about their own parental insecurities, they benefit tremendously," he says. "But I usually don't have that time, especially with all the changes in our health-delivery system."

People in Latin countries are much more relaxed about time, and this attitude affects their relationships with others. They enjoy sitting and talking and philosophizing—even during work hours. The concept of time and efficiency isn't as rigid as it is here. While "time-saving" is valued in the United States, making it seem as if people here are always in a rush, Latino cultures value the everyday experience of friendly interaction. This attitude gives people the opportunity to talk over their problems in a casual way with those to whom they feel close, including their family doctor.

The Local Clergy

The close ties many Latinos form to their church also provide an avenue for dealing with personal and family concerns. The Catholic Church—and churches of other denominations as well—feel like home to many, places where people can unburden themselves of their troubles and find a sympathetic ear. The local member of the clergy is often the person people turn to for guidance and comfort.

Clergy can offer empathy and good moral advice, but there are drawbacks to depending solely on the Church for solutions to your relationship problems. Often an individual's or couple's problems are much more complicated than a simple moral dilemma. Such concerns need to be addressed in greater depth by someone trained in human psychology. Not all clergy have the professional education required to resolve relationship conflicts and/or mental-health problems. And with psychological issues so broadly discussed in the media today, people's expectations about the kind of advice they need have become much more sophisticated.

This does not mean that you should see a psychologist or counselor *instead* of seeking the advice of your priest or minister. One doesn't take the place of the other. Someone with a religious background can help you to think about your problems from a religious and spiritual point of view, which can contribute to working out your difficulties. A family counselor or psychologist can help you understand what is going on in your relationship from a psychological and family dynamics point of view. These professionals' sole purpose is to help you to resolve psychological, marital, or family problems in a way that will be most beneficial to you and to the members of your family.

Curanderos and Naturistas

Traditional healers or curanderos have also played a role in helping Latinos deal with physical illness, psychological problems, and general life difficulties. In his book *Latinos*, Earl Shorris describes curanderismo as "an ancient form of psychotherapy," which, unlike Western medicine and psychotherapy, does not depend on professional training but rather on the curandero's demonstration of knowledge.

Curanderos believe that their healing abilities are God-given and that their profession is a calling from God. They use herbal medicines, massage, prayer, ritual, and other folk practices to heal their patients.

Naturistas are those who recommend natural, herbal remedies for physiological and psychological problems. They know about the beneficial uses of different herbs, and they recommend and sell them to customers in botánicas—specialty stores. This natural approach can be beneficial as long as clients don't neglect to see a medical doctor when such a consultation is warranted. Unfortunately, some naturistas call themselves "doctores en naturismo," misleading people into thinking that they have medical degrees.

Curanderos, naturistas, and others in the healing arts are part of a tradition that can be traced back to most of the world's ancient cultures. The Chinese, for example, have a highly developed system of healing that includes acupuncture, acupressure, and herbal treatments. I think that what these traditional practices offer is both a complement to scientific approaches and a type of spiritual empowerment. People who visit a curandero or a healer feel that they are taking charge of their own mental or physical health by employing the special knowledge and spiritual energy of

that healer. This approach feels much more personal and meaningful than the impersonal system of Western medicine.

Curanderismo works best when the patients firmly believe that
it is within the curandero's power to heal them. Curanderos are
usually closely connected to their clients' extended family, and
they are therefore trusted implicitly. If a family member has recommended you to a respected curandero whom she trusts, you
would tend to believe in the curandero's ability to ease your pain
or make your marriage better, and you would therefore probably
benefit in some way from the treatment.

In addition to feeling spiritually inspired—believing that they
have been called upon by God to heal others—curanderos can
have very special abilities, such as heightened intuition and highly
developed sensitivities. Such healing individuals can often break
through the client's barrier of loneliness to connect with that person's energy and soul, and the results of this connection can be
very therapeutic.

On the other hand, some curanderos can be very damaging to
the clients' psychological health. I have a story to illustrate this
point. A woman I know was having problems with her husband.
Though the problems were not severe, she was unhappy enough
to seek help from a curandera. The curandera told this woman
that her mother-in-law was interfering in her relationship with her
husband, even practicing black magic to try to disrupt the marriage. The woman was advised to go home and confirm this information by noticing anything unusual in her house. The woman
went home and found a sweater that was soaking wet. After in-
terpreting this "sign" to mean that her mother-in-law was trying to
sabotage her marriage, she confronted her husband, and of course,
her husband became very upset. He was offended that his wife
doubted his own mother in this way, especially since the mother-
in-law had so generously helped to take care of their children. Because her husband became so defensive, the woman started to
doubt him as well, believing even more strongly that this behav-

ior was evidence of the mother-in-law's black magic that the curandera had foretold. She fought with her husband and told him
that she no longer wanted her mother-in-law to care for their children. Their whole family structure was imperiled, and the situation grew much, much worse.

Curanderismo isn't always practiced in such an irresponsible
way, but when it is—especially when the curandero tries to identify someone who is doing something wrong—it can be very, very
dangerous. But as many of you know from experience, there are
individuals who really do have special intuitive abilities. Let me
tell you another story, about an amazing experience with a healer
whom my husband and I met in Argentina. We were in a province
called Cordoba and went to visit a man who was very well known
there as a healer. He started talking to us about poetry and went
on for quite a while, when suddenly he looked into Alex's eyes and
asked, "Is the pain in your knee gone?" We were stunned; there
was no way this man could have known that Alex had been experiencing sharp pains in his knee for the past two weeks, but at
that moment, the pain disappeared. We were later told that this
man had very positively affected many others in the same way.

Some Westerners are skeptical about the authenticity and ef-
fectiveness of native healing techniques; but others grant that
such methods contribute an intuitive, spiritual element sorely
missing in traditional psychology and medicine. I believe that a lot
of the process of healing takes place in our minds. It's about being
positive, having faith, and believing in our own healing power.
Our minds have so much potential for healing, and modern society is still in the process of discovering these capabilities. Jay Ha-
ley, Norman Cousins, Dr. Carl Simonton, and others have written
extensively on the mind's healing abilities.

Interestingly, there is a marriage, family, and child counselor I
know of in Los Angeles, named Ignacio Aguilar, who combines
psychotherapy with the healing curanderismo he learned in Mex-

ico. He first has his client go through a limpia—a cleansing—that consists of bathing in special herbs. This procedure is intended to cleanse both body and soul of any negative influences. (He has special facilities in his office for this procedure.) Then he starts the psychotherapy session. Of course, this combined therapy works very well for those Latinos who believe that they will find the answers to their dilemmas within the unique healing process of the curandero.

The Extended Family

As we have discussed earlier, the extended family is very important in the lives of most Latinos around the world, and in the United States as well. Having so many relatives to whom we can relate, with whom we can talk and share our problems, and whom we can count on in a crisis is a blessing we deeply appreciate. Being part of a large, close family makes us feel empowered in a very special way, because we sense that we are more than an individual person, we are connected to something larger than ourselves. This connection to our families may actually contribute to longer life expectancy for Latinos. According to David E. Hayes-Bautista, executive director of the Center for the Study of Latino Health at the UCLA School of Medicine, the life expectancy of Latinos in Los Angeles County is almost four years longer than that of their Anglo counterparts; this discrepancy is due in part to the importance of family in their daily lives and to the opportunity to rely on relatives to meet many of their needs.

Many Latinos living in the United States, however, lack a large extended family. The built-in support system we once took for granted is often merely an idealized concept. Family members are spread throughout the country or still "back home," in our country of origin. Without the cousins, abuelas, sisters, and tíos whom we can automatically trust with our personal problems, we feel isolated and alone. Further, many of us who are used to the idea of family being number one and fulfilling our social needs find creating close friendships an unfamiliar process.

I remember being amazed when I first came to this country that my brother and sister-in-law, who had been in the United States for seventeen years, had created their own surrogate extended family, comprised of friends! To me, this was unusual. They had grown very close to a number of Argentine couples who had emigrated to this country, were about their same age, had children, and had other things in common culturally. So these families gathered together in much the same way an extended family would, on weekends, at holidays, and for other special occasions. They were also constantly and consistently available to one another, sharing problems and common concerns, babysitting, even swapping children's clothing. These people immediately accepted me into their "family" and treated me as my own extended family would have.

It was a lesson for me that our Latino experience of extended family can be modified to include others who may not be related by blood but who are connected to one another by cultural similarities and mutual need. My brother's friends created a family because, having no blood relations in this country, they needed one. Just as in a regular family, they didn't always see eye to eye; there were differences and conflicts among the members—as in any family. But these people were there for one another. And they opened their circle to admit new family members, like me, who needed the support and comfort that only a family can provide.

ASKING FOR HELP FROM NEW SOURCES

We come from a tradition in which bringing one's problems to extended family members, to the family doctor, to the clergy, or to the curandero is the customary way to resolve conflicts. But when those sources aren't available, or when we need answers and solutions that we can't get from these people, we must go beyond tradition and find new sources of guidance and emotional support.

In the rest of this chapter, we will pursue these new options. We'll talk about the importance of therapy when it is called for, but we'll also explore other helpful alternatives, such as support groups, twelve-step programs, and self-help books and tapes. And I will also share with you the experiences I have had with my talk-show listeners and viewers who have reached out to me for help.

Acknowledging that you cannot get through a marital or family crisis alone, that you're unable on your own to resolve a problem that has been holding you back or keeping you from living a happier life, is the first step toward improving your situation. Asking for help can be the beginning of a life-changing process of personal growth.

Why Can't My Best Friend Be My Therapist?

There are many people I know who believe that they need to go no further than their best friend to resolve relationship problems. "Why should I go to a counselor to talk about my marriage problems?" they might ask, "when I can always count on my best friend, Gloria, to help me figure things out? She understands me better than anyone."

Friends are wonderful and extremely important. They give us needed emotional support and love, and they make us feel less alone in the world. They're there for us in countless practical ways as well, from baby-sitting to bringing over a meal when we're sick to helping us move. But when it comes to problems between you and your partner, friends will take sides. And guess whose side they'll be on?

"That's great!" you may say. "I need to hear my girlfriend back-

ing me up and telling me how badly my husband has been treating me!"

It's true, you do need to have your friend on your side to make
you feel supported and loved. But this support won't help you resolve the problem between you and your husband. Let's listen in
on two conversations, one between Lupe and Gloria and another
between Eduardo and Roberto, and you'll see what I mean.

LUPE: You know, Eduardo leaves without telling me where he's going, he never takes me out anymore, and he refuses to talk to
me about what's going on.

GLORIA: No te dejes, girl—don't let him get away with it. Men are
like that, and you shouldn't let him treat you that way. He's
taking you for granted, just like Roberto used to do with me.

Here's how Eduardo and Roberto discuss the same circumstances.

EDUARDO: Lupe has been on my case every day, telling me I don't
take her out enough, I don't do this and I don't do that. She
doesn't appreciate anything I do for her anymore.

ROBERTO: No la dejes, man. Women always want to take advantage of men by crying or through sex or some other thing. If you
let her get away with this, she'll figure you're weak, and she'll
try to pull stuff like this all the time. Don't let her do that to
you. Be strong, man. Show her she can't get to you like that.

What has happened in these conversations is that both sets of
friends—Lupe and Gloria and Eduardo and Roberto—have
turned Lupe and Eduardo's marital problems into a kind of gender
war. It's only natural that when we complain to our friend about
our partner, we present our story in terms of our partner's taking
advantage of us. Our friend (who cares more about us than about
our partner) cannot be objective and therefore instinctively tries

to protect us from this husband or wife who is mistreating us in some way.

The advice a friend gives also tends to be "contaminated" by that friend's own experiences. With the best of intentions, friends project their own conflicts and issues into your situation—so that their advice is geared toward them, not you. In any relationship, there are the issues of one person, the issues of the other person, and then the issues of the relationship, which is a third entity. Our friends don't usually know both sides, and there's no way they can know about the relationship as an entity.

One of the best things a friend can do is simply to listen and to provide empathy and support. But while it makes us feel better to have a friend on our side, we're still left with an unresolved problem. In fact, the kind of "gender bashing" mentality evident in the above conversations creates more obstacles instead of more understanding.

Eduardo and Lupe would be much better served by talking to each other, with the goal of resolving their differences. The problem that many couples face in trying to do so, however, is an inability to get beyond blaming and becoming defensive so that each person can honestly listen to the other and understand their partner's point of view. (Chapter 3 deals with techniques to improve communication between couples.) This is one reason why seeing a professional marriage counselor or therapist is so helpful. Such a professional is an objective "third party," trained to help people see themselves and others in a more impartial and honest light, so that resolution to problems becomes more feasible.

Friends are invaluable in our lives, but we cannot expect them to be objective when listening to our problems or to advise us of the best way to handle our relationships. The role of therapist is not one for which they are either prepared or suited.

Television and Radio Psychology Shows: Learning What It's Like to Share Your Problems with a Professional

Before we discuss when it is appropriate to see a therapist for relationship problems, I think it would be beneficial to examine how television and radio advice shows work, because such shows provide a kind of introduction to what it's like to get help from a professional therapist. Of course, talking to a psychologist on the radio or getting advice from one in front of a television camera is very different from going for private therapy. In private therapy, there is time to fully discuss how you feel about the issues you are dealing with. You can talk in depth about how your personal history may have influenced a particular problem, and this exploration helps shed light on why you're currently going through certain difficulties. And of course, after the hour is up, you usually come back at another appointed time and continue exploring whatever issue you're working on. Even short-term therapy generally involves between ten and twelve hour-long sessions.

With television counseling, you have only two or three minutes to address a particular personal issue; on the radio, you have six or seven minutes. From a technical point of view, it's best for the host and the person who wants advice to complete a topic between commercials, and the time frame is therefore very limited. Such short conversations can give you, as the caller or guest, only a hint about what you should be concerned about in your relationship as well as the motivation to probe more deeply into the particular difficulty you're experiencing. A potential risk to listeners or viewers is that they may be tempted to identify so closely with a guest on the show that they feel the advice is appropriate for them as well, when in fact, such advice is meant only for the individual to whom it is given.

My talk shows provide advice, education, and information for the people who either call in or appear in front of the camera to share their problems with me. As we discussed earlier, without the traditional support system to which Latinos are accustomed, there is a tremendous need for people to talk openly with others about their personal dilemmas.

Talk shows serve a unique function in that, even if you are not the one discussing your problems with the professional or host, you can listen to the concerns of others and thereby feel less isolated, knowing that other people are experiencing similar difficulties. Knowing that you are not alone, that you are not the only one having a particular marital or sexual or family crisis, can provide enormous relief.

About 80 percent of the calls on my radio show are from women between the age of twenty and forty. But those figures do not reflect my entire audience; those are just the callers. The husbands and boyfriends are listening as well, and they're the ones who often tell their wives or girlfriends to call. After all, men don't want to look weak. And what kind of questions do callers ask? Questions about infidelity, sexual difficulties, the role of men and women in a changing society, and parenting problems are among the most typical concerns. Both men and women ask about these issues, but they do so in very different ways.

If I had to characterize these differences, I would say that women "share" and men "intellectualize." For example, Maria might call in with a complaint about her husband, Alberto: "For the last six months, Alberto has not been coming home on time, his moods have changed, he's very irritable, he doesn't want to talk to me, he's nasty. He's nasty even with the kids, he doesn't want to listen to them, and sometimes he becomes too aggressive with them. He tells me that all his time is taken up with work, and that's the excuse he gives for acting this way."

After telling me this much, María will finally say, "And today I found out that Alberto had an affair."

José, on the other hand, may say something like, "Doctora, I would like to know what the chances are that a marriage can survive after an affair."

So a man's and a woman's approach to the same problem tend to be quite different. For the woman, there is the need to disclose, to share her problems. The man needs to remove himself emotionally by posing a more theoretical question. And he wants to get right down to business by determining a solution to that problem. The woman wants to talk about the problem, to open her heart to another human being, and to receive comfort. The man is talking to a doctor, a "scientist"; he wants statistics, facts, and to be told what he is supposed to do.

Once my guests have told me the basic problem they want help with, I usually ask them to describe how this situation came about, so that I can learn more about their lives and the context of their difficulties. María, for example, might begin to elaborate on her husband's infidelity by attempting to justify his actions. For example, she might say, "Los hombres llegan hasta donde las mujeres quieren—Men will go as far as women allow them to go. He's not really responsible, because he's a typical man . . . and you know men are very weak when it comes to sex. If they're offered something, they will go for it."

María's justification of Alberto's behavior tells me that she wants him to remain worthy of her love and forgiveness. She may go even further and blame herself, saying, "Well, I rejected him many times, not wanting to have sex with him. And I took better care of my children than of him. So it's no wonder he wanted another woman for sex."

Interestingly, men also have a tendency to justify their wife's infidelity on the basis of her "weakness." José would typically tell me that his wife's affair means "she was unable to resist the advances of another man, because all women are weak." This explanation is a way of justifying his wife's behavior; she succumbed to another man's advances because she couldn't help herself. "A guy tells a woman something nice about her looks or her personality, and she can't say no to him," is how José might explain it.

Unlike women, men don't usually blame themselves. They might begin with self-blame, but they'll end with a condemnation of their mate. José would mostly likely say something like:

> Well, probably I should have paid more attention to Olga. I recognize that. But in reality I couldn't, because she was always busy with her kids [note that he calls them "her" kids, not his or theirs], or with trying to make the house shine. She was always worried about something. So I didn't ever feel invited to say nice things to her or to come near her. I may not have told her I loved her, but I showed her by working hard. But she's so weak, just like most women. Just because this guy said some nice things to her, she falls for it.

These accounts are typical of the stories I hear on my shows. One of my jobs as a psychologist in this short-term interaction with people is to get women to go from a "complaint" to an "action," and to get men to take the time to understand the feelings and the problem before demanding a quick solution or "action."

Behind all my callers' questions and complaints is a need to take action, but most don't know just what that action ought to be. Women usually feel that they're the ones who are supposed to take care of the problems at home, to be the peacemakers, the ones who settle all the conflicts. When they have done everything they can think of, and no change has occurred, they become frustrated. From that frustration comes the big complaint, "la gran queja." Women expect to have to endure a lot in the way of stress and problems, to put up with what life gives them (aguantar)— after all, that's what our mothers taught us. But getting stuck with the attitude of aguantar, unable to take the appropriate action, means that one's conflicts are never resolved.

With women callers, I first allow them to vent their feelings. By releasing frustrations first, thoughts can become more organized, you can begin to prioritize them, and finally you'll be able to get greater clarity about the problem at hand. Then, we formulate what the problem is together, so that the caller can consider what kind of action might resolve it. After venting and formulating the problem, we can make a plan—and in this way the queja is transformed into an action.

We have an expression in Argentina, "Tenemos que limpiar el campo," which literally means, "We have to clean the ground." If you have a garden with a lot of weeds and bushes and you can't see what's there, you have to clear away the excess growth, to see what you've got. In terms of personal problems, once you've expressed your feelings and "gotten it all out," you can clear away the excess details and emotions and identify the essential dilemma you're facing. That's what I do on my talk shows, so that my listeners and viewers can clearly see the issues they're troubled by. I then help them figure out their options, and after that, they can consider the decisions they might make.

Men are usually very action-oriented; they're anxious to take steps to solve the problem. "Give me the solution, and I'll do it," they may say. But what is often missing is the process of feeling their emotions and taking the time to assess their thoughts. Frequently I must ask them how the particular situation makes them feel, because they've distanced themselves from it to a certain extent by presenting it as an intellectual problem. "Getting in touch with your feelings" may be a cliché, but it's something a lot of men have difficulty doing at first.

I know from experience with many male callers and clients that, for men, approaching difficulties in a relationship can be extremely frustrating and at times demoralizing. Initially, they often don't see that solving relationship problems is a process to which they must dedicate themselves. They're anxious to hear my solution to their problems—but it's not a question of my solution. Their problems with their wives or girlfriends require that they go through a process of expressing and listening to each other's feelings, pinpointing the problem, coming up with options, and then agreeing on their own solutions. I am only there to guide them in that process.

Some men neglect to include themselves as part of the problem they describe. A caller may say, for example, "Can you help my wife? She's here with me, she doesn't want to call, but this is her problem. . . ." This caller has taken himself out of the picture, labeled the problem as his wife's, and put the problem into my hands. He thinks that, because I am a woman therapist, I will understand his wife and tell her, from a woman's point of view, what is the best thing for her to do. The process of conflict resolution doesn't work that way.

Once we start talking about the conflict and how it can be worked on, most men begin to understand that they must take some of the responsibility for whatever the situation is. When there is a problem in any relationship, it involves both people, not just one or the other; and both people must participate in resolving it.

It may appear at first as if men don't want to receive help, but that is not usually the case. Once I invite them to work on the problem, and once they understand that a solution doesn't usually become apparent immediately but involves a longer process, they understand how important it is to participate in that process. Men need to feel reinforced and accepted for doing the right thing in a relationship, for taking steps to improve it. Acknowledging them for doing so is very important.

The following interactions between María and me, and then José and me show how my talk-show guests go from a complaint to defining the issue to thinking about what action they might eventually take. This progression is similar to what takes place in therapy. Of course, these excerpts are brief, and certainly, serious problems cannot be dealt with in a very short period of time. But reading the scenarios will give you some idea of how the process of resolving a relationship conflict is initiated.

Also notice how certain themes we have been discussing

throughout the book—cultural influences on behavior, differences between male and female perspectives, acknowledging feelings, and getting beyond blame—arise as María and José attempt
to sort through their difficulties.

SCENARIO #1: MARÍA TELLS ME ALBERTO HAD AN AFFAIR

MARÍA: Alberto acts like a different person now. He's never at
home, never takes any interest in the kids or me. He's nasty to
me when we do speak, but most of the time he just avoids me.
I feel so upset and angry at him, but I know it's probably my
fault. I just don't know whether I should ask him to leave or
not.

ME: Are things so bad that you would ask him to leave? Has anything happened that you haven't told me?

MARÍA: Well . . . he had an affair—it's over now, and he still wants
to continue our marriage, but do you think I should ask him to
leave?

ME: I cannot make that decision. I think that sometimes people
rush into asking the other person to leave in circumstances like
this, because they feel so much pain, inflicted by the person
who had the affair, that they need to punish that person by asking them to leave. I don't think that is a final solution. If you
need to be alone for a day or two or even longer, it may be good
for Alberto or for you to leave, so that you can have time to
think. But the main issue is not whether or not you should ask
him to leave. The main issue is, Is this a relationship that you
want to keep? Is it a valuable relationship? Is it worth it for you?
Was it good before this happened?

MARÍA: There were a lot of good things. But how can I stay with
someone who betrayed me?

ME: There are so many issues that may be involved in your husband's infidelity. It's impossible for me to tell you whether or

not you should stay with him. You may have many good things in your relationship, but your husband's affair may have caused such a blow to your sense of pride and shame that you think you must get rid of him. It's possible you could work things out with your husband, if you believe the relationship is worth it, and if he is also willing to work on it and commit to earning back your trust. You would both have to talk about why he was seeing another woman, and you would both need to deal with the fact that one of your marriage vows—the promise to be faithful—has been broken.

Some people don't necessarily believe in fidelity as an essential part of marriage. There are some marriages in which both partners feel free to have sexual relationships outside the marriage. In our culture, some Latino men feel that there is a distinction between loyalty and fidelity. They believe in being absolutely loyal, in that they would never leave their wives, but at the same time they have affairs with other women. You need to have a conversation with Alberto in which you both find out how each of you feels about being faithful.

Perhaps Alberto is so self-centered that he has never been— and never will be—able to meet your needs. If that is the case, it may not be worthwhile to work on a relationship that will never provide what you are expecting. If he has been unfaithful to you repeatedly, his behavior may indicate a pattern that is difficult to change. On the other hand, when people have affairs, it's usually not with the intention of humiliating their partner. They act according to their own needs. Perhaps Alberto feels insecure about something in his life and has had this affair to bolster his self-esteem.

These are all issues that need to be confronted by the two of you. You need to talk about them and come to your own conclusions. And again, the bottom line is: Do you feel that your marriage is worth the effort it will take to work things out?

MARÍA: So I have to learn more about why he had the affair and what's going on between us, and figure out if this relationship is worth it for me? If the good outweighs the bad?

ME: That's right. And the answer won't come right away, because you are in pain. Alberto has hurt you by what he has done. You have to live with that pain a while before you make any final decisions. That hurt will be there whether you stay together or break up. Divorce or not, the pain will be there, because overcoming infidelity involves a lot of pain. So the two of you should take the time to deal with this issue of betrayal before you can answer the question, "Is this relationship worth it or not?"

SCENARIO #2:
JOSÉ TELLS ME THAT OLGA IS HAVING AN AFFAIR

JOSÉ: What is your opinion, Doctora, about what a husband should do when he finds out that his wife has had an affair?

ME: Are you referring to your wife, José?

JOSÉ: Yes. Should I ask her to leave? Should I keep the children, because she obviously has no morals?

ME: It sounds as if you want the answer right now, but it takes time to think about what has happened, why it has happened, and how you feel about it. Are you willing to spend some time thinking about this, José?

JOSÉ: Yeah, but I didn't do anything wrong, Olga's the one to blame.

ME: Well, I think there's more to the situation than blame. You need to give yourself time to vent your feelings and thoughts. Review what has happened in your relationship through all the years you've been together. See if this is really a question of morals, or if it might have been something else that was happening in your relationship with your wife that led to her being unfaithful. You should allow yourself to feel the anger or the sadness or whatever else you're feeling, and then you need to talk to your wife, to find out what has gone wrong between the two of you.

JOSÉ: But how can I stay with a woman who has done such a thing?

ME: The bottom line is that you need to answer the question, Is the relationship valuable? If it is valuable for you, and for your wife, and the two of you want to work on the relationship, the second step will be to determine the issues that led to Olga's having the affair. Usually, infidelity is not about sex. There are many reasons people are unfaithful: sometimes it's power, or control, or feeling insecure about yourself, or escaping from something in the relationship that you don't want to face, or injecting excitement and drama into the marriage. These are questions you need to discuss with your wife. Both of you need to learn more about your relationship and see if it can be healed, by providing each other with what is missing between you. That's the only way you can get over the pain from this affair. Otherwise, the superficial steps you might take to make things better will be just like a Band-aid, and rifts between you will happen again.

JOSÉ: So I should take my time to learn more about what's been going on in our marriage, before I can figure out if our relationship is worth it for me?

ME: Yes. That is what you need to do.

When Is It Appropriate to See a Therapist for Relationship Problems?

In the course of reading this book, you have, hopefully, begun to gain a new understanding of the issues that most concern you in your relationship. As you responded to the questionnaire at the end of Chapter 2, you had an opportunity to identify the specific concerns you would like to work on, and as you read through the subsequent chapters, you probably focused on specific problems in your relationship, perhaps taking notes or writing down your thoughts. By now, you have had a chance to consider the ways in which your cultural and family background has influenced your relationship with your partner, how communication between the two of you could be improved, what you might do to prevent taking out your stress on the person you love. You may have identified particular exercises or techniques that might be appropriate for you to try. Becoming more conscious of what you can do to bring about a change in your relationship and employing the right strategies to make those changes happen can be very helpful. But sometimes new insights and self-help techniques are not enough.

When you feel that the connection between you and your partner is blocked in some way, or that your relationship is getting in the way of your personal growth, or that there are conflicts between the two of you that you cannot solve on your own, consulting a marriage counselor or psychologist is a good idea. Of course, all of us experience ups and downs in our relationships. But constant conflicts, blaming, and emotional pain are signs that your relationship is out of touch with its reason for existing, which is to nurture both you and your mate.

If your relationship no longer makes you feel cherished and nourished and strengthened, it's time to do something about it. If you and your partner have tried to resolve your conflicts, and your efforts have been futile, consulting a professional could make the difference between remaining stuck and moving on with your life.

It may be that you need only one consultation to get the two of you on the right track, so that you can keep going and growing. Or you may require more sessions to work out more serious problems. Perhaps your partner doesn't want to go to therapy, because of the cultural prejudices against what this process is all about (see "Misconceptions About Psychological Therapy" on page 221). You can still see a therapist on your own. If you are willing to work on your problems and are open to learning about new choices and possibilities in your life, the experience will be a positive one—and it will most likely cause your partner to change as well. Because when one person in a relationship alters their awareness and behavior, the other person has to adjust to that. And as that adjustment takes place, the relationship changes.

Do most people resist the idea that they need help with solving their problems? Yes, many people do. It's hard for most of us to admit that we can't figure out our problems for ourselves. And when we can't, we may deny that the problem exists, or we blame our partner, or we blame something or someone else. Actually, having enough of a perspective on ourselves and our relationship to acknowledge the need for help is a sign that we are reacting to our difficulties with courage and intelligence.

The following story of Veronica and Arturo shows how consulting a therapist can help avert more serious problems by addressing relationship difficulties before they escalate.

When Veronica and Arturo came to me for their first appointment, they were seated at opposite sides of the couch, looking at each other in a very hostile way. After I asked them to tell me what the problem was, the session continued as follows:

ARTURO: We have problems with communication and satisfying each other's needs. We've been married for eight years, and I'll admit I nag a lot. I complain when there's a problem. And right now the emotional bond is not there.

VERONICA: I am the opposite. If something bothers me, I keep it inside. I walk away from problems. I can't take the pressure he gives me. I have to constantly do things on his demand. I have to be a wife, work, take care of our two kids—and he's asking me about communication! I know I hold things in a lot, and I get into mood swings, but it's because I have too many things happening at once.

As we talked further, I found out that one of the things that was happening in Veronica's life was that her parents were having serious marital difficulties, and they were using her as a sounding board for their problems. Arturo resented the time Veronica spent addressing her parents' problems rather than facing their own. Veronica not only feared that her own marriage would deteriorate as her parents' had and that Arturo would one day cheat on her as her father had cheated on her mother; she also grew exasperated at Arturo's constant criticism.

VERONICA: I feel like just dissolving our marriage! I don't have the energy to keep going. I don't feel secure about myself—physically, the way I look, the way I feel. Maybe I'm not thinking right. I know I just withdraw, which makes things worse, but I have too many pressures!

ARTURO: I'd like to establish communication again. These problems can be solved. I'm a jealous man, and I know that. I yell, and I make it worse. But I'm trying just to make her realize that there is a problem. I talk and talk, and she simply answers, "Are you finished?" And then I ask her, "Why aren't you cariñosa—affectionate—to me? How come you aren't spontaneous with me?"

This part of the conversation led to a discussion of their sex life; Arturo said that it was not satisfactory.

VERONICA: How can I be cariñosa with you in bed, when you tell me that I'm fat? I'm not the same as I was when I was eighteen years old.

ARTURO: Well, I'm honest.

VERONICA: Yes, but you're hurting my feelings.

Up to this point, the session had consisted of complaints and defenses. It was also evident that Arturo was there to figure out a way to solve their problem quickly, which he identified as Veronica's failure to attend to his emotional and sexual needs. Like many men, Arturo is very solution-oriented, and he seemed to be most concerned with reaching that solution as soon as possible. Veronica, on the other hand, felt overwhelmed by Arturo's demands, by the pressures of her daily life, and by the problems of her parents—to the extent that she was tempted to give up on her relationship completely.

What I told Veronica and Arturo at the end of that first session was that each of them needed to understand that there was a middle ground between immediately finding a solution and giving up completely. This middle ground involved listening to each other's side of the story, expressing their feelings without blaming the other person, identifying the underlying problems, and then trying to come up with appropriate solutions.

Veronica and Arturo's problems are not unusual or unsolvable, but if they had let them go unattended much longer, they might have led to divorce. Veronica's quiet resentments and Arturo's "nagging" demands had been part of an ongoing situation that had already lasted eight years. Veronica was feeling pressured and overwhelmed, and Arturo was feeling rejected and unloved. Who knows how much longer they could have lived together with such distressing feelings?

Arturo and Veronica couldn't resolve these particular problems on their own, and they had begun talking about divorce. I think their decision to seek outside help when they did was a very wise one.

Misconceptions About Psychological Therapy

Although psychological therapy has been practiced for nearly a hundred years by various kinds of medical practitioners and others, many myths and misconceptions still surround it. Here are some of the most widespread misconceptions, along with my thoughts on these issues.

1. *Only locos go to a therapist.*

As reflected in the quote from José at the beginning of this chapter, probably the greatest misconception Latinos (and others) have about therapy is that only locos—crazy people—consult therapists. This attitude stems from the belief that we ought to be strong enough to take care of our problems ourselves. Pride is a major factor. To many Latinos, seeking help from a psychiatrist or psychologist for psychological difficulties means that you're either very weak or that you have extremely serious problems—like paranoia or schizophrenia—that require medication. As for a marriage, family, and child counselor (MFCC), most people are not familiar with this specialized professional, since there is no such profession in Latin America. So there is a skeptical attitude toward them as well. "What is it exactly that they do?" many Latinos may ask. Once they find out that MFCCs help people with their relationships, many have a response similar to their view on psychologists and psychiatrists: "Why should we have someone else help us solve our problems? We can resolve them by ourselves!"

The fact is that millions of people in the United States consult counselors, psychologists, and psychiatrists for a variety of personal, marital, and family difficulties, ranging from not so serious to very serious. And some go to these professionals, not for any particular problem, but for their own personal growth. Certainly the majority of these clients would not be deemed loco by any professional standards.

2. *If I go to a therapist, I will be forced to live in the past and talk endlessly about my childhood.*

Many people think that going into therapy is like entering an intensive, highly emotional state of turmoil. They fear that they will have to discuss all their painful childhood memories at once, like going into surgery and opening up all the wounds of the past. They are very afraid of feeling uncomfortable in the process.

On the contrary, the main focus of therapy is to learn about your past so that you can have a more comfortable present and a better future. We don't ever want to live in the past or to be so overwhelmed by memories of it that we cannot cope. Actually, the goal of therapy is to be able to let go of the negative or unpleasant patterns that we may be stuck in and to open up to new experiences. When we don't acknowledge our past, we can remain stuck in it. But when we're aware of our personal history, we can begin to change in positive ways.

3. *A therapist is just another "authority figure," who won't understand me but will tell me what to do.*

For the therapist-client relationship to work, the client must always feel that the therapist understands the client's circumstances. The therapist must be familiar with and sensitive to the client's cultural background, and the client must trust the therapist enough to be able to talk openly and honestly. For Latinos and other ethnic groups especially, it is essential that the therapist understand the unique cultural factors that influence our lives.

The therapist's role is not to "tell clients what to do," but rather, to help clients understand their problems and the options and opportunities available for solving them. It's very important that the therapist explain in the first session how the therapy is going to work, since there are so many misconceptions about what therapy entails. It's also crucial that clients feel free to voice any kind of discomfort they might feel in the course of their therapy. For therapy to be effective, the client has to trust both the therapist and the therapeutic process.

4. *I can't afford therapy. It's much too expensive.*

While some private therapists do charge high fees for their services, there are others who charge on a sliding scale, based on the client's ability to pay. Additionally, most cities have mental-health clinics that cater to low-income clients who wish to consult a counselor or psychologist.

There are also a number of ways you can qualify for assistance in paying for the services of a private therapist. Many people don't know that many medical insurance plans cover psychological services. EAPs (Employee Assistance Programs) also often cover psychological therapy. Sometimes it is totally covered, sometimes a copayment is offered. Medicaid and Medicare provide coverage for psychological consultation as well.

In addition, victims of crime—domestic violence, assault, robbery, or rape—are covered for psychological services by state-sponsored Victim Witness Assistance Programs. Children who have been exposed to domestic violence are covered under these programs as well. Various community mental-health programs also provide psychological help in crisis situations.

5. *Psychotherapy requires that I spend many years in treatment.*

The therapeutic process has been adjusted over the last several decades to accommodate those who want to deal with just one particular issue. Such short-term therapy can be very effective. For example, if someone is suffering from anxiety or depression as a reaction to a specific stress, it is possible to learn about how to relieve most of the symptoms in twelve to twenty sessions. It's not necessary to go into treatment for years. And for certain marital problems, you may need only a few sessions to get to the point where you understand the root of your difficulties and know what you need to do to work on them.

6. *If I get started with therapy, I will end up depending on a therapist forever.*

Some people think that if you're seeing a therapist, you lose control over your own life, that you always have to check with your therapist before doing anything. This is not true. Again, good therapists don't make decisions for their clients. They give the clients the tools they need to make appropriate decisions for themselves.

7. *A therapist will try to sell me on his or her "weird ideas," which will only interfere with my relationship to my partner.*

The fear that a therapist will introduce notions that are foreign to the couple and to their relationship is not based on fact. Good therapists work within the value system and philosophies of the person or couple they're helping. They never try to force their own ideas on a client.

8. *If my spouse and I go to a therapist, the therapist will take sides and tell us who is right and who is wrong.*

A therapist's role is not to take sides or to say who's right or wrong. A therapist is not a judge. He or she is someone who objectively looks at what's happening from both people's points of view and then helps both people discover how to accommodate each other so that the relationship can become more functional. Each relationship constitutes its own world; it is not up to a therapist to change that world. Rather, a therapist helps both partners to make their world happier and more workable.

How Support Groups Can Help

Getting together with other people who share the same kinds of problems has become a very popular way to cope with personal crises and concerns, especially in this country. Support (or self-help) groups are formed to deal with a wide array of physical and emotional situations and issues. Al-Anon (for family and friends

of those with drinking problems), Divorce Dialogue, Incest Sur-
vivors Anonymous, Narcotics Anonymous, and Parents Without
Partners are only a few of the many support groups that exist.

Central to self-help groups is the idea of sharing feelings, perceptions, and problems with others who have had the same experiences. Self-help group members:

* feel less isolated knowing that others share similar problems;
* exchange ideas and effective ways to handle problems;
* actively work on their attitudes and behavior to make positive changes in their lives;
* gain a new sense of control over their lives and feel less overwhelmed by their problems.

Research has shown that self-help groups substantially improve
the quality of life of their participants and promote better physical
and/or mental health. Much of the strength of self-help groups de-
rives from their emphasis on empowerment, self-determination,
and mutuality. Help comes primarily from the efforts, skills,
knowledge, and concern of the members themselves. A group
member is both the helper and the one to be helped.

Although a professional may sometimes be present as a re-
source, groups are organized and led by their members. Many people who are in support groups also attend individual or group
therapy sessions with a psychiatrist, psychologist, or counselor.
Getting support from people like yourself does not preclude seeing
a therapist, and vice versa.

Remember Rosanna, cited at the beginning of this chapter? She
joined a support group when the quarrels with her husband became so troubling to her that she would cry herself to sleep every
night and could barely concentrate at work the next day. She had
prayed for things to get better, but they didn't. So she tried something new. Here's how she tells her story:

A friend at work, who noticed how unhappy I was, recommended that I come with her to a meeting of Emotional Health Anonymous, a support group for people suffering from any kind of emotional problem. I thought it was a pretty strange idea to sit in a group and tell everyone your problems. I had always tried to work things out myself and to get comfort by going to church. But at that point, the way I was feeling, I was willing to give it a try.

I was real scared to talk at first, so I just listened. I remember that at the second meeting, a woman got up and started talking about her marriage. She said she felt constantly put down by her husband, that he criticized her and made her feel worthless. She had lost her job and had been without work for about six months, which made her feel even worse about herself. She broke down and started to cry, and I began to cry too—for her and also for me. Her story was so similar to mine.

At that point, I realized that I wasn't all alone. Hearing the stories of other women and men in the group—especially this one woman—I learned that there were other people who were having a hard time coping with their moods and their relationships.

I found out from members of the group about how they had become stronger, how they had gone about building self-esteem. As I began to do this myself, talking to my husband about our problems wasn't as upsetting as it always had been for me. I knew that, whatever happened, I felt stronger about myself. Now, without so many emotional lows and with the support and love I feel from the group, I believe I can face my problems with my husband and feel more confident about myself.

Another benefit Rosanna and other support-group members report is the experience of camaraderie *after* the meetings. Following most twelve-step program meetings, there is an informal "fellowship" gathering, usually held in the hall where the meeting takes place or, sometimes, in a nearby coffee shop. This is a period of socializing with other members in smaller groups over coffee. Talking on a more informal basis with people who are dealing with similar life problems is a very nourishing, self-affirming experience, which can help you face the process of change that lies ahead.

If you are interested in joining a support group for a particular problem or situation, the first place to look for a list of existing groups in your area is your local telephone directory's listing of social services, usually found at the front of the telephone book. Or, look in the Yellow Pages under the heading of "Self-Help" or "Community Services" or "Community Information Referral." Another source of general information about existing groups is your local branch of the United Way. Many self-help groups are conducted in Spanish.

Self-Help Tapes and Books

Not all problems require you to consult with a therapist or join a support group. There are many situations in which you can help yourself, given the appropriate information or the input of new ideas by qualified authors of self-help books and/or tapes.

Psychologist Abraham Maslow, regarded as the founder of humanistic psychology, stated that all of us have a natural tendency to look after our own well-being. But so often, with life's many pressures, we neglect to take care of ourselves and our relationships with those we love. Self-help books and tapes can help us to refocus on what our needs are and motivate us to look for the answers. As Latinos, we have so much pride that sometimes it's hard to ask for help. So, if we want to help ourselves, books and tapes are a good way to begin that process.

Because all of us seem to be so short of time in this country, listening to self-help or educational tapes as we drive to and from work is a great idea, I think. For this reason, I decided to create a series of tapes dealing with the emotional issues that are predominant in Latino culture. The titles of these tapes appear on page 230.

GETTING THE HELP YOU NEED

In this chapter, we've been exploring the many different ways to get help with a personal or relationship problem. When you realize that you need to confront a difficult situation in your life, the first step may be to talk with a trusted family member, member of the clergy, or doctor. For Latinos, it is always comforting to reach out to the people who know us well and whose experience and advice we trust. Often their input is enough to help us to come up with an appropriate solution or plan. Sometimes just being listened to by a close friend or writing down your thoughts in a journal enables you to "get things off your chest," so that you can gain a clearer perspective on what's troubling you.

Reading a book or listening to a tape that addresses the issue that concerns you can also be helpful. Finding out what experts have to say can give you useful new ideas and insights. Books and tapes often suggest relevant exercises and techniques that target the problem areas you are attempting to deal with, and such self-help strategies can prove very worthwhile.

In some cases, joining a support group whose members share your problem can be the best way to cope with your difficulties. You will not only feel genuinely understood, but you'll also receive advice and get answers from those who have "been there" and want to help. And in turn, you'll have the opportunity to help others by listening to their stories and offering your emotional support.

When such measures don't seem enough, however, and you're faced with a distressing situation that prevents you from fully enjoying your life, going for psychological therapy is a wise decision. No longer something to feel self-conscious about, therapy can provide the needed guidance to allow you to better understand what's troubling you and to take the necessary steps to do something about it.

Wherever you decide to turn for help, taking action to resolve your personal and relationship problems means that you respect yourself and those you love and will do whatever it takes to make the necessary changes in your life.

RELATIONSHIP SUCCESS STORIES: BLENDING THE BEST FROM BOTH WORLDS

When I chose Diana as my wife, part of my decision related to the fact that I wanted to share my life with someone from my same background. In college, I continually had to explain myself to friends, because the "Mexican" aspects of my behavior, my ways of feeling and thinking, were foreign to them. There are enough unknowns in marriage—at least with Diana, we both know that we're coming from the same place culturally, and we both want to carry on certain traditions.

On the other hand, there's a lot about our lives that is typically "American." Diana is a professional career woman, we share housework and child care, and I actually do much of the cooking. We both try very hard to treat our son and daughters equally, because we want our daughters to have the same opportunities as their brother. I think we've created a good balance between what the two cultures have to offer. But I confess that there are times when my Mexican machismo comes out, and I need to be taken care of and catered to.

—Martín, a prominent attorney and leader in the Latino community

Throughout this book, we have been exploring the many ways in which our cultural background influences our personal relationships. We've seen how being both Latino and "American" affects how we perceive ourselves, how we fall in love, how we relate to our partner or spouse, how we raise our children.

For newcomers to this country, straddling two different worlds often feels like a difficult balancing act, holding on to the familiar customs from our countries of origin, while at the same time adapting to the United States lifestyle. To those born here, Latino values sometimes seem more foreign than those of the mainstream culture they've grown up in. Most of us, however, wish to retain what is beloved and valued in both cultures.

So how do we manage to live successfully in these "two worlds" at once? The success stories you'll read about in this chapter will reveal the answers. You're going to meet some very special women and men, who have learned to incorporate into their lives the most meaningful aspects of both worlds. Comfortable and happy with the choices they have made, and yet not without their daily struggles, these people have ultimately enriched and strengthened their relationships by embracing both the "Latino" and the "American" that reside within them.

MARTÍN AND DIANA

Martín was raised in a single-parent family. His mother worked hard to earn an income and raise her children at the same time. Since Martín's father did not live with them, it was up to Martín, as the oldest son, to help out in a number of ways. He cooked, did housework, and often supervised his younger brothers and sisters. He learned at an early age that every member of the family has to do their part if the family is going to survive.

In spite of the family's hardships, Martín's mother instilled in him the will to overcome whatever obstacles stood in the way of his goals. A second-generation Mexican-American, Martín was not intimidated by the racist teachers at his public school in East

Los Angeles, who didn't believe that a Mexican boy could excel in his studies and go on to college. As a child, Martín reacted to their prejudice with anger and determination. He told himself that he was just as good as any other child, that he was not going to limit himself because he was Mexican. He was going to make it.

And he did. Martín went on to college and then to law school and became a prominent attorney in the Los Angeles area. Today he is deeply involved with the Latino community, dealing primarily with issues of discrimination and the media.

Martín's decision to marry Diana was influenced by his wish to share his life with someone from a similar background. Although he dated non-Mexican women before he was married, he felt that it would be too hard to have a lifelong relationship with a woman who was not intimately familiar with the culture that partly defines who he is. With Diana, he doesn't have to explain his "Mexican" ways of behaving, as he had to with his friends in college. He told me that, because they have the same cultural roots, he and Diana agree on countless issues concerning their marriage and family life.

For example, they have preserved the strong ties to the Catholic Church, in which each of them grew up. Baptizing their children was an automatic decision on which they wholeheartedly agreed. And they made a decision, after their first child was born, that they would attend church regularly in order to give their children both a "moral compass" and the "cultural tie-in" the Church provides. Martín explained the importance of the Church in their lives.

> The Mexican culture is very much tied into the Catholic
> Church. You almost can't be Mexican without being a Catholic, in
> my view. Our children were baptized in the church, they have had
> their first holy communions, and these are occasions for wonderful
> celebrations. People think of a Mexican baptism as almost a generic
> event. It has the religious aspect, a fifteen-minute ceremony, but

*then the baptism's over, and you go to a seven-hour party, or an
all-night party, with the family and friends and everybody. There
might be only six or eight people at the actual baptism ceremony,
but you go to the baptism party, and two hundred people will be
there. Still, you can't get away from the religious basis that's at the
root of it.*

*In college I used to have these discussions with friends. We were
all very involved with the Chicano movement and with defining
ourselves as Mexican-Americans. Some of those people rejected
religion totally, and I felt that they didn't understand the crucial
tie-in between the Mexican culture they were trying to retain and
the religious part of it. I don't think you can have one without the
other.*

In addition to Catholicism, certain Latino customs help to
strengthen the bond between Diana and Martín. "Living with
someone from the same culture makes everything much easier,"
Martín says, "because there are so many decisions that you don't
even have to think about. You just know your spouse wants what
you want, because you have the same cultural mind-set." Birthday
festivities are a perfect example of this. Martín and Diana reject
the typical American ritual of "kids only, cake and ice cream"
birthday parties and instead invite their entire extended families
for their childrens' birthday celebrations, providing guests with a
full-course Mexican buffet dinner. If all the cousins, aunts, and
uncles, great-aunts and great-uncles weren't there, the kids
wouldn't feel that their birthdays were being properly celebrated.
Martín and Diana remember the many times their relatives gathered to celebrate birthdays, anniversaries, and graduations when
they were children, and continuing this tradition brings them
closer to their families and to each other.

If these are just a few of the ways in which Diana and Martín
incorporate Latino customs and values into their family, what are
the more "Americanized" aspects of their relationship and home

life? Perhaps the most significant is their shared commitment to equality between the sexes and to instilling this belief in their children. Martín says that he's grateful that he has a wife who is intelligent, has her own opinions, can speak her mind freely on any subject, has a fulfilling career as a banker, and will not be criticized for any of these attributes as she might be in Mexico or any other Latin country. He also appreciates the opportunity to be a fully participating father, without anyone telling him that he's usurping a role exclusively reserved for mothers.

Martín acknowledges that his attitude about these matters was shaped by his exposure to mainstream American culture. But he also remembers that, when he was first married to Diana, he initially expected her to handle all the "female" duties in the home. This expectation is especially interesting, since Martín was not unfamiliar with domestic chores, having had to cook and clean and take care of his siblings when he was a boy. Still, he had expected Diana to be the sole "homemaker." This is what Martín has to say about why he had these traditional expectations, and what made him change his mind:

> I think it had to do with the changing times. Women like Diana were beginning to question why they needed to be solely responsible for housework and child care, especially when they were also working outside the home. For me, I started thinking and realized that I knew how to do all those domestic things—in fact, even better than Diana did. I wondered why I had automatically expected her to assume this role. I had helped my own mother in the house, and I hadn't been in a home where the wife serves the husband, because my father wasn't even around. This expectation that the woman should cook and clean for the man must have been handed down to me through the culture. Perhaps being in the homes of my aunts and uncles and seeing how they lived together.
>
> In any case, it finally made sense to me that doing household chores and taking care of the children should be shared

responsibilities. And although it was a bit hard to get into it at first, now I am quite comfortable doing these things.

When it comes to raising their children, the issue of equality between the sexes also arises. Martín and Diana have one son and three daughters. Martín says that he makes an effort not to treat the boy and the girls differently, because he wants his daughters to have the same chances in life as his son. Diana and he have discussed the fact that, if their son is given special privileges or comes away with the feeling that he is in some way superior to his sisters, this attitude will have a detrimental effect on the girls' self-esteem as well as on their son's. "To have the misguided notion that somehow he's better than girls would be a terrible thing for my son to grow up with," Martín says. "It would be something he—and the women around him—would suffer for his entire life." Knowing how difficult it has been for women, especially Latinas, to get ahead, Diana and Martín are committed to giving their girls the emotional support and guidance they need to achieve whatever they want in their lives.

"We're trying to raise our children with the best traditions of both the Mexican and American cultures," Martín emphasized. "The sense of family, of sharing and caring about each other— those are very strong Mexican values we want to impart. But we also want to draw from the American ideal that everyone is created equal and everyone should be treated equally. So we want to give our children the opportunities to develop into the best that each of them can be."

Martín says that he appreciates the more modern, "American" aspect of his parenting role: that he can be a fully participating parent without the stigma, without society telling him that "this is not a man's responsibility." He appreciates this element not only because he didn't live with his own father, but also because he grew up in a culture where fathers kept their emotional distance and generally left child rearing to women. Martín has been actively involved in his children's lives from the moment of birth, taking care of them, witnessing their daily spurts of growth, helping them solve problems, guiding them, having fun with them. He feels free to express his feelings to his children and his wife, and this experience has made him a more fully developed human being.

As Martín and Diana describe it, their lives embody a blend of the cultural values that matter most to them. They have taken from both the Latino and mainstream American lifestyles those elements that fit with who they are, both as individuals and as a couple, and they have rejected the aspects of both cultures that don't suit them. They love socializing with their extended families, participating in Church events and rituals, using Spanish terms of endearment in bed. They're equal partners when it comes to raising their children and maintaining their home, and they want both their son and their daughters to pursue "the American Dream" of fulfilling their personal potential.

Although they are a very modern Mexican-American couple, Martín says that there are still days when he wants to be catered to as the man of the house, in the old, conservative Latino way. He wants Diana to cook for him, take care of him, pamper him. Because Diana trusts Martín's commitment to a basically equal relationship, she has no problem with occasionally indulging Martín's "traditional macho" needs. On such occasions, Diana tells him, "This is your day," and Martín gets to satisfy the yearning he kiddingly admits was handed down to him through his Mexican genes.

When he and Diana sit down with their family to celebrate the "very American" holiday of Thanksgiving, Martín appreciates the chance to say, "Gracias" for all he has been given. He also remembers the difficulties he had growing up in a racist community, where his teachers looked down on him because he was Mexican and never held out any hope that he would amount to anything. He is now thankful to the very country that once ostracized him for also giving him and his wife the opportunity to succeed.

SAL AND NANCY

Sal and Nancy beautifully embody the concept of blending the best from both the Latino and American cultures. Sal is an immigrant, and Nancy was born in this country, but both had similar experiences of losing touch with and then regaining their cultural identity.

Sal is a mental-health professional who comes from Bogotá, Colombia. Ten years ago, when he was nineteen, he came to California "just to have an adventure." He also wanted to learn English and to attend college here, but he never planned to make the United States his home. Feeling at home in the United States has been a gradual process for Sal.

Sal's girlfriend, Nancy, is also a professional in the mental-health field. She is twenty-seven and was born and raised in southern California. Her parents are from Argentina, but Nancy grew up feeling very immersed in American culture. It may seem natural that she found someone like Sal, since both come from middle-class South American families and work in the same field. But Sal is actually one of the few Latino men Nancy has ever dated. She admits that she once believed a fairly negative stereotype of Latin guys—that they were insincere Casanovas who liked to string many women along at once. Being involved with Sal has had a lot to do with Nancy's unlearning this unfair stereotype.

Nancy and Sal met in my office during the aftermath of the 1994 Northridge Earthquake. As mental-health professionals, we were all involved in helping the Latino earthquake victims in our area. Neither Nancy nor Sal had had much previous contact with the southern California Latino population. Meeting other Latino professionals, getting to know the Latino families they were serving, and finding and falling in love with each other were pivotal experiences in both their lives. These experiences marked the beginning of their realization that being Latino is part of their identity. Both are now deeply committed to maintaining a strong connection to their roots.

Sal had attended a college of only 2,500 students, and only 50 of these were Latinos. He was therefore exposed to mostly non-Hispanic people when he first arrived in this country. He dated non-Hispanic women, got hooked on American music, ate American food, and wanted to learn everything he possibly could about how life worked here in the United States. He wanted to "Americanize" himself as quickly as he could, so that he would fit in with the mainstream and live the kind of life he wanted for himself.

Wishing to belong to the exciting new culture he had come here to experience, Sal lost touch with the country he had once called home. If he had stayed in Colombia, he would have had to follow in his father's footsteps; here, he could do whatever he chose to do, and there was no one to pass judgment on him.

Sal explained that his parents' life was conservative and based on strict class and gender roles. These were patterns he wanted to avoid in his own life. His mother's dependence on his father was something Sal had always disliked, and he told himself that he didn't want that kind of relationship for himself. He wanted the woman he chose to live with to have a life of her own, beyond un hogar—the home.

Like Nancy, Sal confesses that he had a bit of a prejudice when it came to Latinos of the opposite sex. "Too often Latinas don't say what's on their mind, because they're afraid they'll be judged by others," Sal told me. Before he met Nancy, what he was looking for in a woman was someone who knew who she was and what she wanted. Someone who could understand him. Someone creative and fun.

Sal found all these traits in Nancy. He says that she has all the positive qualities of an American woman—confidence, sincerity, honesty—and in addition, she is hogareña, cariñosa, y comprensiva—warm, caring, understanding, and very attached to the idea of family, although it is not her whole life.

Having grown up in primarily non-Latino neighborhoods, Nancy had generally dated non-Latino men. She enjoyed the guys she went out with but never quite experienced from them the sensitivity and "gentlemanly quality" she wanted in a man.

> *What I like about Sal is that he is in touch with his intuitive, emotional side. He's goal-oriented and concerned about his career, but he's also able to talk about what's going on in his mind and his heart. He's open and honest with me, he has a great sense of humor, and he's gentlemanly.*
>
> *I don't like guys who are too macho or into male bonding with their friends all the time—watching football games, all that stuff. Even though Latino guys have a reputation for being too macho, I found that the American guys I dated were the ones who fit this picture. Before I met Sal, I thought all men were like that. I was becoming resigned to Monday Night Football.*

Until Nancy started working with other Latinos on the earthquake project, she never really thought of herself as a Latina. It was then that she realized how much she had in common with others, including Sal, who shared various aspects of her cultural background. Before then, for example, she never paid attention to the fact that she could speak Spanish. She speaks with an accent, but she can communicate in Spanish very well, and she grew to appreciate her ability to talk to new immigrants about their needs and concerns. After working with the earthquake victims, she got a job working for another Latino agency and found that she fit in there as well. "I realized I am a Latina, too," Nancy told me with pride.

After that point, she even began to explore facets of her cultural roots she had ignored all her life. She got into Latin music, for example. Having grown up listening to tangos when she was a little girl, she disliked her parents' music when she was a teenager and a young adult, preferring rock. Like many children of immigrants, Nancy may have wanted to deny whatever it was about her heritage that would define her as anything but "purely American." There is such pressure to blend in with mainstream culture that children whose parents or grandparents still retain cultural tastes and habits from "back home" are often embarrassed or ashamed of who they are. But in her twenties, Nancy discovered that she didn't want to neglect the Latina part of herself anymore.

Sal was a part of Nancy's cultural reawakening. As an immigrant, he had initially felt similarly about wanting to immerse himself in the mainstream culture, only to find out that he missed the music, the language, and the values he was raised with. He began to value the cultural aspects of the life he had taken for granted and left behind. As he and Nancy began their life together, they looked forward to sharing many of the traditions they both loved.

Sal and Nancy have been living together for about a year and a half now. They currently reside in Oregon and are waiting until Nancy finishes her Ph.D. to marry. Although they have not yet stood before a priest or judge to take their marriage vows, and they do not have wedding bands on their fingers, they "feel married" anyway. Both tell me that they have the same responsibilities and commitments to each other that a married couple does; they feel that they don't have to "sign a piece of paper" to be faithful. It's not that they are against marriage, they just want to make sure they know each other very well before they take the final step in solidifying their commitment to each other.

Part of Nancy and Sal's process of learning about themselves and each other has been their rediscovery of their cultural roots. Enjoying that part of their identity, and at the same time enjoying whatever they have taken from American culture, contributes to their closeness and strengthens the bond between them.

ANGELICA

Angelica is thirty-one, divorced, the mother of a six-year-old daughter, an executive assistant, and a student of broadcasting. During our conversation, Angelica talked about how she had changed over the last several years since her divorce. She had grown stronger and "more secure in who I am," and this is having a very positive effect on her relationships with men.

She has come a long way, because in her marriage, she had usually deferred to her husband. Although she had been raised within the context of equal rights for women and worked outside the home, within her marriage, Angelica more or less conformed to the traditional woman's role accepted by many Latinas. She described how she used to feel and behave with her ex-husband.

> I always thought I had to be the subservient woman and just be quiet about things. Growing up, I had been taught this. Don't rock the boat. That's what caused a lot of problems, because I wasn't communicating what was wrong or what I felt was wrong in the relationship. If my ex-husband did something I didn't agree with, or acted disrespectfully toward me, I would just let it pass.
>
> Also, I wasn't part of making any financial decisions, or any other big decisions—like where we lived or what we did—so the only way I had any power in that relationship was with sex. When things weren't going right, I refused to have sex with him. I would say, "Well how do you expect me to be warm and affectionate and loving to you when I'm mad at you?" I didn't realize it then, but now I see that it was a power play. It was the only power I had.

From the mainstream culture in which she grew up, Angelica said, she had learned that a woman should be strong and "really kind of manlike" when it came to business. "With the new equal rights that women supposedly have in this country," she explained, "you're supposed to play down some of your feminine traits, be more cutthroat and more shrewd in the working world." For Angelica, this essentially self-serving philosophy is the antithesis of her parents' strong belief in sacrificing your own needs for the sake of the family.

Wanting to be both a successful career woman and a loving partner and mother, Angelica has struggled to balance her belief in self-assertiveness with her respect and love for family. She acknowledges that in the past, in her marriage, she associated subservience with love, because that had been part of her Latino upbringing. But today, her relationships are clearly based on mutual respect, and she demands that respect by standing up for herself. As an example, Angelica told me about a recent experience at a dinner dance she went to with a man she's dating—and how this experience contrasted to her prior behavior with her ex-husband.

In my marriage, we'd go to an event, and my husband would flirt with other women, but I would never say anything. Of course we'd go home that night and not have sex, but I wouldn't be forthright about it. I wouldn't express myself. Things are really different now. A couple of weeks ago, I was at a dinner dance with the man I'm currently dating, and I had excused myself from the table to go to the ladies' room. When I came back, my date was dancing with this young, lovely little gal, and I was really upset by it. I thought it showed a great disrespect for me.

Rather than just keeping it inside like I used to, I said something right away—not in a mean, bitchy way, not angry or lashing out, but I just said flat out, "I think that was very disrespectful. This is where I draw the line. I don't like being treated like that at all." He made excuses, saying, "Oh, she was just somebody who asked me to dance, she was just being bold. What was I supposed to say, no?" And I said to him, "Yes. You tell her no. You say, I'm with my girlfriend, and she'll be right back. Thank you, I'm flattered, but no, I can't dance with you. That's what you say."

We talked about it, and at first he defended himself, being kind of macho and saying, "Oh, you're just being jealous." But I didn't back down. I said, "It's not about jealousy, it's about respect and what is acceptable to me." And I put the shoe on the other foot. I asked him, "What if it had been me, and you came back from the men's room and I was dancing with some handsome man? Wouldn't you find that was a total slap in the face in front of your friends and business associates?" He admitted I had a good point and said, "You're right. That was a sign of disrespect, and I apologize."

I felt so good that I had spoken up for myself. If you stick to your guns on something where you know you're right, something that's a respect issue, the right kind of man will back down—not because he's weak, but because he's understanding and sensitive. And this man was sensitive to what I was feeling. And I appreciated that. The rest of the evening was wonderful. No bad feelings. When we went home that night, we had great sex! And a fun time the next day too!

Having dated both non-Latino and Latino men, Angelica finds herself more attracted to Latinos, for a number of reasons. While she says that they can be overly domineering and macho at times, she appreciates both their strength and their affectionate, loving qualities. She likes the fact that they're not afraid to physically demonstrate their affection—hugging, touching, kissing. She loves to hear words of love spoken in Spanish. She also believes that Latino men "are more respectful of me as a woman, and that's a loving gesture." The fact that Latino men value family so highly is also crucial to Angelica.

What I like about Hispanic men is that there's an importance placed on the family. The Anglo men I've dated don't seem to understand why my family is so important, and why my family's opinion is so important to me. They don't understand why I want to talk to my mom once a week. Certain non-Latino guys I know don't have a problem not talking to their family at all, or not being with them on big family occasions. Whereas, Hispanic men, they know why it's important. It's your family!

I think I'll be sixty years old and I'll still want my family's approval. And it's not that my decisions are contingent on what they think, but they gave me my foundation for right and wrong. They have given everything for their children—heart and soul, body and mind. So I seek their approval—when it comes to my relationships, my studies, my work, whatever I do.

Angelica sees herself as a modern young American woman, who is also deeply connected to her Hispanic roots. She is critical of "chauvinistic men," who lack respect for women by attempting to hold them back from educational and career goals. She feels proud of the fact that she is currently striving to meet her own career challenges. "I know it is always in my power to achieve better for myself," she tells me. She is also proud that she has learned to be more open and fair in her relationships, to speak up and say what she means—and to demand the same from her partners.

Because she feels more secure in herself as a person, Angelica says that sex is a much more pleasurable experience now, "much more fun, much closer." It's no longer an activity she uses to control her partner, because she has learned to tell a man how she's feeling and what she wants in a relationship. Because she has developed the inner power to create the kind of life she wants for herself, Angelica no longer has to use sex as her only outlet for exerting her influence.

As "liberated" as Angelica is, she is also a devoted mother and daughter, who treasures her family and the culture in which she was raised. It is very important to her that the man she chooses to share her life with be someone who also values strong family ties and an attachment to the Hispanic culture.

I think the beautiful thing about being a Hispanic-American woman is that I can pull together both sides of what might seem like opposite values. I can be a strong woman intellectually and emotionally, I can be brave and bold and stick up for myself. But I can also be very feminine and soft. I can be romantic. I can feel passionately about my family and not have to apologize for it. And I really like sharing these things with a man who understands my culture and my beliefs.

ANTONIA AND MIKE

Antonia Hernandez is a lawyer and the president of MALDEF, the Mexican-American Legal Defense and Education Fund. She was born in Mexico and grew up on an ejido in El Cambio, Coahuila. Antonia says that she always felt her parents had a very equal relationship. Although her father was the head of the household and was respected as the ultimate power, he collaborated fully with Antonia's mother. Antonia's mother was creative, people-oriented, assertive, and the one who would always say to her children, "You can do it!" For these reasons, she served as a very powerful role model to Antonia.

Many other women in Antonia's family were strong and assertive as well. She had an aunt who was the principal of a school at a time when very few women held such positions in Mexico. And both of her grandmothers were widowed at an early age and therefore had to raise their families by themselves. One grandmother inherited an ejido from her husband, and it became a cooperative enterprise for all of the extended family members. Antonia also has many female cousins who are professors, doctors, and nurses, and all are very, very strong women.

Antonia came to the United States when she was eight years old. Her father had been born here and moved back to Mexico.

But he wanted to return to the United States with his family, because he believed that they would enjoy a better quality of life here. Antonia says that the hardest adjustment for her and her family was going from ejido life to city life—from a town with a very small population to a major metropolitan area. There were also difficulties in learning a new language and in adjusting to the many ways in which the cultures differed. Her parents had a particularly hard time getting used to the fact that Antonia's mother worked outside the home. Her father was a laborer, and her mother worked as a gardener in a nursery. In Mexico, Antonia's mother had worked on the ejido, but that work did not take her away from her children. She and her husband both felt sad that her job in this country meant that she couldn't always be near her kids.

Antonia was a good student, and it wasn't hard for her to get into college. After attending two years at East Los Angeles College, she transferred to UCLA. Through grants, scholarships, and loans, she was able to finance her education. The product of affirmative action, Antonia explained that, although this program opened the door for her by giving her the opportunity to pursue a higher education, she always got good grades and did very well in college. She appreciates the educational and professional opportunities that were open to her in this country, though she admits that law is still a very male-dominated profession.

Antonia met her husband, Mike, when he was a legal-aid attorney, serving the farm worker population in Santa Maria, California. Mike is Jewish and not Latino, but Antonia says that she doesn't see him in terms of his ethnic roots. "He could be Chinese or Jewish or Mexican or black or white. The most important thing for me is to have someone who is supportive of me, and Mike is." It was also important that she share her strongly held beliefs with the man she chose to marry. Mike's commitment to the cause of workers' rights goes as deep as Antonia's. When Antonia met him, she saw that Mike not only was doing a job he believed in, but that he had a good relationship with the field workers, he spoke Spanish, and he respected Antonia's cultural background.

Mike and Antonia are raising their children in the Catholic faith, though Mike did not convert to Catholicism. They have an ongoing agreement to respect each other's differences, be they cultural, religious, or personal. As Antonia puts it, "I won't change him, he won't change me."

Antonia still feels very Mexican, and her home life with Mike reflects many of the traditions she grew up with in Mexico. The children are taught to respect their elders, as Antonia was taught to do when she was a child. They eat the kind of Mexican food Antonia's family prepared back in Mexico. Because extended family is very important, they live very near Antonia's parents and siblings, and family gatherings include grandparents, uncles, aunts, cousins.

As for Antonia and Mike's personal relationship, it is built not only on love but also on mutual respect. Although both have an equal say in the raising of their children, Mike is often the primary parent, because Antonia's job requires her to travel a lot. Their relationship certainly does not conform to the traditional Mexican marriage in this regard, but the couple's trust in each other's values and competence as a parent allows this special arrangement to work for them. When the tables are turned and Mike has to travel for his work, Antonia takes over.

Antonia is proud of her professional success. She fights hard for the causes she believes in, and she is perceived as a very strong feminist. But there is a side to her that most people outside her family don't get a chance to see. In her private life, Antonia profoundly enjoys many aspects of the traditional female role. She loves to sew and cook and act as hostess at family parties.

I enjoy being with my family and sharing in family activities. I love to do things with them. I'm proud that my career involves working with my mind, but I'm also proud that I can work with my hands—as my mother did. It's very rewarding to go home and to bake a loaf of bread and to serve it to my family. It gives me pleasure to bring my family pleasure.

What does Antonia believe to be the secret to her good relationship with Mike? And what does she especially value in her marriage?

Mike and I see each other as friends and as partners. We have the same goals and objectives regarding our children, We respect each other, and we're there for each other—in the good and the bad times. It's so important, I think, that we accept each other for what we are, not what we expect the other one to be. We both realize that we have a good relationship, but we also realize that it takes nurturing and work. And we're very committed to that.

SUE AND LOUIS

An associate television producer in Miami, Sue came to this country from Cuba when she was thirteen. The story of Sue and Louis' relationship represents several types of success. First of all, in building a committed relationship with Louis, Sue has been able to successfully overcome her mistrust of men and her reluctance to marry. (She and Louis are currently engaged.) The other aspect of their "success story" relates to how well they have made their intercultural relationship work. Louis' family are Euro-Americans, from an area in the southern United States where few Latinos live. Sue's parents were initially skeptical about her dating a non-Latino. Yet these circumstances have not prevented Sue and Louis from creating a strong, loving bond, not only between themselves, but also with each other's family as well.

Sue has always been a very independent woman, and before she met Louis, she felt fine about living on her own. For her, being in a relationship had always "seemed like work."

> *In previous relationships, it took so much of my energy. It was actually a job—I had to be constantly thinking about the other person, calling and checking in with him, making sure my work schedule fitted in with his need to be with me. It was too much. It was like a sacrifice. So I decided I wasn't going to marry anyone; I didn't want to hurt anybody, and I wasn't willing to give up my career.*

What happened to change Sue's outlook about a serious involvement with another person? And how did these two twenty-somethings from very different backgrounds happen to meet? Like a growing number of contemporary couples, Sue and Louis met on the Internet—but the occasion was not as lacking in romance as you might think. Here's how Sue describes it.

> *I came home late from work one night and was just going to pick up my E-mail and go to bed. But then I noticed an open window on my screen, and I don't know why I picked up on this one, because there were many others wanting to communicate with me. I think it was just destined to happen. Anyway, it was Louis, and we went immediately into a private room on the computer. I loved that he was a fast typist. A lot of times I get bored waiting for the person to respond, but Louis kept up with me, and the conversation came so easily for both of us.*
>
> *After about an hour and a half on the computer, we decided to talk on the phone and actually hear each other's voices, because we both felt good about what was going on between us. We talked from two until five in the morning. And as much as we talked, we wanted to talk more. We found out there were some things we didn't agree on, but we enjoyed listening to each others' different points of view.*

After that initial marathon phone call, Sue and Louis planned to meet in person to see if they were physically attracted to each other. Both agreed that there would be no pressure to stay if things didn't work out. When Sue saw Louis, she found him to be exactly as he had described himself. Because Louis had not misrepresented himself, Sue realized at that initial stage in the relationship that she was dealing with a basically honest person, someone she could trust. And as their relationship progressed, this trust—along with their ease in communicating with one another—became one of the key elements that enabled the two of them to grow close.

Trust was especially important to Sue, because she had had a number of disappointing relationships that had led her to become mistrustful of men.

I had so many bad experiences, I began to doubt that I would ever have a partner for life. I never felt the kind of companionship I feel with Louis. I dated mostly Latino guys, and they seemed to have a problem with the way I live my life. In my work as a TV producer, I sometimes have to go to bars and discos dressed kind of flashy, or to the beach in a tiny bikini. And my previous boyfriends were all so jealous of any attention I got. They never trusted me, and I couldn't trust them to see me for who I really am. They couldn't seem to appreciate that I am an independent woman, with my own career, my own opinions, my own life.

With Louis, Sue says, she can be herself—he doesn't want to change her, he doesn't want her to live her life any differently than she would on her own. She had always felt that a serious relationship or marriage should not involve sacrifice, but she had just about given up on finding someone who agreed.

Thanks to Louis, Sue has also become more vulnerable to romance. She says Louis vive para complacerme—he lives to make her happy—and she feels it in how he touches her, how he kisses her, and how he is romantic in little ways. "He calls me at odd times during the day, just to tell me what he's doing, and I like that. I wasn't used to it before, but I'm learning to be romantic in this relationship."

When Louis first raised the subject of marriage and children, Sue told him that she wasn't ready. She was honest and confided in him that she had pushed marriage out of her mind, because she didn't "have much faith in men." But after some further discussions, Sue agreed to "talk about the concept" of getting married and having a family together.

> I finally realized that being with Louis is like having completed a cycle. I went from wanting a committed relationship but distrusting that a man would let me be myself, to not wanting a committed relationship at all, to now trusting and loving someone very much and knowing that I can get to my goals in life much more easily with him.
>
> Many of my friends got married just because they reached the age when it was the thing to do. I didn't want to do that. My mom married at nineteen, and my grandmother at fifteen, so when I reached twenty-five I said, "Hey, wait a minute, I haven't met anybody yet." Still, I didn't want to go with the flow of getting married just because it was time.

Sue says that it was a good thing she didn't feel pressured to marry earlier, because not only had she not met the right guy, she also needed time to mature. With the guys she used to date, she became jealous when they looked at other women. She feels much more secure now, and she trusts Louis so much that he can look at beautiful women at the beach or the park, and Sue doesn't feel at all threatened. In fact, she told me that, recently, someone sent him a special edition of a magazine called *Latino Lover Playboy*, and he called to ask her if she had sent it. She hadn't, but the gift didn't bother her. She calmly told him that they could look at the magazine together.

When I asked Sue if their different ethnic backgrounds presented any problems, she said that there are no actual problemas with the fact that she is Cuban and Louis is Anglo—but some interesting situations arise. The biggest difference is the language, because English is her second language. She thinks in Spanish, and all her friends in Miami speak Spanish—so when she's with Louis, she has to be aware that he doesn't understand the language. The Cubans in Miami, she says, tend to all speak at the same time, and it's hard for her to translate when everyone's talking at once. But Louis is trying to teach himself Spanish, and learning very quickly. "He can already ask for an 'empanizado' when we go out to eat!" she says good-naturedly. Speaking Spanish is something Sue is very proud of. "It's my language, and I love my accent. I don't want to change it. I want to speak all my life with my accent!"

Both Sue and Louis are very family-oriented. He has become close to her parents in Miami, especially her father. "My father always wanted to have a son," Sue told me. "In the beginning, he was skeptical about Louis, because he wasn't from the same culture, but now they spend a lot of time together, doing things together like father and son, which they both really enjoy."

As for Sue being accepted by Louis' family, they have demonstrated a strong willingness to make her feel welcome. The first time she met Louis' father and stepmother, they hugged her, and Louis' stepmother said, "We're looking forward to getting to know you, and we're happy about your relationship with Louis."

Sue was initially concerned because she was a "foreigner" in their lives.

Sometimes, with his family, as with many other non-Latinos, I feel like I have to explain myself. Some people think that all Latinos are "mariachis"! So I have to explain where I'm coming from—

*that my background is caribeño. Louis' grandparents are from
Mississippi, where very few people of color live, so initially I asked
him, "Are you sure your family knows I'm a Latina?" But they've
already made an effort to understand me, to learn about me, to the
point that I introduced his family to los frijoles—almost like when
Christopher Columbus introduced American specialties to Europe!
Now I regularly send his family five packages of Sazón Goya and
frijoles negros and café cubano. They like these things so much
now.*

Sue is grateful to her future in-laws for being so warm toward
her. She corresponds with her future mother-in-law via E-mail,
and they speak on the telephone frequently as well. Louis' parents
are helping plan the wedding, and his grandmother is making
them a quilt as a wedding gift. Sue feels that she and Louis are integrating the "Cubano" and the "Americano," and she jokingly
refers to their upcoming wedding as a "spic and hick wedding."
She is obviously pleased that Louis' relatives are easy-going people, who look for the things that they have in common with Sue,
rather than being pessimistic about the differences. For example,
when Sue and Louis came to visit Louis' mother and stepfather,
Louis' mother asked Sue what they liked to eat, and Sue responded, "We eat rice, beans, meat." And Louis' mother said,
"Oh, we eat the same things." Because she wants to pick up more
of her future daughter-in-law's language and culture, Louis'
mother now watches Spanish programs on television every day.

A less serious issue: Sue loves to dance, and Louis doesn't know
how to do the merengue or salsa. But Louis makes such an effort
to please her and to be with her—with joy, not in a self-sacrificing
way—that he is willing to go dancing with Sue and to stand while
she dances around him. He's open to trying new things because
that's who he is, and because he loves Sue.

A hundred and fifty people, from two different cultures and
speaking different languages, will be at Louis and Sue's upcoming

wedding. Sue is happily looking forward to the event, but she's also concerned that the two families may separate into two groups, or that some of her friends may not accept Louis' friends and relatives. A few of her Cuban friends have said things like, "Hey, what are you doing with that gringo?" as if she had betrayed them. "It's not like I'm going to 'convert' into anything," she explained to me. "I am an independent Cuban-American woman, and I'm marrying someone who respects me for exactly who I am." Still, she's afraid that her wedding guests may not get along—that there will be some who will misinterpret how the other culture behaves, that certain people may offend other guests. "I'm a control freak," she says. "I want to control everything. But I cannot control how other people act. What I do know is that I love Louis, and that his parents and mine are trying very hard to make us all feel like family."

Sue's and Louis' families' efforts—to break down barriers, to think about what they have in common rather than what separates them, and to genuinely welcome their new son- and daughter-in-law—testify to their openness and love. What beautiful gifts to give a couple as they begin their married life!

LETTING LOVE SUCCEED

The successful relationships we've looked at in this chapter reveal some interesting differences and similarities. Martín and Diana made a conscious decision to choose a mate from the same ethnic background, because they feel that this choice makes marriage much easier, and they enjoy having "the same cultural mind-set," as Martín put it. Antonia and Mike come from different ethnic backgrounds but share a deep commitment, not only to Latino social causes, but also to equality within their marriage. Sal and Nancy went through the experience of regaining the cultural identity they had never quite valued before they met each other.

Angelica has always valued her Latino identity and chooses to date men who, like herself, can combine Latino warmth and family values with respect for a woman's right to determine her own goals. And Sue and Louis are about to begin their married life with enthusiasm and excitement about blending their Cuban and Anglo roots.

All these women and men incorporate into their relationship, in their own unique way, not only respect and love for their partner, but also an appreciation of their own cultural traditions and a belief in those "mainstream American" values that help them become who they want to be. None of these relationships is free from occasional problems and conflicts, and yet all are strong because the individuals who have joined together are dedicated to working out their differences with honesty, fairness, compassion, and amor.

THE TEN MOST FREQUENTLY ASKED QUESTIONS ABOUT AMOR, SEXO, AND RELATIONSHIPS

During my twenty years as a psychologist working within the Latino community, I have listened as women and men told me about the problems in their relationship that most troubled them. In my private practice, in clinics and workshops, and on my radio and television talk shows, husbands, wives, single people, abuelas, teenagers, even children, have shared their personal concerns with me. They have talked to me about clashes between Latino and "Americanized" lifestyles, about the inability to communicate with their partner, about infidelity, sexual difficulties, parenting problems, domestic abuse, and many other important issues, such as the ones we have explored in the last nine chapters. I have given them the kind of information, insight, and advice that I have shared with you throughout this book.

Of course, reading a book is not the same as going into therapy or participating in a workshop. But I hope that I have addressed some of the troubling issues you may be facing at the moment within your own family or relationship. Hopefully, reading about people who have already confronted what you're currently going through will help you begin to understand and resolve your situation. Should you feel that you need additional help with your problems, I want to encourage you to find the help that is most appropriate, be it a personal therapist, a support group, or further reading concerning the particular difficulty you are having.

In this chapter, I want to answer some of the most frequently asked questions about love and marriage, sex and intimacy, parenting and family matters. As you read these questions, you will probably hear your own voice or that of your partner or another family member asking about similar concerns. I hope that in my answers you can begin to identify a solution that might work for you and your family.

1. Why does my husband pay more attention to his family—his mother, his father, his sisters and brothers—than he does to our family, me and our children?

Loyalty to our family of origin is very strong in the Latino culture, so your husband's closeness to his parents and siblings is not at all unusual. Being a son, his ties to his original family may be particularly related to the attachment between him and his mother. One reason Latino mothers establish such an intense bond with their sons is that their relationships with their husbands aren't always as close as they'd like them to be. So there is a very close relationship between sons and mothers, and often when the sons grow up, they feel responsible for their mothers and sisters. And they are proud of that responsibility.

As wives, we cannot just say, "Forget about your mother, forget about your sisters, forget about your extended family, because I am your family now"—even though that may be what we want. You can't try to pit your family against your husband's family, because that's not what love is. Instead, you need to find a way to accept the importance of his family and to incorporate it into your life, while at the same time creating the intimate time for you and your husband and your children to be together.

The key is to create a balance. I think that, if we are open to our in-laws, it doesn't matter who they are or what they're like, whether they are poor or rich, educated or not—we can learn something from them. I have learned a lot from my husband's family, even though, at first, I didn't feel that I had much in common with them. I come from the city, and they come from a rural environment. I'm from Argentina; my husband was born in California. His parents were field workers of Mexican origin; my parents were middle class. But I realized that originally my in-laws were immigrants, as I am an immigrant and my parents were immigrants to Argentina. Although my parents were middle class, my mother told me that there were times before I was born when she didn't have enough milk to give to my older brother. My husband's family was lower middle class in Mexico, but when they came here, they had to start all over—and this starting all over is an experience both our families have gone through. Both of our families worked hard and stayed together so that the children would benefit.

I admire the strength of both my husband's family and mine. I admire my mother-in-law for being strong and telling her children, "Never give up. There is always something that we can strive for." Even though my husband and his siblings worked in the fields with their parents during their childhood, my mother-in-law had the strength to tell them, "You're no different from anyone else. You can do it." And the four of them are college graduates. So her strength, and that of my father-in-law as well, made a difference. My father-in-law took his children to museums, read them history, and regardless of the economic situation they found themselves in, he communicated the sense of "Let's go and do it!" and "There's always something else we can learn," with a great heart and a great kindness and a wonderful spirit.

So, it's important to appreciate every member of our extended family, and for our children to get close to their grandparents, so that they can have a sense of pride and belonging and can realize their own personal history. Thinking of our family in a narrow way—just the two of us and our children—is not the Latino way. Our spouse's family and our own family—we are one. Being together is what gives us strength.

If you want your husband to have a greater role in the lives of your children, help him realize how important he is in their lives by reminding him how much he wanted to be with his father when he was a child. Since, in the past, men were not as involved with their children as they are now, many Latino boys (and girls) didn't get this kind of attention. So this is a lack your husband can rectify in his own child's life. Give him permission to participate in the parenting role, since many men feel that this job is primarily for women. And remind him that successful men and women are usually those who have had emotional support from both parents. Finally, always give him positive feedback about the time he spends with you, to let him know how great it feels to be together.

2. Why is my wife so demanding? How can I get her to stop treating me like she's my mother?

Is it possible that your wife's "demands" are actually reasonable requests or wishes? Often the things women ask of their husbands are very important and meaningful to them. But some men are a bit defensive about having to account to a woman for their behavior—perhaps out of fear that their wife will assume a mothering or authoritarian role.

Rather than getting into a "demanding and rebelling" situation with your wife, ask her to make a list of what she is asking of you. Sometimes the many demands you may feel she is making of you can be boiled down to a few simple requests. After she has made the list, ask her how important each request is to her. How will it make her feel to have what she is asking for? If she really is demanding that you do certain things, ask her to change her demands into requests. No one likes being bullied or treated like a child; but if a reasonable request is made, you can respond in a reasonable manner.

One request women often make is that their husbands let them know where they'll be during the day or in the evening, and when they can expect to see them back at home. This simple request seems to cause lots of problems, however. I hear so many men say, "My wife always has to know exactly where I am every minute, and what I'm doing. Why is she so insecure and so demanding? Why should I have to report to her every single thing I do? She's not my mother!"

Such a conflict usually reflects a problem with trust. The husband wants his wife to trust him, but for any number of reasons, she may not be able to. Perhaps he has violated that trust in the past by being unfaithful. Perhaps she grew up in a family where one of her parents betrayed the other, so that she finds it hard to trust her own husband. Some women say, "It's not that I think he's doing anything wrong when I don't know where he is, I just feel more comfortable if he would tell me, 'I'm going to come home two hours late because I have to go to such and such place.' I would like him to let me know rather than just show up two hours late."

Both you and your wife need to be open with each other regarding this issue of "demands." She needs to tell you why the things she is asking of you are so important to her or why your current behavior makes her feel uncomfortable or insecure. And you need to listen respectfully to what she has to say, try to understand her feelings, and then explain to her how you feel about the situation. Most wives do not want to be mother figures to their husbands, and they do not want to be perceived as nagging or demanding. The fact is that you are two people who share a life. When one partner knows that the other is suffering or hurting, that partner needs to do everything possible to make the other partner's life easier and more comfortable. Why would you not want to do this for the person you love and are married to? I think you will find, for example, that if you give your wife information about where you are going when she asks, she will feel more secure, and she won't have any reason to nag you. And you'll feel better, too.

If each of you can turn your demands into requests, and if you can promise to address each other's requests with respect for the other person's feelings, neither of you will feel unduly insecure or pressured. Bringing requests out into the open and dealing with underlying feelings will make your relationship much more relaxed—and stronger. (See the exercise entitled "Exercise for Feeling Stuck: Asking For What You Want, Giving What You Can Give" in Chapter 3.)

3. I am single and want very much to find a husband/wife. What is the best way to meet someone to marry?

First of all, I want to say that sometimes, when we're very eager to be in a relationship, we end up in the wrong one. A relationship is something that has to come about naturally; it doesn't happen by going out and frantically searching for one. This kind of obsessive searching and pushing ourselves to find a husband or wife can not only result in making the wrong choice, but it also prevents us from developing our own lives. Often we are impatient and want a relationship to materialize right away, but in fact, we are not ready for one. Usually, when we are ready—that's when we meet someone.

Love happens in its own time. You want to be open to a relationship, but you shouldn't structure your life around meeting "Señor or Señorita Right." Being open means that you acknowledge that you want to find someone to love; you may even let friends and family know that you would like to meet someone, in case they know of a person they could introduce you to. But rather than searching for your soul mate, search inside yourself to make your life as fulfilling as you can.

Being open to a relationship means being around people, but not in a compulsive effort to zero in on a potential mate. Being involved with people at work, in classes, at church, or at neighborhood functions brings you closer to those with whom you have things in common. And sometimes, these relationships can lead to a deeper friendship. Very often, the right man or woman is much closer than you think, but in the frenzy to find "the ideal mate," you may overlook someone in your daily life who may be a suitable companion for you.

The key is to be open but to put your energy into creating your own life and developing yourself. Don't ever put your life on hold until you find the "right person" to share it with. Invest your time in yourself. Develop yourself into the best that you can be, so that you are happy with who you are. Think about what you want, and go after it. And as you immerse yourself in pursuing your own path, you will find the love you are looking for.

4. My husband tells me that I'm too inhibited sexually. How can I feel more free?

Our education, culture, and religion tend to be very repressive when it comes to sex, especially in regard to a woman's sexual role. Consequently, many women receive the implied message that females are supposed to be sexually passive. But we don't have to accept this old-fashioned way of thinking. If you give yourself permission to develop your sexuality, and if your husband is patient and gentle with you, you should have no problem becoming more open and more sexually expressive.

When men become too demanding, however, it makes women feel more afraid, and they tend to shut down their feelings rather than opening up. Your husband therefore needs to reinforce your desire to become a more sexual person by refraining from making specific demands upon you. Instead, he needs to tell you how much he enjoys you, compliment whatever he likes about you, and become more aware of your sexual relationship's deeper meaning: an encounter between two souls coming together through the experiences of the body.

Without pressures or demands, you'll be able to feel much more in tune with your own body—what feels good to you and what excites you—rather than worrying about what is expected of you. Many of our sexual fears are related to satisfying our partner's expectations. On the one hand, women want to be lovable and to make their partner feel good; yet, they worry that if they are overly passionate, they might be judged too "whorish." Again, Latino women's inhibitions are often tied to the Church and to the ideal of the virginal mother figure. The message many Latinas receive is that feeling too sexual is sinful or sleazy, and that women ought to keep their passion in check.

You need to acknowledge how such cultural taboos may have affected your sexual development and then practice forgetting them. Forget what's expected of you, stop thinking of sex in terms of a particular role you must play or a forbidden territory you must avoid. Instead, learn to trust your own feelings.

Sexuality is an expression of your inner feelings, including fears and love, trust and doubts. So, as you and your husband build trust and love in other ways, your sexual relationship will reflect that development. By being yourself, and by developing trust between yourself and your husband, you will feel more free to express and enjoy your sexuality. (See the exercise entitled "Slowing Down and Intensifying Your Sexual Encounter" in Chapter 4.)

5. How can my wife expect me to devote more time to raising our children when she knows I have too many responsibilities already, supporting our family as well as helping support extended family?

It's a question of prioritizing what is most important. Supporting your family financially is obviously very important. And if there is a need to support your extended family as well, that is also important. But so is the opportunity to share your values and your life with your children. So you need to figure out how much time you're investing in making money, and ask yourself if you need that much money—or would some of your time be better spent with your family? How many hours do you have to invest to make the money to buy luxury items? Are those things really worth giving up the time to help your children with their homework? If it is impossible to cut back on your time at work, what about the time spent after work? Is it more important to have a beer with friends after hours or to read a story to your daughter before she goes to bed? It is a question of balance.

Once the time we have with our children is gone, once they are grown up, that time never comes back. Your son or daughter will only be five years old or ten years old or sixteen years old for a short time, and then that young person moves on, and that time is gone forever. So we have to reassess how we are investing our time. Time is certainly very limited, especially in this country. But our time with our children is also limited—and we need to make sure that we are there for them as they grow.

The opportunity to be a father is a unique one. Our children need to be with their fathers, and perhaps you can remember how much you needed or wanted the attention of your own father when you were growing up. Fathering allows a man to develop a tenderness, a sensitivity, a new emotional context for discovering himself. And being a child again with your children is a very invigorating and renewing experience. It's one of life's opportunities that too many men pass by, often without realizing it. Those who take advantage of the chance to be there for their children, cherish their role as father and realize how much more important it is than other aspects of their life.

When we decide to invest time in anything, we have to ask ourselves, "What am I gaining, and what am I missing?" We all know that men enjoy activities that are going to make them look good in society—achieving, striving, competing. Fulfilling society's role of a "successful man" doesn't always blend so well with giving a child what he or she needs. Relationships with children require nurturing, flexibility, understanding, patience, a sense of humor, and time. But participating in the life of his children gives a man a priceless benefit. It allows him to balance his life in the best sense. And at the same time, his children grow up having the best of two worlds: their mother and their father.

6. How can we give advice to our teenage children without being told by them that we don't understand—because we're from another generation? Or another country? Or another culture?

As Latino parents, not only are we of a different generation from our children, but often we are also from very different cultural backgrounds—even different countries. Even those of us who are not immigrants are the children or grandchildren of immigrants, and we have to acknowledge that our childhood experiences were usually quite different from our own children's. We have to talk openly with our daughters and sons about the differences between our experiences as young people and theirs.

The key is to talk *with* them rather than *to* them, so that we can listen when they tell us how their lives are different in this country as teenagers today. More than likely, we have a lot to learn about that experience. If we don't know what their lives are really like, if we are coming from a place of limited information, we will just be imposing our own experience on them, and we will be wrong. Two-way communication is crucial.

Still, we have to remember that we are the parents, we are the adults, and we are the ones who are supposed to be more flexible and more understanding and more tolerant. Tolerance is a very important ingredient in parenting. Obstacles can become challenges. If there's something that we don't understand about our teenager, we can approach this lack of understanding as an opportunity to learn. It's an invitation to gain a greater insight into each other's lives.

Sometimes we feel that we talk and talk to our children, and that they are not hearing us. They complain that we don't understand them, but we feel that they're not listening to us. I think that it's important to keep in mind that the time we invest in them is never wasted. Our input may not inspire an immediate positive reaction on their part, it may not result in their doing exactly what we want them to do. But if we think about the effect it will have in the long run, we will realize that everything we say, all our advice and guidance, all our interaction with our children, are filed away in their minds and their experience.

It might seem that they're not paying attention or that they're discarding what we say, but sooner or later, they will understand what we're talking about. We can recall this effect with regard to our own parents. Do you remember what your parents used to tell you? The advice they would give again and again? Aren't many of those things still with you, even though at the time you may have thought that your parents were crazy, or old-fashioned, or antiquated, or didn't understand you?

What our parents tell us stays with us. Similarly, when we communicate our values to our children, this information stays with them. We just have to be patient; we will see the fruits of our relationship with our children in the long run, even if they seem to be ignoring everything we say now.

There are so many pressures on our young people today: worries about school, sex, jobs, college, drugs, violence, racial prejudice. Perhaps we need to be more understanding about what adolescents have to go through nowadays. They can't always do everything we want them to do, just because we want them to. So, we have to be supportive, forgiving, patient, and trusting, and we have to trust that our relationship with them will continue to develop over time. We hope that our essential values will become integrated into their own value system; in fact, that's usually what happens. Sometimes, they may take a direction we don't want for them, and as they grow older, we have to be able to accept that outcome as well.

It may be necessary to adjust the way that we give advice, especially to teenagers. If we're always telling them what to do, they may think that we don't believe they are smart enough or moral enough to think for themselves, to make decisions for themselves. And they may react—or sometimes overreact—with behavior intended to shock us. We therefore need to give teenagers the opportunity to solve their own problems, so that they can develop the confidence they need to become competent adults.

Communicating our values to teenage sons and daughters, being available to talk with them, letting them know that we care what happens to them, and allowing them to test their decision-making abilities is the best we can do for them, once they reach this stage. Rescuing or attacking them, or trying to resolve problems for them, only prevents them from being able to find their own way in life.

When we do give advice to our teenage children, we need to let them know that being from another generation, from another country, or from another cultural background has value because they can learn from us. Our differences are not a minus, they're a plus. When we tell them how different it was for us growing up in another generation or in another country or culture, they have the benefit of comparing our experiences with theirs. If they add this information to their own experience, the sum can help them determine what direction to take and can give them options that can enrich their life.

Unfortunately, we can never protect our children from all the dangers of the world. But we can prepare them to live wisely by setting a wise example, listening to their problems, and sharing what wisdom we have gained in our own life.

7. How can we prevent our children from drinking alcohol and taking drugs?

Again, my advice is to engage your children in a serious two-way conversation about this very important problem. Ask them to tell you what they have learned about the dangers of drug and alcohol abuse, and what they believe. Then tell them what you know about the risks involved with these substances. Giving our children accurate information about how damaging alcohol and drugs can be is very important. This information can be in the form of books, newspaper articles, or television programs about the consequences of drug and alcohol use. Even more compelling are personal stories concerning friends or family members who have been in car accidents caused by drunk drivers, who have destroyed their lives with drugs, or who have contracted a fatal condition as a result of smoking cigarettes (cigarettes are a drug, too!). Usually children learn more from witnessing something firsthand, so if you know someone who has lived through the destructive consequences of alcohol and drug abuse, arrange for that person to talk to your children about his or her own or a family member's mistakes. Rather than just telling your children, "Alcohol and drugs aren't good for you, so stay away from them," give them concrete information and personal examples that will really make them think.

Of course, the most important thing for you to do as parents is to set a good example. How many parents do you know who tell their children not to use drugs but who themselves drink too much or smoke cigarettes? I frequently hear from my teenage patients how much they resent their parents for telling them not to do harmful things to their body, while the mother or father is smoking a pack of cigarettes a day. Cigarettes kill millions of people by causing lung cancer, heart disease, emphysema, and a host of other diseases, and we now know that tobacco companies intentionally get people "hooked" on cigarettes by assuring that certain levels of nicotine will create an addiction in the user.

Children are therefore correct in pointing out the hypocrisy that exists when their cigarette-smoking parents tell them not to take harmful drugs.

Nowadays, many parents themselves had experience with drugs when they were young, so they may give mixed messages to their children, such as, "I experimented with marijuana when I was your age, but I don't want you to do it." Children are very sensitive to the issue of hypocrisy, so we have to be very clear about the messages we are transmitting to them. "Do as I say, not as I do" has never been an effective way to teach children how to behave.

Another consideration that is very significant in communicating with your children about alcohol and drugs is young people's concern with "fitting in." Teenagers especially don't want to be different from their friends. We can help them understand, however, that it's always good to think for yourself and to be yourself. Paradoxically, since rebelling and being different are also perceived as positive attributes by many young people, perhaps you can explain abstinence from drugs in terms of rebelling against the norm.

It's also important to know your children's friends. Invite them over. Know who they are, who their parents are. Listen to what your children's friends have to say, and don't criticize them. Teenagers identify so strongly with their friends that if you come down on their pals, they will feel that you're criticizing them and will distance themselves from you even more. So be careful about what you say and how you choose to guide your children. Let them know what you think without making them feel criticized.

The best way to do this is to ask *them* questions. For example, "Why do you think your friend is doing that? What do you think is in his mind? What do you think happened to him to make him act this way?" Asking your children questions and engaging them in a discussion will have a much greater impact than simply warning them about what *not* to do. You'll be teaching them to think about what's going on with their friends and the ways unhealthy behavior can be related to such issues as lack of self-esteem and lack of personal direction.

Finally, be aware that when people become involved in any kind of substance addiction, they are usually searching for something. As parents, we have to ask ourselves, "What is it my child is trying to find?" "What is he trying to avoid?" "What is she feeling that she's trying to cover up with drugs or alcohol?" Helping our children search for the answers to such questions can go a long way toward preventing and/or overcoming the devastating problems associated with drug and alcohol abuse.

8. *My husband was always a "Latin lover" with me when we were dating and in the early years of our marriage. But the romance seems to have gone out of our marriage. How do I get him to be more romantic with me again?*

This is a very typical situation, which many married women describe to me. What I would like to ask you first of all is, Are *you* still romantic with your husband? Do you continue to do the little things that you know he enjoys? Do you cultivate the passion within yourself and express it to him? Sometimes, once we get married, we contribute to a lack of romance in our marriage without being aware of it. We get so caught up in all the work we have to do around the house, and we become so preoccupied with the children and our jobs, that romance is neglected. Instead of continuing to be the woman for our husband—the one he married—we become his mother. Being constantly concerned about the house, preparing meals, and doing the laundry is not romantic. So we have to consider what is lacking that we had before and how we can make time for romance again.

You might start by thinking about the history of your relationship. What kind of romantic life did you have in the past that you don't have now? Go back to the time when you and your husband first fell in love. How did you feel? What was it like to be with him? What were you feeling as you looked forward to being with him, when you were waiting for him to pick you up for a date? That anticipatory feeling that you found so exciting—how might you recapture it? How did you look at him? What expression was in your eyes? With what kind of touch did you express your love for him? How did you feel when he touched you? What kinds of words did you use to welcome him? What types of activities did you do together in those days? When he was upset, what did you do for him? In what ways did you ask him to be with you when you needed him?

If you want your husband to be more romantic, start by developing that sense of romance within yourself. When you create romance, you attract it. As your husband senses the intensity of your emotions, he will be inspired to help re-create the passion that once existed between the two of you.

I am a very romantic person myself. What I do to keep my marriage romantic is to always remember how it was when I met my husband, Alex. When I look into his eyes, I always have in mind how our love began, and I bring that memory to our experience in the present. I don't consider it an effort to keep the romance in our relationship; I enjoy thinking about the two of us in this way. I know that, when that feeling is not there, it's because there are so many activities and distractions that have taken over our lives. But I never want to give up the romance. It's very important to me and to our relationship.

As women, we also need to remember that romance is not always the same for us as it is for men, even though we both want to be loved and appreciated all the time. The psychologist John Gray says, "Men are motivated and empowered when they feel needed, and women are motivated and empowered when they feel cherished." So maybe we need to understand that this is one way we're different, and we may therefore perceive the concept of romance differently. Once we have an appreciation of these differences, perhaps we can learn to romance each other in new ways. What do you do to make your husband feel special and needed?

When you do these things, is he more likely to make you feel cherished?

What Latinos have in common is the feeling that romance is something very passionate and very intense. Romance, for us, isn't only candlelight and roses; it's an intense experience of emotions. Feeling this intensity on a daily basis, however, is probably expecting too much. Remember, when you and your husband were dating, you were spending only a few nights or days together each week. Now that you are together all the time, it's unrealistic to think that every moment will be filled with passion.

What you can do, though, is set aside times of the week to be together for romance. You set aside time for your social life, to be with friends or family, right? So you can set aside this time for yourselves. During this time together, you can choose whatever you want to do to be in touch with your passion, to reconnect with that Latino lover within each of you. You will find that having these experiences will not only be enjoyable in the moment but will also create memories that will resonate and bond you to each other. These shared romantic experiences will deepen your intimacy and help you to get through life crises together.

Creating a special time for romance is very important to your marriage. Just as you water your plants and flowers to enable them to grow, you have to nurture your relationship with romance to keep it alive. We can't forget about the kiss, the look into each other's eyes, touching, massaging each other, walking hand in hand, having intimate conversations, laughing, being playful, leaving a loving note for the other to receive, having a special lunch or dinner, watching a romantic movie, dancing with the lights out. You can make a list of the special romantic expressions of love that you really enjoy and share this with your husband. Remind him of the things he used to do that make you feel passionate or romantic. Or suggest new ways to be together that would feel romantic to you.

We all need passion in our lives. It is a tribute to life, and it should be a natural part of our marriage. Passion keeps us alive, intimately connected, and young in spirit. Don't ever allow it to escape!

9. *We have been in the United States for several years, and now that the political and economic situation in our native country is better, I want to go back. But my wife doesn't. She says that she has found a new way of life here, and she loves it. She has a career she enjoys, and now she feels she is more than "just someone's wife." Although we have a more comfortable life here in the United States, my joy in life is gone. I miss my family and close friends. This just doesn't feel like home to me. My wife and I argue about what to do, how differently we feel. And yet we don't want to separate. What should we do?*

As you can see, this troubling question cannot be stated briefly, because there are two deeply felt "sides" to the issue and a number of different questions to consider. But this is a dilemma that I hear very often from my clients and talk-show guests. Adjusting to a new country and adapting to the many ways in which life is different from what we knew at "home" is never easy. Nor is compromising your own desires and goals for the sake of your partner's happiness.

As Latino immigrants, we have strong roots in our countries of origin. Getting used to our new home takes a lot of courage and strength. There are many reasons why so many people want to live in the United States, and it's not just that we want to live more "comfortably." It's not comfortable to feel different. It's not comfortable to be unable to speak the language and to integrate yourself into a new society. It's not comfortable to have to accept work that requires much less skill than the jobs we did back home. All these aspects of an immigrant's life are very uncomfortable and irritating. At times, people try to humiliate us. For example, Latinos are often accused of trying to take advantage of the benefits of this country; but in fact, we work very hard for what we get. Being falsely accused does not feel comfortable.

But each of us has very important reasons for choosing to come here—otherwise we would not go through so much to get here and to survive here. Each of us invests so much of ourselves in coming to this country—and that includes the illegal immigrants, who spend their life savings to cross rivers and mountains, risking arrest and sometimes their lives.

Neither you nor your wife will be happy, nor will you be able to make each other happy, if you can't make peace with your choice to either remain here or move back to your native country. Somehow, the two of you are going to have to spend some time considering all the pros and cons of life here and back home, factoring in not only how you feel but also how the person you have chosen to spend your life with feels.

Your wife has to find out if opportunities back home have improved since you left. Is it possible for her to transfer what she has learned here in the United States to your home country, so that she might have as satisfying a career there as she has here? And have you considered that you may find it difficult to readjust to your home country, after living in the United States for several years? Sometimes, people go back to their country of origin, only to find out that they don't quite fit in as they did before. Have you honestly given your friends in this country a chance? Or have you been so homesick that you haven't been open to new possibilities for friendship?

You and your wife have only been married for a few years and you have no children yet, but you should also consider what would be best for the children you may one day have. Weighing the opportunities for them both here and there, the extended family they have back home and the new choices they might have here—all these considerations will certainly figure in your decision.

Ultimately, your decision should be made with a view of the long term; it should not be based solely upon what you are experiencing at this moment in time. Are things likely to get better for you here, as you make more friends and accommodate to this way of life? Would your wife eventually enjoy living back home, once she established a career there? Where will your future children be more likely to have a happier and more fulfilling life?

Being in a loving relationship is what gives you the strength to deal with life's changes and difficulties. Nurturing and being there for each other provide the stable foundation upon which your lives can flourish. Whatever decision you make, wherever you decide to make your home, realize that your love and support for each other is what matters most.

10. My children seem to be so "Americanized." How do I teach them to love our culture?

First of all, we have to love our culture ourselves. If we don't know anything about it, if we are secretly (or openly) prejudiced against or critical of our own people, as some Latinos are, how can we teach our children to love that part of themselves? So we must start with ourselves. We can acknowledge our prejudices and opinions and try to understand why they exist. Has the mainstream American culture and media influenced the way we think about our own people? Are we reluctant to identify with those who are less fortunate than we are?

On the positive side, what can you share with your children that would excite and interest them about their roots? Are there books and magazines, as well as movies that the family could enjoy together, that would better educate you and them about Latino culture or the rich and varied history of your country of origin? (See the Suggested Reading Lists at the end of Chapter 6.) Are there certain areas in your town or city that contain elements of Hispanic history, and could you visit these? Does your city have a cultural museum or art museum that might feature Latino arts and artifacts? Do you ever take your children to special concerts featuring Latin-American music? Have you visited your country of origin with your children, and if so, have you shown them interesting cultural sites, neighborhoods, museums, and murals?

There is no more meaningful way of connecting to our cultural roots than through contact with our elders. Keeping your children in touch with grandparents or great-grandparents, great-uncles and great-aunts gives them a very personal sense of their cultural history. Sometimes we take for granted the stories our parents or grandparents tell over and over again of what life was like back in their country of origin, how it was for them coming to the United States for the first time, the hardships they went through, and the adjustments they had to make. But once these relatives are gone, it would be a tragedy if their stories were not remembered and passed on. These stories help us understand, in a very personal way, how history and culture shape who we are. I know some families who have taken the time to make tape recordings and videos of their elderly relatives as they tell these stories, so that they will be preserved for future generations.

I would also like to share with you some information about a wonderful group in southern California that was founded by two actors, Tony Plana and Ada Maris, to expose young children to Latino culture. It is called La Escuelita, and I encourage you to start a similar group in your own community. La Escuelita teaches Spanish to Latino children who may not speak the language or be fluent in it. The group also cooks Latin-American foods with the children, organizes craft projects related to the culture, plays games that originate in Hispanic countries, and teaches Spanish songs and folk dances related to the traditional cultures of Latin America. My husband and I look forward to our daughters' participation in La Escuelita as a fun and enriching experience for them.

However you choose to do it, bringing your native culture into your children's lives in a meaningful way is an invaluable gift to them. It will help them understand who they are and where they come from, and it will provide the basis for sharing this understanding with their own children one day.

INDEX

Abortion, 151, 152
Abusive relationships, 108–33
  alcoholism and, 109–15
  child abuse and neglect as, 117–18,
    121–23
  domestic abuse as, 118–21
  resources for overcoming, 129–33
  respect and overcoming, 128
  self-directed prejudice and racism
    in, 123–28
  stresses and violence in, 115–18
Actions, expressing feelings through,
  14
Aguilar, Ignacio, 202–3
Al-Anon, 113, 114, 129, 225
Alcohol abuse, 111–15
  facts on, and help for, 129
  preventing, in children, 269–71
Alcoholics Anonymous (AA),
  113–15, 129, 225–26
American-born Latinos

  cultural double identity of, 1, 2, 3,
    8–10
  successful relationship between
    Latino immigrant and, 238–41
  successful relationship between
    two, 231, 232–38
American culture, mainstream
  blending into, vs. retaining Latino
    roots, 7–10
  blending Latino values with values
    of, in successful relationships,
    231, 232–38
  casualness in, 17–18
  characteristics of, vs. Latino
    culture, 21–22
  expression of feelings in, vs. in
    Latino culture, 13–16
  freedom of choice in, 43–45
  parenting in (see Parenting)
American Dream, hope and reality in,
  for Latinos, 4–7

Anger and resentment
  changing, in relationships with
    family, 188–94
  communication affected by, 58
  racism and, 111
  sex affected by, 80
  unresolved, and threat of violence,
    119
Anglo-American(s), successful
    relationship between Latinas
    and, 246–55
Animals, abuse of, 119
Argument, overcoming feeling stuck
    in same, 66–69. See also Conflict
    in relationships
Asking for What You Want, Giving
    What You Can exercise, 68–69
Audio tapes, 228–29, 230
Authority
  of parent, 140–42
  of psychotherapists, 223
Aztec culture, 19
Aztec Thought and Culture (Leon-
    Portilla), 19

Barbach, Lonnie, 102
Bedtime problems for children,
    137–39
Behavioral traits of families
  asking partner about, 194–95
  assessing negative and positive,
    186–88
  changing, 188–94
  child's unexpressed feelings to
    parents and, 175–84
  legacy of infidelity as, 168, 170–72
  unhealthy emotional alliance
    between parent and child as,
    184–86
  woman's role and parents' unhappy
    relationship as, 168, 172–74

Belonging, factors contributing to
    Latino sense of, 10–13, 30–31
Berbosa, Henry, 163–64
Birthday festivities, 234
Blended cultural values, Latino and
    mainstream American, 42
  in single-parent woman, 242–46
  in successful marriage relationships,
    231, 232–41, 246–55
Blended families, problems of
    parenting in, 137–39
Blending into mainstream American
    culture vs. retaining Latino
    roots, 7–10

Catholic Church
  decision to leave, 43–44
  Latino culture and sense of
    belonging linked to, 12–13, 44,
    164, 233–34
  on role of women, 27
  seeking help for relationship
    problems from, 199–200
  sex roles and taboos and, 80, 81,
    96–97
Celibacy, 41
Child abuse, 117–19
  getting help for, 131–32
Children, 134–67
  abuse of, 117–19
  communicating with teenaged,
    143–48
  cultural clashes over parenting of,
    135–36
  discipline for, 137–39, 142–43
  education of, 157–59
  effects of domestic abuse of,
    119–21
  family favoritism toward light-
    skinned, 123–26
  fostering respect for authority in,
    140–42

Latino value for family and, 8
love as greatest gift to, 164–65
motivating, 154–57
neglect of, 121–23
parenting and guiding teenage, 148–54
permissive parenting of, 142–43
protecting, from drugs and alcohol, 269–71
questions to identify conflicts about rearing, 49
racism directed at, 159–61
reading list for, 165–67
role of extended family in rearing, 6
teaching Latino culture to, 276–78
teaching tolerance to, 161–64
unhealthy emotional alliance between parent and, 184–86
Clergy, seeking help for relationship problems from, 199–200
Cohen, Angela, 102
Communication in relationships, 50–78
conversation vs., 54–57
different ideas about perfect marriage and, 69–74
gender differences and, 51–54
guidelines for healthy, 57–61
life expansion and personal growth through, 76–77
questions to identify conflicts about, 48
overcoming distance from partner through, 61–66
overcoming feeling stuck in same argument, 66–69
seeking help from psychotherapist for, 219–20
sex as, 79–81, 106–7
with teenagers, 143–48
value of disagreements for, 75–76
wish list visualization exercise for, 74–75
Compromise, 67
Conflict in relationships, 23–49, 108–33. *See also* Abusive relationships
communication and (*see* Communication in relationships)
demands leading to, 260–62
about desire to return to native country, 274–76
as family legacy, 172–74
freedom of choice and, 43–45
identifying areas of, 45–49
infidelity and, 36–42, 116, 168, 170–72, 210–11, 214–17
keys to resolving, 51
overcoming feeling stuck in same argument, 66–69
about parenting, 134, 137–39
role of extended family and, 30–36
role of women and, 24–30
Conversation
communication vs., 54–57
imaginary, with parents, 176–82
preparing for actual, with parents, 182–84
Cultural double life, xii, 1–22
American dream and, 4–7
blending in vs. Latino roots and, 7–10
blending values of, 42
characteristics of Latino culture vs. mainstream U.S. culture and, 22
conflict in relationships and (*see* Conflict in relationships)
formality vs. casualness and, 17–18
ideas about perfect marriage and, 69–74
"macho" vs. "liberated" males and, 18–21

parenting and, 135–39
self-expression and, 13–16
sense of belonging and, 10–13
Curanderos, seeking help for
    relationship problems from,
    200–203

Defeatism in Latino children, 154–57
Disagreements in relationships, value
    of, 75–76
Discipline and routines for children,
    137–39, 142–43
Distance from partner, remedying
    feelings of, 61–66
Doctor, seeking emotional support
    from family, 198–99
Domestic duties, sharing, 91–92,
    235–36
Domestic violence, 20, 116–21
    getting help for, 133
    signs of, 132–33
Double life of Latinos. See Cultural
    double life
Double standard, 36–42, 48. See also
    Infidelity
Drug abuse
    facts on, and help for, 130
    preventing, in children, 269–71
    by teenagers, 149–50
    use of, as form of infidelity, 170–72

Economic abuse, 121–23
Education
    on Latino culture, 276–78
    Latino value for, 157–59
Emotional Health Anonymous, 227
Emotions. See Feelings
Erotica, 101–2
Erotic Interludes (Barbach), 102
Erotic Pleasures: Women Write Erotica
    (Barbach), 102

Escuelita, La, 277–78
Exercises
    assessing negative and positive
        family behavioral traits, 187–88
    communicating and remedying
        distance from partner, 62, 63–66
    on different ideas about perfect
        marriage, 71–74
    exploring fear of your or your
        partner's success, 28–30
    on feeling stuck in same argument,
        68–69
    forgiving parents, 190–94
    imaginary conversation with
        parents, 177–82
    intensifying sexual encounters,
        93–95
    wish list visualization, 74–75
Expressing, Listening, and Repeating
    Exercise, 62, 63–66
Extended Latino family
    conflicts about appropriate role of,
        30–36, 46–47, 258–60
    help for relationship problems
        from, 203–4
    loss of, by immigrants, 5–7
    role of, in rearing children, 6
    sense of belonging created by,
        10–13

Family. See also Extended Latino
    family
    birthday festivities in, 234
    blended, 137–39
    conflicts about role of extended,
        30–36, 46–47, 258–60
    disapproval of, 32–33
    help for relationship problems
        from, 203–4
    loss of extended, by immigrant
        Latinos, 5–7

positive and negative aspects of behavioral traits in, 186–88

sense of belonging and Latino, 10–13, 244–45, 253

time spent with members of, 34–35, 258–60

weddings in, 254–55

Family doctor, seeking emotional support from, 198–99

Family history and relationships, 168–95

acknowledgment of negative and positive aspects of, 186–88

asking partner about, 194–95

changing legacy of behavioral and emotional patterns, 188–94

effect of parents' unhappy marriage, 172–74

legacy of infidelity, 37–38, 168, 170–72

"unfinished business" with parents, 175–84

unhealthy emotional alliance with parent, 184–86

Fantasies, sexual, 102–6

Fathers, parenting by, 236–37, 260, 264–66

Fear

of changing role of women and of her success, 24–30

child's, and bedtime problems, 138–39

child's, of parents' authority, 140–41

of communication, and "opening up," 54–57

Feelings

distance from partner as, 61–66

expression of, in Latino culture, 13–16

expression of, to parents in imaginary conversation, 176–82

gender differences in expressing, 54–57

overcoming feeling stuck in same argument, 66–69

teenagers', sexual activity and, 152–54

Fools Rush In (film), 11

Formality, Latino, 17–18

Fox, Sarah Gardner, 102

Freedom of choice in United States culture, 43–45

Friends

loss of childhood, for immigrant Latinos, 5

problems of getting help from, for relationship problems, 205–7

as replacement for extended family, 204

Gangs, teenage, 148–49

Gender differences

in communication, 51–54

in seeking help for relationship problems, 209–17

sexual, 82–87, 88–90

Hayes-Bautista, David E., 203

Healing systems, traditional, 200–203

Help for relationships, 196–230

for alcohol and drug abuse, 129–30

best friends and, 205–7

for child abuse, 131–32

from clergy, 199–200

from curanderos and naturistas, 200–203

for domestic violence, 132–33

from extended family, 203–4

from family doctor, 198–99

from self-help tapes and books, 228–29

from support groups, 196, 225–28
taking action to get, 229–30
from television and radio
    psychology shows, 207–17
from therapists and marriage
    counselors, 217–25
Hendrix, Harville, 62
Hernandez, Antonia, 246–49
Hispanic Condition, The (Stavans),
    20
Honor, Latino sense of, 19–20
    work life and, 112–13

Immigrant Latinos
    American Dream for, hope and
        reality, 4–7
    conflict with partner over desire by,
        to return to native country,
        274–76
    cultural double identity of, 1, 2–3
    value of, for education, 157–59
Infidelity, 116, 210–11, 214–17
    legacy of parent's, and effect on
        relationships, 168, 170–72
    relationship conflicts and double
        standard on, 36–42, 48
    successful relationship between
        American-born Latina and,
        238–41
Internet, romantic relationships on,
    250

Labor practices, unfair, 121–23
Latino(s). *See* American-born Latinos;
    Immigrant Latinos; Men
    (Latinos); Women (Latinas)
Latino culture
    expression of feelings in, 13–16
    formality in, 17–18
    machismo in, 18–20

male role in providing for family in,
    112–13
parenting values in, 134–36 (*see
    also* Parenting)
reestablishing relationship to
    Latino roots and, 238–41
reluctance to seek professional help
    in, 196, 197
retaining roots in, vs. blending into
    mainstream culture, 7–10
sense of belonging in, 10–13
sexuality and values of, 80, 84,
    88–90, 95–98
teaching, to children, 276–78
value for education in, 157–59
values of, vs. mainstream American
    values, 21–22
values of, blended with Anglo
    mainstream American values in
    successful relationships, 231–41
Latino heritage, teaching, 163–64
Latinos (Shorris), 19, 200
Leon-Portilla, Miguel, 19
Life expectancy for Latinos, 203
Listening
    exercise on speaking and, 63–66
    guidelines for effective, 59
Love. *See also* Relationships
    finding marriage partner, 262–63
    parents' greatest gift to children,
        164–65

Machismo, 18–21, 26, 237
    double standard on infidelity and,
        36–42, 48, 170–72 (*see also*
        Infidelity)
    sex in relationships and, 38
Mainstream culture. *See* American
    culture, mainstream
MALDEF (Mexican-American Legal
    Defense and Education Fund),
    246

Maris, Ada, 277
Marriage, different ideas about perfect, 69–74
Marriage counseling
    misconceptions about and prejudice against, 196, 218, 221–25
    seeking help for relationship problems from, 217–21
Maslow, Abraham, 228
Men (Latinos). *See also* Gender differences; Women (Latinas)
    changing role of women and fears of, 24–30, 47
    communication by women vs. communication by, 51–57
    competition and role of, 52
    double standard on infidelity and role of, 36–42, 48, 170–72 (*see also* Infidelity))
    expression of feelings by, 15
    father role of, 236–37, 260, 264–66
    "macho" vs. "liberated," 18–20 (*see also* Machismo)
    role of, in providing for family, 112–13
    sexual activity among teenage, 153–54
    sexuality of, and stereotypes about, 82–84, 87–90
Mothers
    effect on children of domestic abuse of, 119–20
    emotional alliances between son and, 184–86, 258
    role of, in double standard and infidelity, 40
    role of, in sex education, 153–54
Motivation, encouraging in children and teens, 154–57

National Committee to Prevent Child Abuse, 131
Naturistas, seeking help for relationship problems from, 200–203
Neruda, Pablo, 102
Northridge Earthquake of 1994, 238
Nuclear family, 11

Parent(s). *See also* Fathers; Mothers
    as examples, 269–70
    exercise for forgiving, 190–94
    expressing feelings to, in actual conversation, 182–84
    expressing feelings to, through imaginary conversation, 176–82
    unhealthy emotional alliance between child and, 184–86
    "unfinished business" with, 175–76
Parenting
    communicating with teenagers, 143–48
    cultural clashes over, 134, 135–39
    discipline and, 134, 137–39, 142–43
    education of children and, 157–59
    by fathers, 236–37, 260, 264–66
    fostering respect for authority, 140–42
    gender roles and equality in, 236
    love as greatest gift to children in, 164–65
    motivating children, 154–57
    permissive, 142–43
    racism and, 159–61
    teaching tolerance, 161–64
    of teenagers, 148–54, 266–71
Patterns, changes in sexual, 98–102
Permissive parenting, 142–43
Personal growth through relationships, 77–78

Plana, Tony, 277
Play, importance of sexual, 81–87
Pornography, 101–2
Powerlessness, feelings of, 19
Pregnancy, teenage, 150–52
Prejudice
    against seeking professional help
        for relationship problems, 196,
        218, 222–25
    effect of, on personal relationships,
        109–15
    racial, directed toward children,
        159–61
    racial, within families, 123–28
Pride, Latino sense of, 17–18, 41–42,
    222
Privacy, cultural idea of, 31–32
Psychotherapy
    curanderos as form of traditional,
        200–203
    misconceptions about, and
        prejudice against, 196, 218,
        221–25
    seeking help for relationship
        problems from, 217–21

Questionnaire on relationship
    conflicts, 46–49
Questions asked most frequently
    about relationships, 257–78
    on author's radio and television
        psychology shows, 209
    about childrearing responsibilities,
        264–66
    about demands from partner,
        260–62
    about finding marriage partner,
        262–63
    about guiding children away from
        drugs and alcohol, 269–71
    about loyalty to family, 258–60

    about parenting teenagers, 266–68
    about returning to native country,
        274–76
    about sex and romance, 271–74
    about sex and woman's role,
        263–64
    about teaching Latino culture to
        children, 276–78

Racism
    direction at children, 159–61
    effect of, on personal relationships,
        109–15
    within families, 123–28
Radio psychology shows, seeking help
    for relationship problems from,
    208–14
Refugee immigrants, 5
Relationships
    abusive, 108–33
    with children, 134–67 (see also
        Children)
    communication in, 50–78
    conflict in (see Conflict in
        relationships)
    cultural clashes causing conflict
        within, 23–49
    effect of family history on, 168–95
    getting help for problems in,
        196–230
    finding partners for marriage,
        262–63
    Latinos' cultural double life and
        affect on, 1–22
    most frequently asked questions
        about, 257–78
    racism and dating in, 127–28
    sex and, 79–107
    stories of successful, 231–56
    value of disagreements for, 75–76
Religion. See also Catholic Church
    freedom of choice in, 43–45

Latino sense of belonging and, 11–13, 44, 233–34
Reserve and modesty, Latino, 15
Role models, lack of positive, 154, 155
Romance
    reestablishing passion and, in relationships, 271–74
    machismo and, 20

Self-acceptance, sexual, 85
Self-expression in Latino culture, 13–16
Self-help tapes and books, seeking help for relationship problems from, 228–29, 230
Self-image
    ability to provide for family and male, 112–13
    counteracting, negative, in children, 154–57
    machismo and, 19–20
Sex education, 151–54
Sex in relationships, 79–107
    changing patterns of, 98–102
    as communication, 79–81
    disagreements over frequency of, 87–95
    erotica, pornography, and, 101–2
    fantasies and daydreams about, 102–6
    giving permission to touch and explore, 95–98
    infidelity and, 36–42, 48, 116, 168, 170–72, 210–11, 214–17
    machismo and, 38
    questions to identify conflicts about, 48
    rediscovering and revitalizing romance and, 81–87, 271–74
    seeking help from psychotherapist for, 220–21

sensual dimension and, 106–7
shyness about, 80, 263–64
stereotypes about women and, 40–42
women's role and inhibition about, 263–64
Sexual activity among teenagers, 150–54
Shorris, Earl, 19, 200
Smoking, 269–71
Spanish language, 253, 254
Speaking
    exercise on listening and, 63–66
    guidelines for effective communication through, 57–59, 60
Spousal abuse. See Domestic violence
Stavans, Ilan, 20
Stress, abusive relationships linked to, 115–18
Suarez-Orozco, Marcelo, 157
Success, exercise on fears about, 28–30
Success stories in relationships, 231–56
    blending Latino and Anglo families as, 249–55
    incorporating Latino and mainstream U.S. values, 231, 232–38
    love and, 255–56
    reestablishing relationship with Latin roots, 238–41
    shared Latino and Anglo goals and values, 246–49
    single-parent woman and, 242–46
Suicide, threat of teenager's, 147–48
Support groups
    Alcoholics Anonymous as, 113–15, 129, 225
    seeking help for relationship problems in, 196, 225–28

Taking it out on each other in
    relationships. See Abusive
    relationships
Teenagers, parenting of, 143–54,
    266–71
  education and, 157–59
  gangs, drug abuse, and sexual
    activity in teens and, 148–54
  importance of communication in,
    143–47, 266, 268
  importance of tolerance in, 266–67
  promoting drug and alcohol
    abstinence in, 269–71
  threat of teen suicide and, 147–48
Television psychology shows, seeking
    help for relationship problems
    from, 208–14
Therapy. See Psychotherapy
Time
  amount of, spent with family
    members, 34–35, 258–60
  idea of, in Latino culture, 198–99
Tolerance, teaching to children,
    161–64
Trust in relationships, 251, 261
Twenty Love Poems and a Song of
    Despair (Neruda), 102

Unfair labor practices, 121–23
United States culture. See American
    culture, mainstream

Values. See Blended cultural values,
    Latino and mainstream
    American
Violence in relationships
  child abuse, 117–18, 131–32
  domestic abuse, 115–17, 118–21,
    132–33

Weddings, 254–55
Wise Woman's Guide to Erotic Videos
    (Cohen, Fox), 102
Wish list visualization exercise, 74–75
Women (Latinas). See also Gender
    differences; Men (Latinos);
    Mothers
  blended cultural values in, single-
    parent life of, 242–46
  communication by, vs.
    communication by men, 51–57
  complaints by husbands about
    demands made by, 260–62
  conflicts with partner about role of,
    24–28, 47–48
  connections, relationships, and role
    of, 52
  domestic duties and role of, 235–37
  expression of feelings by, 14–15
  fears of, and changing role of,
    26–27
  good-girl, bad-girl sterotype about,
    40–42
  partner's infidelity and role of,
    37–39 (see also Infidelity)
  pressures affecting, and role of,
    8–10
  sexuality of, and cultural values,
    40–41, 88–90, 263–64
  sexuality of, and fantasy, 102–6
  sexuality of, and sexual self-
    acceptance, 85–87, 105–6
  sexuality of, and sexual self-
    pleasuring, 95–98
Work
  motivating children toward self-
    fulfilling, 156–57
  racism against Latinos at, 109–15
  unfair labor practices at, 121–23

Dr. Ana Nogales' Self-Help Psychology Audio Tapes

1. Overcoming Your Past
2. Learning to Love Yourself
3. Combating Depression
4. Using Anger in a Positive Way
5. Understanding and Resolving Your Fears
6. Managing Anxiety
7. Loving Your Body
8. Becoming "The Ideal Couple"
9. Understanding the Opposite Sex
10. Enjoying a Healthier Sexual Life
11. Finding True Happiness
12. Learning How to Relax

(The set of twelve audio tapes also includes a videotape and a self-help book.)

For information on how to order, please contact:
Dr. Ana Nogales
3550 Wilshire Blvd., Suite 670
Los Angeles, CA 90010
Telephone: (213) 413-7777
Web site: www.drnogales.com

Printed in the United States
by Baker & Taylor Publisher Services